Variation in electoral support explained

Rajiv Sharma

Table of Contents

Preface and Acknowledgements ii
List of Tables xi
List of Figures xiii
Abbreviations xiv
Map of India xv

Chapter 1. Introduction 1
    Research Questions 6
    Research Contribution 10
    Ethnically Mediated Retrospective Voting 11
    Research Methods 14
    Research Findings 15
    Chapter Summaries 18

Chapter 2. Setting the Context: The Rise of the Bharatiya Janata Party (BJP) 20

Chapter 3: Ethnic Politics and Urban Voting Behavior in India 34
    Indian Electoral Politics and Voting Behavior 34
    Review of Literature 41
        Ethnic politics and voting behavior 41
        Retrospective Voting and Voter-Party Linkages 50
    Ethnically Mediated Retrospective Voting Theory (ERV) 57
    ERV's Testable Implications 66
    ERV's predictions to explain urban voter support for the BJP 85
        ERV's predictions for Delhi and New Delhi 86
        ERV's predictions for Gujarat and Ahmedabad 87

Chapter 4: Research Design and Methodology 88
    Nested Analysis Research Design 91
    Large-N Analysis 92
    Case Study Analysis 101

Chapter 5: Ethnic Politics and Voting Behavior in Delhi and New Delhi 108

    Delhi 109
    Delhi: Indian National Election Survey Analysis, 1999, 2004 and 2009 115
        Delhi, 1999 Election 116
        Delhi, 2004 Election 122
        Delhi, 2009 Election 135
    New Delhi: Case Studies Analysis, 1999-2009 145

Chapter 6: Ethnic Politics and Voting Behavior in Gujarat and Ahmedabad 161

    Gujarat 163
    Gujarat: Indian National Election Survey Analysis, 1999, 2004 and 2009 177
        Gujarat, 1999 Election 177
        Gujarat, 2004 Election 185
        Gujarat, 2009 Election 192
    Ahmedabad: Case Studies Analysis, 1999-2009 202

Chapter 7: Conclusion 223

    Summary of Research Findings 226
    Contributions to the study of Indian Politics 231
    Final Thoughts 233

List of Tables

Table 1.1 Summary of Election Results: BJP, Congress, NDA and UPA, 1999-2009 3
Table 1.2 Number of BJP Seats Won in Delhi and Gujarat, 1999-2009 3
Table 3.1 ERV's predicted generalized scenarios of voting behavior and voter support for an ethnic party in different social and economic conditions 67
Table 3.2 Scenarios of Individual Voting Behavior: based on differences in the way in which ERV's mechanisms impact individual vote choice 71
Table 3.3 Levels of political economy of development and ethnic conflict in Delhi and Gujarat, 1999, 2004 and 2009 elections 75
Table 3.4 Sectoral Composition of Delhi Economy: 1993-2009 78
Table 3.5 Sectoral Composition of Gujarat Economy: 1993-2009 81
Table 4.1: Ethnic Group Identity and Interest Indicators 94
Table 4.2 Retrospective Programmatic Interest Indicators 96
Table 4.3: New Delhi Cases 105
Table 5.1: Party Winner of Delhi Elections at the National and State Levels 113
Table 5.2 Delhi National Election Results, 1999-2009 115
Table 5.3 Differences of sample proportions for Ethnic and Retrospective Programmatic Indicators for BJP voters, Delhi 1999 election 118
Table 5.4 Delhi Voter Priorities in 1999: central versus state level government 120
Table 5.5 Logit Regression Results, Delhi 2004 election 124
Table 5.6 Predicted Probabilities: Delhi 2004 election 126
Table 5.7 Logit Regression Results, Delhi 2004 election with interaction terms 128
Table 5.8 Marginal effects of development, Delhi 2004 election 130
Table 5.9 Differences of sample proportions for indicators of caste and religion for BJP voters, Delhi 1999 and 2004 elections 132
Table 5.10 Delhi Voter Priorities in 2004: central versus state level government 133
Table 5.11 Logit Regression Results, Delhi 2009 election 137
Table 5.12 Predicted Probabilities, Delhi 2009 election 139
Table 5.13 What should be built at the Ayodhya site? (Delhi 2009) 140
Table 5.14 Differences of sample proportions for indicators of caste and religion for BJP voters, Delhi 1999, 2004 and 2009 elections 142
Table 5.15 Delhi Voter Priorities in 2009: central versus state level government 143
Table 5.16 Summary of socio-economic characteristics of New Delhi case studies 145
Table 5.17 New Delhi Cases Summary 146
Table 5.18 New Delhi Cases: Vote Choices, 1999-2009 elections 147
Table 5.19 Summary of Vote Patterns: All New Delhi cases 148

Table 6.1 Gujarat National Election Results, 1999-2009...176
Table 6.2 Logit Regression Results, Gujarat 1999 Election..179
Table 6.3 Predicted Probabilities: Gujarat 1999 Election...180
Table 6.4 Differences of sample proportions for select indicators for BJP voters,
    Gujarat and Delhi, 1999 election..183
Table 6.5 Gujarat Voter Priorities in 1999: central versus state level government.........184
Table 6.6 Logit Regression Results, Gujarat 2004 Election..187
Table 6.7 Predicted Probabilities: Gujarat 2004 Election...189
Table 6.8 Differences of sample proportions for ethnic indicators for BJP voters,
    Gujarat 1999, Gujarat 2004 and Delhi 2004 elections..190
Table 6.9 Logit Regression Results, Gujarat 2009 election 194
Table 6.10 Predicted Probabilities, Gujarat 2009 election..195
Table 6.11 Gujarat Voter Priorities in 2009: central versus state level government......197
Table 6.12 What should be built at the Ayodhya site? (Gujarat 2009) 198
Table 6.13 Differences of sample proportions for indicators of caste and religion for BJP
    voters, Gujarat 1999, 2004 and 2009 elections 200
Table 6.14 Summary of socio-economic characteristics of Ahmedabad case studies.....203
Table 6.15 Ahmedabad Cases...205
Table 6.16 Ahmedabad and New Delhi Cases: number of BJP voters...........................206
Table 6.17 Summary of Vote Patterns: Ahmedabad and New Delhi Cases 208
Table 6.18 Vote Patterns of BJP voters in Ahmedabad and New Delhi, 1999 & 2009...208

List of Figures

Map of India xv
Figure 3.1 Ethnic Group Conflict and Shifts in the Political Salience of Ethnic Group Identity and Interests 61
Figure 3.2 Political Economy of Development and Shifts in Retrospective Programmatic Demands by Voters 63
Figure 3.3 ERV: Theorizing Emerging Linkages between Voters and Parties in India 65

Abbreviations

BJP	Bharatiya Janata Party
BJS	Bharatiya Jana Sangh
INC	Indian National Congress
JD	Janata Dal
NDA	National Democratic Alliance
OBC	Other Backward Classes/Backward Castes
RSS	Rashtriya Swayamsevak Sangh
SC	Scheduled Caste
ST	Scheduled Tribe
UPA	United Progressive Alliance
VHP	Vishwa Hindu Parishad

Map of India

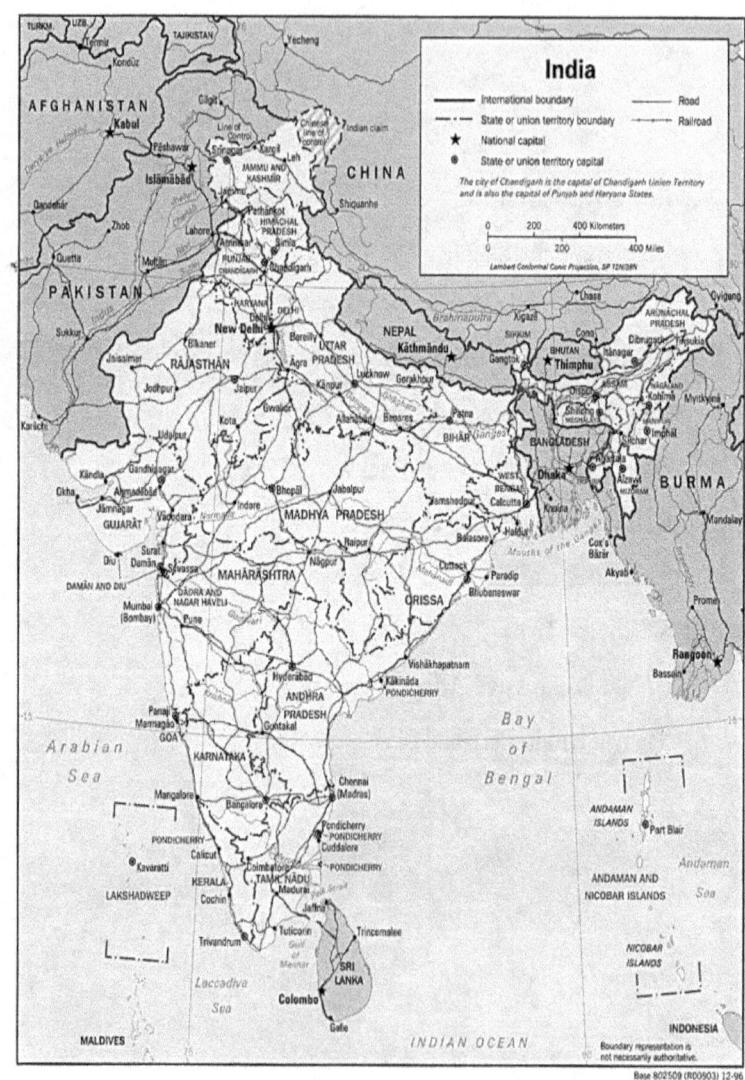

Source: Map "Base 802509 (R00903) 12-96," Washington, DC, Library of Congress, 1996.

Chapter 1. Introduction

> "Free India will be no Hindu raj, it will be India raj based not on the majority of any religious sect or community but on the representatives of the whole people without distinction of religion." -- Mahatma Gandhi

For many Indians, the rise of the Bharatiya Janata Party (BJP) in the 1990s was and continues to be a highly controversial addition to Indian electoral politics. The BJP has advocated a vision of Indian national unity through the concept of *Hindutva*, which many believe does not equally embrace or represent all ethnic or religious groups, and contrasts sharply with India's constitutional mandate as a secular democratic republic.[1]

The BJP's electoral strategy in the late 1980s and early 1990s to mobilize social and political support for building a temple for the Hindu deity, Lord Ram, in Ayodhya, in particular has been deeply criticized for inciting violence between Hindus and Muslims. In December 1992, following a *yatra* (religious pilgrimage) and *kar seva* (religious services) organized by the BJP and other Hindu organizations to initiate the construction of the Ram temple, thousands of Hindu nationalists tore down the Babri mosque in Ayodhya, triggering months of communal violence and rioting throughout the country.

The BJP's advocacy of *Hindutva* and its mobilization efforts to build the Ram temple has thus earned it the reputation as being *an explicitly pro-Hindu party*. More specifically, since the BJP's inception in 1980, the party has typically been associated with traders, shopkeepers, professionals and civil servants, which predominantly includes

---

[1] The Preamble of India's Constitution states, "We, the people of India, having solemnly resolved to constitute India into a sovereign socialist secular democratic republic..." The Constitution of India, available at http://india.gov.in/govt/constitutions_india.php.

upper caste Hindus living in urban areas.[2] For this research project, the BJP is defined as an ethnic party, in that it "overtly represents itself as a champion of the cause of one particular ethnic category or set of categories to the exclusion of others."[3]

The Bharatiya Janata Party's rise to power culminated in its sweep of the 1999 National (Lok Sabha) election: the party won 182 parliamentary seats and built a 270-member National Democratic Alliance (NDA) coalition government for a full five-year term. Yet, within three election cycles, the party's precipitous rise to power at the national level was followed by a rapid decline. In the 2004 election, the Indian National Congress (INC) led United Progressive Alliance (UPA) defeated the BJP, which lost over 40 parliamentary seats. In the 2009 Lok Sabha election, the BJP fared even worse: the Congress party gained an additional 60 parliamentary seats while the BJP was reduced to 116 seats.[4] Table 1.1 summarizes the national election results by the number of parliamentary seats won for the BJP, the Congress and the two national coalitions, (i.e., National Democratic Alliance and the United Progressive Alliance) in the 1999, 2004 and 2009 Lok Sabha elections.

---

[2] Falcao, Vanita Leah, "Urban Patterns of Voting and Party Choices," *Economic & Political Weekly*, September 26, 2009, p. 101. Chhibber, Pradeep, "Who Voted for the Bharatiya Janata Party," *British Journal of Political Science*, 27(4), 1997, p. 638. Chhibber shows that the variables of caste (i.e., being upper caste) and urban residence were associated with a higher likelihood of voting for the BJP in the 1991 national election.

[3] The term, ethnic party, is based on Kanchan Chandra's description that an ethnic party "overtly represents itself as a champion of the cause of one particular ethnic category or set of categories to the exclusion of others, and that makes such a representation central to its strategy of mobilizing voters." Chandra, Kanchan, *Why Ethnic Parties Succeed: Patronage and Ethnic Head Counts in India*. Cambridge: Cambridge University Press, 2004, p. 3. The Bahujan Samaj Party is an example of an ethnic party representing lower caste Hindu interests in the state of Uttar Pradesh, India. However, unlike the BJP, the BSP has generally not been associated with ethnic violence.

[4] Despite the BJP's electoral decline in the 2009 election compared to the two past elections, it remains the second most popular party in India, garnering nearly twenty percent of the popular vote.

Table 1.1 Summary of Election Results: BJP, Congress, NDA and UPA, 1999-2009

Party/Coalition	1999 Election	2004 Election	2009 Election
BJP	182	138	116
National Democratic Alliance*	270	181	159
Congress	114	145	206
United Progressive Alliance**	156	218	262

*BJP-led coalition
**Congress-led coalition

In addition to this variation in electoral support for the BJP over time, at the state level, Delhi and Gujarat, two highly urbanized states, present two different political trajectories for the BJP. In Delhi, the BJP came to dominate politics in the 1990s, and won all of Delhi's Lok Sabha seats in the 1999 election. However, the party's electoral success was followed by a rapid decline, such that the BJP could not win a single Lok Sabha seat in the 2009 election. This pattern of a precipitous rise followed by a steep decline in political support for the BJP broadly mirrors the national pattern described above. By contrast, the BJP in Gujarat also rose to dominance in the 1990s but has remained the dominant party in power for nearly two decades. Table 1.2 shows the number of parliamentary seats won by the BJP in Delhi and in Gujarat in the 1999, 2004 and 2009 Lok Sabha elections. Delhi has a total of seven parliamentary seats, while Gujarat has a total of twenty-six parliamentary seats.

Table 1.2 Number of BJP Seats Won in Delhi and Gujarat, 1999-2009

State	1999 Election	2004 Election	2009 Election
Delhi	7	1	0
Gujarat	20	14	15

Source: Election Commission of India

The emergence of the Bharatiya Janata Party to become the second most popular party in the world's largest democracy, and the subsequent variation in the party's electoral popularity over space and time during the 1999-2009 timeframe pose important questions for understanding the factors underlying voter support for an ethnic party in a rapidly developing country. In the fall of 2010, I moved to India to explore this further.

In March 2011, in the city of Ahmedabad, Gujarat, I met Professor "P," a Public School Principal, who agreed to be interviewed about her political choices. I listened as Professor P explained why she voted for the Bharatiya Janata Party in the 1999, 2004 and 2009 national elections. The most important factor in her vote choice, she said, was her opinion that the Ram temple should be built at Ayodhya. She consistently voted for the BJP because of the party's advocacy for building the Ram temple.

A few days later, I interviewed Mr. "B," a mid-level clerk in a government office in Ahmedabad. Mr. B had also voted for the BJP in the past three national elections. In the 1999 election, Mr. B supported the BJP primarily because of its advocacy of *Hindutva*. He did not mince words in expressing his belief that the Congress party gives more attention and support to Muslims. However, in the 2004 election, he said that rising prices were becoming a bigger concern for him. While Mr. B continued to vote for the BJP in the 2004 and 2009 election, he noted that *Hindutva* had taken a back burner to programmatic concerns about rising prices.

Several months earlier, I had heard a somewhat similar story to Mr. B's from a voter in New Delhi. I interviewed Mr. "S," an owner of a magazine stand in an outdoor market. In the 1999 election, Mr. S was a strong supporter of the BJP and its leader, Atal Bihari Vajpayee. At that time, Mr. S recalled that seeing the Ram temple built was the most important political issue for him. However, in the following two national elections, Mr. S voted for the Congress party, noting that while the Ram temple was still important to him personally, it was no longer affecting his political choices. Economic growth had become the driving factor in his vote choice, and he felt that the Congress party would do a better job on this issue.

Mrs. "M" provided a quite different story from the previous three voters. Mrs. M is a highly skilled human resources professional working for a multinational company in New Delhi. In the 1999 election, she was a strong supporter of the BJP and its leadership under Vajpayee, based on her assessment that the party would be able to do better on policies relating to economic development and dealing with corruption. However, by the 2009 election, Mrs. M felt that the Congress party had performed well at the national level, and she switched her vote to the Congress in hopes that it would continue to deliver high levels of economic growth. Additionally, she expressed strong concerns that the BJP's advocacy of *Hindutva* could divide the country, noting, "We are a secular country and that's what it should be."

These examples of urban voters in New Delhi and Ahmedabad suggested that both ethnic interests, such as *Hindutva* and the Ram temple, and programmatic interests, such as economic growth and corruption, are critical factors for understanding urban voter support for the BJP. In addition, voters like Mr. S and Mr. B. also suggest variation in the political salience of ethnic and programmatic interests over time. This variation in urban electoral support for the BJP over space and time led me to ask the following research questions.

This chapter follows by introducing the research questions motivating this dissertation project and briefly discusses the literature informing these questions. I then discuss how these research questions contribute to the study of ethnicity and electoral politics, through expanding knowledge of the reasons why voters vote for an ethnic party in a rapidly developing country context like India. Next, I present my theory, Ethnically Mediated Retrospective Voting (ERV), which offers a framework for understanding the way in which both ethnic and programmatic interests factor into explaining voter support for an ethnic party, and the conditions under which each of these factors increase in salience in voters' political choices. I then outline the research design used to test the applicability of this theory to explain urban voter support for the BJP over space and time, and provide a summary of the research findings. I conclude with an outline of the following chapters.

Research Questions

In the study of ethnicity and electoral politics, scholars have highlighted the ways in which political elites use ethnic identity strategically for political gain. Early scholarship on ethnic politics and conflict highlighted the mechanism of ethnic outbidding, in which ethnic parties make increasingly more extreme ethnic appeals leading to polarization and political instability. In the context of India, Wilkinson's work posits the conditions under which politicians will support or prevent ethnic violence in order to win votes. Related research by Jaffrelot argues that the BJP's support for building the Ram temple was an instrumental use of ethnic mobilization for gaining Hindu votes.

This dissertation research project seeks to contribute to this research on ethnicity and electoral politics by focusing on voting behavior and the factors affecting voter support for an ethnic party, the Bharatiya Janata Party, in a rapidly developing country context. Recent research by Birnir on the nature of ethnic political participation argues that voters use ethnic identity strategically as a means of achieving ethnic group objectives, and that ethnicity can provide an information short-cut for voters' political choices. Birnir's research highlights that under certain institutional contexts, an ethnic party can serve as a means to promote peaceful and productive ethnic political participation. Related research by Chandra argues that voters in a patronage democracy choose a party that best represents their own ethnic category through conducting ethnic head counts.

Thus, we can posit that a voter such as Professor P, an urban upper caste Hindu in Ahmedabad, votes strategically for the BJP primarily based on the ethnic objective of electing the party most likely to support the construction of the Ram temple in Ayodhya. Likewise, we can posit that other Hindu voters I interviewed who indicated that they voted for the BJP because of the party's advocacy of *Hindutva,* or support for building the Ram temple, do so based on a strategic assessment that it is the party most likely to support and reward their ethnic group interests.

Yet, for some voters we find variation in the propensity to focus on ethnic interests when voting over time. The voting behavior of Mr. B in Ahmedabad and Mr. S in New Delhi are examples of urban voters who are strongly influenced by ethnic group identity and interests related to *Hindutva* or the Ram temple to vote for the BJP in the

1999 election, but are more influenced by programmatic interests when voting in later elections.

Specifically, in seeking to explain variation in voter support for the BJP, an important question to consider is the following: why is it that the bitterly disputed site of the Ram temple at Ayodhya, a critical rallying point in the BJP's Hindu nationalist mobilization strategy throughout the 1990s, appeared by the fall of 2010 with a landmark court decision dividing the site between Hindus and Muslims, to no longer evoke as intense *political* passion by the Indian electorate?[5]

This variation in the relative influence of ethnic interests in explaining voter support for an ethnic party suggests the need to examine the conditions which influence variation in the salience of ethnic group identity and interests upon voters' political choices.

In the literature on Indian politics, existing theories put forward to explain the surge in electoral support for the BJP tend to focus on either ethnic identity issues or programmatic issues. One predominant theory of electoral support for the BJP focuses primarily on ethnic/religious factors. This explanation posits that Hindus felt threatened by the changes taking place in the social and political order, and thus were attracted to the BJP's discourse of a unifying Hindu nationalist vision particularly through its advocacy of *Hindutva*. But this explanation has difficulty explaining why some voters vote for BJP for principally programmatic reasons.

---

[5] On September 30, 2010, after sixty years of litigation, the Allahabad High Court (state Supreme Court of Uttar Pradesh) ruled that the land at the disputed Ayodhya site would be divided between Hindus and Muslims. The entire country was put on high security alert before the verdict for fear that the ruling would spark nationwide Hindu-Muslim riots. However, there were no reports of riots or other major public acts of violence, and most notably, neither the Congress party nor the BJP publicly capitalized on the ruling. See "Land Divided, India United," *The Economic Times*, October 1, 2010, front page.

Two other explanations have focused primarily on programmatic factors to explain electoral support for the BJP. A second explanation argues that the BJP's electoral success in the late 1990s was the result of the party's economic position of a reduced role for the state in the economy. A third explanation focuses on issues of governance and corruption and argues that electoral support for the BJP, particularly from the emerging upper middle class, was primarily driven by concerns about corruption and a desire for more effective government. In contrast to the first explanation, these explanations have difficulty explaining why some voters vote for the BJP primarily for ethnic reasons. All of these three explanations of electoral support for the BJP have been applied in particular to explain middle class support for the BJP.

Each of these existing theoretical explanations focus primarily on either ethnic factors or programmatic factors to explain the upsurge in voter for support for the BJP in the 1990s, and do not address the subsequent variation in electoral popularity of the BJP over space and time. However, the examples of voting behavior in Ahmedabad and New Delhi indicate that some urban voters, such as Professor P, support an ethnic party such as the BJP primarily based on ethnic group identity and interests, while other urban voters, such as Mrs. M, vote for an ethnic party based primarily on programmatic interests.

These examples also suggest the need to examine the conditions which influence variation in the salience of programmatic issues upon voter's political choices, and the need for a theory of voting behavior that can account for the ways in which both ethnic and programmatic interests influence voter support for an ethnic party such as the BJP over space and time in a rapidly developing country like India.

From this discussion, three questions can be identified that guide this research project going forward. First, how do ethnic and programmatic interests influence voting behavior and help us understand variation in voter support for an ethnic party, such as the BJP? Second, what conditions increase the salience of ethnic interests in voters' political choices? Third, what conditions increase the salience of programmatic interests in voters' political choices? Next, I will address how focusing on these questions contributes to the study of ethnicity and electoral politics and why it is useful to study them in the context of Indian politics.

Research Contribution

The study of ethnicity and electoral politics has become a well-established field of inquiry. This literature has shown the ways in which ethnic parties can function as a stabilizing or a destabilizing presence to democratic politics. The literature has expanded our understanding of party behavior and the conditions under which politicians strategically support or prevent ethnic violence in order to win votes.

In the context of India, existing explanations of voting behavior either focus on the role of ethnic identity or performance on programmatic issues to explain voter support for an ethnic party. However, less attention has been paid to the way in which ethnic interests and programmatic interests influence voter support for an ethnic party, and the conditions under which each of these factors increase in salience in voters' political choices.

In developing and testing a theory of voting behavior which posits the conditions under which ethnic interests and programmatic interests influence voter support for an ethnic party, this dissertation broadens our understanding of voting behavior and the factors influencing voter support for an ethnic party in a rapidly developing country context

For nearly half a century, India has functioned as a patronage democracy. Yet, since the early 1990s, as the country undergoes major structural socio-economic change, India is also an example of a rapidly developing maturing democracy in which multiple political parties compete for votes.

A study focusing on voter support for the Bharatiya Janata Party, the only national ethnic party in India, offers a unique opportunity to undertake a structured comparison of voting behavior and voter support for an ethnic party over time and space in a rapidly developing country context.

Ethnically Mediated Retrospective Voting

To answer the above research questions, I put forward a theory, *Ethnically Mediated Retrospective Voting (ERV)*, which posits the conditions that influence the salience of ethnic interests and programmatic interests in voters' political choices in order to explain variation in voter support for an ethnic party such as the BJP.

ERV can be understood as a theory of retrospective voting which is adapted to explain voting behavior and voter support for an ethnic party in a rapidly developing country context, that seeks to account for the impact of 1) changes in the perceived level of ethnic group conflict, and 2) changes brought about by rapid economic growth and reforms, on voters' political choices.

I start with the assumption that in many poor countries, voters often sell their votes in exchange for access to state-provided material goods and services, such that the party-voter relationship is often based on an expectation of votes in return for patronage.

ERV first posits that under conditions of a heightened level of perceived ethnic group conflict, ethnic group identity and interests increase in salience for voters' political choices. Drawing from Karen Kaufmann's research on urban voting behavior in a developed country context, this claim is based on the idea that changes in the level of perceived ethnic group conflict have a corresponding influence on the political salience of ethnic group identity and interests.

Contextual factors, such as institutional environment, party program and campaign strategy, and socio-political history, can influence perceptions of ethnic conflict, which in turn increases in-group identification and cohesiveness. Drawing from Birnir, ethnic group identification is viewed as both fluid and as something that can be used strategically by voters as a means of achieving ethnic group objectives. This mechanism provides a means of explaining relative changes in the political salience of ethnic group identity and interests.

Second, ERV posits that under conditions of economic growth and reforms, an increasing number of voters can make programmatic demands on government and political leaders. This mechanism draws from Herbert Kitschelt's idea that structural changes associated with a strong political economy of development support programmatic voter-party linkage formation.[6] This mechanism focuses on the impact of structural changes resulting from rapid economic growth and economic reforms in a developing country context, which create the conditions for new opportunities and

---

[6] I use the phrase, the political economy of development, to refer to the structural changes associated with economic reform (such as changes in economic openness and the size of the public and private sectors) and economic development (such as changes in citizen income and level of affluence, etc.) in a developing country context. This term is defined in the theory chapter.

expectations by voters, which in turn creates the possibility for an increasing number of voters to make retrospective programmatic demands on government and political leaders.

Whereas poor citizens discount future rewards and rely on clientelistic exchanges, increasing levels of affluence and expanding economic opportunities put citizens in a position to be able to demand indirect collective goods, which in turn creates the opportunity for an increasing number of voters to make retrospective programmatic demands on government and political leaders.[7]

This mechanism provides a means of situating programmatic linkage formation between voters and parties in a developing country context historically characterized by clientelistic exchanges, and in turn, explaining the conditions under which an increasing number of voters could vote for an ethnic party based on programmatic interests, such as employment or economic growth.

With these two mechanisms, ERV conceptualizes the way in which changes in the level of ethnic conflict influences the political salience of ethnic group identity and interests, and changes in the level of economic growth and reforms influences programmatic voter-party linkage formation and increases retrospective programmatic demands on government and political leaders. In doing so, ERV provides a framework for explaining how *both* ethnic and programmatic interests influence voter support for an ethnic party, such as the BJP, in a rapidly developing country like India.

---

[7] I use the term, retrospective programmatic voting, to mean voting based on an assessment of incumbent performance as well as an assessment of future incumbent and opposition party performance on programmatic issues of concern. It is similar to Fiorina's definition of retrospective voting, but emphasizes the programmatic element of political exchange (i.e., indirect, based on a package of policy positions, etc.). This term is defined in the theory chapter.

Research Methods

In order to test ERV as a means of answering the research questions identified in this introduction, and its ability to explain variation in voter support for the BJP over space and time, this dissertation utilizes a mixed-methods research design strategy combining statistical analysis of national election data, with an investigation of case studies of individual voting behavior.

From a research design perspective, India's urban population, which has functioned as an engine of economic growth, provides a useful location to situate a comparative analytical study of the impact of socio-economic change on voting behavior and the factors affecting voter support for an ethnic party, such as the BJP, in the context of a rapidly developing country.

Using a most-similar research design, the large-N analysis focuses on comparing voting behavior in Delhi and Gujarat over three Lok Sabha (national) elections: 1999, 2004 and 2009. The states of Delhi and Gujarat share several commonalities, such as relatively large urban populations compared to the rest of India, and increasingly higher levels of economic growth. Additionally, Gujarat and Delhi have been dominated by a two-party system comprised of the Congress and the BJP, with very little influence from other regional political parties.

However, Delhi has experienced moderate to low levels of ethnic conflict, whereas Gujarat has had a recent history of severe violent ethnic conflict. Thus, while Gujarat and Delhi share some similar characteristics, the states diverge significantly in their experience of ethnic conflict.

The data used for the large-N analysis comes from the Indian National Election Study (NES) post-poll surveys for the 1999, 2004 and 2009 Lok Sabha elections. This dissertation benefits greatly from this relatively new and evolving collection of data on Indian voters' political preferences.

The second component of research for this project entails in-depth case studies of urban voters and their voting behavior in the cities of New Delhi, Delhi and Ahmedabad, Gujarat, two of the largest cities in India. Similar to Gujarat and Delhi, the cities of Ahmedabad and New Delhi share similar characteristics (i.e., a political landscape dominated by two-party system and increasingly higher levels of economic growth). Yet, Ahmedabad has experienced major episodes of Hindu-Muslim violent conflict during the 1999-2009 timeframe, whereas New Delhi did not. I conducted research on a total of 72 case studies, including 35 in-depth voter interviews in New Delhi, and 37 in-depth voter interviews in Ahmedabad.

By conducting in-depth case studies of urban voters in these two large cities, the research design seeks to generate a structured focused comparison of urban voting behavior and voter support for the BJP, which complements the large-N analysis of voting behavior in Delhi and Gujarat.

Research Findings

In this dissertation I posit the need to examine both the role of ethnic interests and programmatic interests to understand voter support for an ethnic party in a rapidly developing country context like India. Focusing only on ethnic interests or on programmatic interests only tells half of the story of the nature of voter support for an ethnic party, such as the Bharatiya Janata Party.

Ethnically Mediated Retrospective Voting hypothesizes that heightened levels of perceived ethnic group conflict in turn increases the salience of ethnic group identity and interests for voters' political choices. Second, ERV hypothesizes that under conditions of rapid economic growth and economic reform, an increasing number of voters are able to make retrospective programmatic demands on government and political leaders. This study tests ERV's ability to explain how ethnic and programmatic interests influence variation in urban voter support for the Bharatiya Janata Party over space and time.

The findings from the large-N research in Delhi and Gujarat provide support for these propositions and are corroborated from the case study research findings in Ahmedabad and in New Delhi. First, the research findings suggest that the condition of a high level of perceived ethnic conflict is associated with a heightened salience of ethnic group identity and interests in voters' political choices

During the 1999 national election, which was influenced by the Kargil conflict with Pakistan, and the BJP's decade long political mobilization strategy emphasizing *Hindutva* and building the Ram temple, the relative influence of ethnic interests on vote choice and explaining voter support for the BJP was markedly higher in both Gujarat and Delhi than compared to in the 2004 and 2009 elections.

In Gujarat, which has had a history of ethnic conflict between Hindus and Muslims, the relative influence of ethnic group identity and interests in explaining voter support for the BJP is comparatively higher than in Delhi, which has experienced low to moderate levels ethnic conflict between Muslims and Hindus.

Second, the research findings suggest that the condition of a strong political economy of development is associated with an increase in retrospective programmatic demands guiding voters' political choices. During the 2009 national election, in which both Gujarat and Delhi experienced a high political economy of development, the relative influence of retrospective programmatic interests on vote choice and explaining voter support for the BJP is higher in both Delhi and Gujarat compared to in the 1999 election.

In addition to finding evidence of the effects of ERV's individual propositions on voting behavior, the findings of voting behavior over time in Delhi and Gujarat provide evidence to support the proposition that ERV's combined mechanisms are able to explain changes in the relative influence of ethnic interests and programmatic interests on voting behavior and voter support for the BJP at the societal level under different socio-economic conditions

The findings from the case study analysis of individual voting behavior in New Delhi and Ahmedabad suggest that differences in an individual voter's assessment of the potential threat from ethnic group conflict and the reward from economic growth and development have a subsequent role in the relative influence of ethnic group identity and interests or retrospective programmatic interests on vote choice and explaining individual voter support for an ethnic party.

I identify four patterns of individual voting behavior, i.e., 1) Retrospective Programmatic Voting, 2) Weak Ethnic Voting, 3) Strong Ethnic Voting, and 4) Party Loyalty, to explain individual voter support for the BJP. These patterns of voting behavior illustrate differences in an individual voter's assessment of and relationship to ethnic group conflict and economic growth and development, which in turn result in differences in the relative influence of ethnic group identity and interests and retrospective programmatic interests on vote choice and explaining individual voter support for an ethnic party.

Chapter Summaries

This dissertation is comprised of seven chapters. Chapter Two introduces the Bharatiya Janata Party (BJP). This chapter provides a historical context of the creation of the BJP in 1980 and its rise to power over the following two decades. I include a discussion of the party's use of ethnic political mobilization strategies, particularly its actions to support the construction of the Ram temple, and its advocacy of *Hindutva*. This chapter provides a contextual background to study the nature of voter support for this ethnic party over space and time.

Chapter Three begins with an overview of the literature on ethnic politics, voting behavior and voter-party linkage mechanisms. The chapter outlines Ethnically Mediated Retrospective Voting theory (ERV) and develops scenarios for testing ERV as a means of explaining urban voter support for the BJP both at the societal level and at the level of the individual voter.

Chapter Four describes the research design and methodology used to test ERV. I start with a brief discussion about the use of mixed-methods in comparative politics research, and also highlight the recent interest in using surveys in the study of Indian politics. I introduce the "nested analysis" research design, describe the research plan for data collection and analysis of electoral survey data, including a description of the ethnic and programmatic indicators used in the large-N analysis, and describe the strategy for conducting structured and focused case studies of individual voting behavior.

In Chapter Five, I introduce the first case, which includes a large-N analysis of voting behavior at the state level in Delhi, and case study analysis of individual voters in New Delhi. The chapter begins with an overview of the political landscape in Delhi. Delhi represents a highly urbanized state, characterized by conditions of low to medium levels of ethnic conflict and very high levels of economic growth. Through an analysis of Indian National Election Study (NES) survey data of Delhi voters in the 1999, 2004 and 2009 national elections, and case study analysis of individual voters in New Delhi, I test ERV as a means of explaining variation in electoral support for the BJP.

Chapter Six presents the second case, which includes a large-N analysis of voting behavior at the state level in Gujarat, and case study analysis of individual voters in Ahmedabad. I begin with a discussion of the political context in Gujarat. Gujarat, like Delhi, is a highly urbanized state with increasingly higher levels of economic growth. However, unlike Delhi, Gujarat, and Ahmedabad in particular, is characterized by conditions of high levels of ethnic conflict. Through a similar analysis of NES survey data of Gujarati voters in the 1999, 2004 and 2009 national elections, and case study analysis of individual voters in Ahmedabad, I test ERV as a plausible means of explaining variation in electoral support for the BJP.

Chapter Seven provides a summary of this dissertation study and its main findings. I conclude with a discussion of the implications of these findings for the study of Indian electoral politics, and final thoughts for further research on voting behavior and the nature of voter support for ethnic parties in a developing country context.

Chapter 2. Setting the Context: The Rise of the Bharatiya Janata Party (BJP)

This chapter introduces the reader to the Bharatiya Janata Party in order to provide a historical context of the party's rise to power to become the second most popular party in India, and a springboard to study the nature of voter support for this ethnic party over space and time.

India's political system is governed by a constitutional commitment to secular democracy. For decades, democratic stability in India was often perceived in part as a by-product of the Congress party's long-standing dominant role in politics as a multi-ethnic party advocating for a secular social democracy and socio-economic development.[8] During the 1980s, however, the Congress party began to advance ethnic themes in its political discourse. Shortly thereafter, Indian electoral politics experienced the rise of the Bharatiya Janata Party (BJP), the first national rival to the Congress party.

Since the early 20th century, Hindu nationalism has constituted a social and political presence in India, with the creation of Hindu movements such as the Rashtriya Swayamsevak Sangh (RSS) in 1925. The first RSS leaders were deeply influenced by the ideas of Vinayak Damodar Savarkar, a contemporary of Nehru and Gandhi, whose vision of Indian national unity was expressed by the concept of *"Hindutva."* Savarkar identified three elements of *Hindutva* or "Hindu-ness", which included 1) a geographical area

---

[8] For many decades, the Indian National Congress was associated with Prime Minister Nehru's vision of building a modern India based on pluralist secular social democracy and technologically driven development (Misra, 1961; Imtiaz and Reifeld, 2002; Deshpande, 2002).

known historically as Hindustan, 2) a common blood, and 3) a common shared civilization or Sanskriti.[9]

Despite the historical presence of Hindu nationalist movements, Ashutosh Varshney notes that at no point before 1989 did a Hindu nationalist party receive more than ten percent of the national vote.[10] The Bharatiya Jana Sangh party (BJS or Jana Sangh), the precursor to the BJP, was created in 1951 and was deeply connected with the Hindu nationalist organization, RSS. The Jana Sangh party built its electoral support base from urban traders, shopkeepers, civil servants and the professional class. However, the Jana Sangh was never able to garner more than nine percent of the vote.[11]

In 1980, after a dismal electoral performance in the Lok Sabha election, leaders of the Jana Sangh created a new party, the Bharatiya Janata Party (BJP).[12] The BJP drew from the support base of its predecessor, the Jana Sangh, and was thus associated with the

---

[9] Savarkar was deeply opposed to Gandhi's attempts at Hindu-Muslim unity, and claimed that only those who could claim *Hindutva* have the moral-political right to constitute the nation. This view advanced the perception that Muslims in India were a religious community that constituted a threat to the stability and unity of the state. Nehru and other leaders of the Indian Nationalist Congress at the time considered the Hindu nationalist organizations both fascist and communal. See Andersen, Walter and Shridhar Damle, *The Brotherhood in Saffron: The Rashtriya Swayamsevak Sangh and Hindu Revivalism*. Boulder: Westview Press, 1987. Deshpande, Satish, *Contemporary India – A Sociological View*. New Delhi: Penguin Books India, 2003. Frankel, Francine, *India's Political Economy 1947-2004*, second edition. Oxford: Oxford University Press, 2005.

[10] Varshney, Ashutosh, "Contested Meanings: India's National Identity, Hindu Nationalism, and the Politics of Anxiety," *Daedalus*, 122(3), 1993, p. 232.

[11] Jaffrelot, Christophe, *The Hindu Nationalist Movement in India*. New York: Columbia University Press, 1996, pgs. 114-149 and Appendix D, "Performance of the Jana Sangh and the B.J.P in Lok Sabha Elections 1952 to 1991." The following background discussion draws in particular from Jaffrelot's comprehensive account of Hindu nationalism in India. See also, Frankel, Francine, *India's Political Economy*, pgs. 206 & 589.

[12] In response to Indira Gandhi's imposition of a National Emergency, a group of opposition parties, including the Jana Sangh formed to create the Janata Party. The Janata Party came to power briefly in 1977, but its diverse political interests, ranging from the Socialist Party to the Jana Sangh, ultimately made the Janata Party an unstable amalgam of political entities. See Jaffrelot, *The Hindu Nationalist Movement*, pgs. 282-313.

interests of traders, shopkeepers, professionals, and civil servants. This constituency disproportionately included *upper caste Hindus living in urban areas*.[13]

The creators of the new BJP initially wanted to distance the new party from the Hindu nationalist leanings of the Jana Sangh, and to focus instead on issues such as promoting a more decentralized economy and combating political corruption. However, this strategy was not electorally successful in expanding the party. Jaffrelot notes, "The [BJP's] tactic of openness, intended to make it…an alternative to Congress by virtue of a socio-economic 'people-oriented' programme, had not enabled it to enlarge its base."[14] In the 1984 national election, the BJP won only two parliamentary seats, receiving 7.4 percent of the national vote.[15]

While the newly created BJP initially aimed at a strategy of openness and moderation, Indian politics in the first half of the 1980s experienced a shift toward ethnic politics and ethnic social and political mobilization on multiple fronts. The early 1980s marked the revival of the Vishwa Hindu Parishad (i.e. World Hindu Council), a Hindu nationalist organization created in 1964 by the RSS. In 1981, the VHP and the RSS galvanized in response to perceived threats from proselytizing religions after a series of religious conversions of lower caste Hindus took place across India.[16] In the effort to

---

[13] Heath, Oliver, "Anatomy of BJP's Rise to Power: Social, Regional and Political Expansion in 1990s," *Economic & Political Weekly*, August 21-September 3, 1999, pgs. 2511-2517.
[14] Jaffrelot, *The Hindu Nationalist Movement*, pgs. 318. In the early 1980s, a small number of Muslim politicians joined the BJP in the state of Madhya Pradesh. Jaffrelot notes that the RSS was highly critical of the BJP for playing down its Hindu character, and did not like the party's efforts to attract Muslims. See pgs. 325 & 327.
[15] Ibid., pgs. 318-319.
[16] Ibid., p. 340. In February 1981, approximately 1000 lower caste Hindus were converted to Islam in Meenakshipuram, Tamil Nadu. The number of alleged religious conversions that took place at this time ranges widely from 2,000 to 22,000.

mobilize and unify Hindus, the VHP employed *yatras* (a religious pilgrimage to a holy site), and emphasized Hindu symbols such as water from the Ganges, or Hindu deities.

In 1984, the Dharma Sansad, the religious parliament of the VHP, passed a resolution to "liberate" the site at which Lord Ram was born in Ayodhya in the state of Uttar Pradesh, in order to construct a temple dedicated to the most revered Hindu deity.[17] According to local tradition, before the Muslim Mughal expansion into India, several Hindu temples existed in Ayodhya, of which the most important was a temple located at the birthplace of Ram. In the 16th century, a mosque was built at the site of the destroyed Hindu temple believed to be the birthplace of Ram.[18]

Several months after passing the Ram temple resolution, in September 1984, the VHP launched a procession through India to gather support for building the Ram temple in Ayodhya. The procession was both religious in nature, with a truck carrying statues of the Lord Ram and his wife, as well as political: members of the audience were asked to "give their vote only to those parties which explicitly promised to give the Hindus their sacred places back."[19]

During this time, the Congress party, under the leadership of Indira Gandhi, began to veer away from a secular political discourse and to advance and support ethnic themes in order to gain political advantage against rivals in several states, such as in Jammu and Kashmir, and Punjab.[20] The event commonly referred to as the "Shah Bano Affair," is

---

[17] Ibid., p. 363.

[18] Van Der Veer, Peter, "'God Must be Liberated!' A Hindu Liberation Movement in Ayodhya," *Modern Asian Studies*, 21(2), 1987, p. 285. The mosque was built by the first Mughal emperor, Babur, in 1527 after the destruction of an existing Hindu temple believed to be the birthplace of Lord Ram. Archeological excavation at the site has indicated the remains of a large Hindu complex.

[19] Van Der Veer, *"God Must be Liberated,"* pgs. 291 & 293.

[20] Ibid., p. 330. For example, Congress used Hindu themes to counter Farooq Abdullah's National conference in the 1983 state election in Jammu and Kashmir.

often considered the most blatant example of the Congress party's turn toward "communal" or identity-based politics.[21]

The Shah Bano affair took place a year after Indira Gandhi's assassination, when her son, Rajiv Gandhi assumed leadership of the Congress party. In 1985, Shah Bano, a divorced Muslim woman, sued her husband in order to obtain financial support from him.[22] Her husband in turn appealed to the Supreme Court on the grounds that under the Muslim customary law of *Iddat*, he was not required to continue financial support after a certain period of time designated by *Iddat*. The Supreme Court rejected the husband's appeal on the basis that Indian law related to alimony and financial support applied to all faiths.

In response to the Supreme Court's decision, several prominent Muslims petitioned Prime Minister Rajiv Gandhi to change the Indian law related to alimony, such that it would exempt Muslims. Following large demonstrations, Prime Minister Gandhi reversed the Supreme Court's decision and agreed that the Indian law would be amended. Subsequently, in early 1986, the Muslim Women (Protection of Rights on Divorce) Act was passed by parliament, which specified that divorced Muslim women would be provided maintenance (alimony) based on a period defined by Muslim customary law.[23] This political decision, arguably more than any other, instigated criticism of Congress as having a pro-Muslim bias.

---

[21] The term, communal politics, is often used in the context of Indian politics, and refers to politics based on religious-identity, particularly Hindu versus Muslim identity.

[22] Ibid., p. 334. Shah Bano invoked Section 125 of the Code of Criminal Procedure arguing that it established her right to maintenance (i.e., financial support).

[23] Full text of the bill is available at http://www.helplinelaw.com.

Yet, at about the same time, Congress appeared to yield to the Hindu nationalist Vishwa Hindu Parishad's demands to unlock the padlocks at the gate of the disputed Babri Masjid mosque in Ayodhya.[24] This allowed a new level of access to the disputed religious site, which had previously only been accessible once a year to a Hindu priest. Thus, Jaffrelot notes that in the first half of the 1980s, while the newly created Bharatiya Janata Party sought a "strategy of moderation at the price of distancing itself somewhat from the RSS...Congress opted to exploit religious identities."[25]

The second half of the 1980s, however, witnessed the BJP's move toward Hindu nationalist themes. Under pressure from the RSS and local party activists, and in response to poor electoral performance in the 1984 election, BJP party strategy shifted. In various speeches in 1986 and 1987, BJP president, L.K. Advani, spoke of the danger of "pseudo-secularism," a criticism of Congress actions, including the Shah Bano affair, and called for the imposition of a uniform civil code.[26]

In a decisive move, the BJP's National Executive Meeting in June 1989 adopted the "Palampur Resolution," in which the party formally embraced the "Ram Janmabhoomi movement" to build the Ram temple at Ayodhya.[27] Through this decision,

---

[24] Frankel notes that Rajiv Gandhi adopted Indira Gandhi's notion of secularism in the Indian context as giving equal recognition to all religions. However, his implementation was more tactical and lacking in foresight. After the Shah Bano affair, Rajiv Gandhi looked for a similar concession for Hindu nationalists. The Vishwa Hindu Parishad's petition to unlock the gates at the disputed site in Ayodhya was just such an opportunity. Later, Rajiv Gandhi tried to strike a bargain with the VHP that would both mollify Hindu nationalists while not alienating Muslims. In 1989, the central government and state government agreed to allow the VHP to carry out a foundation-laying ceremony for a Ram temple at a location near the disputed site if the organization agreed in turn not to proceed with a march to the Ayodhya site in relation to its *Ram Shilas Pujans* processions (see the following page). Frankel calls this an approach to communalism as a vote-getting strategy that was naïve and cynical. Frankel, *India's Political-Economy*, pgs. 684-685.

[25] Jaffrelot, p. 336.

[26] Ibid., p. 376.

[27] The Palampur Resolution, drafted by BJP leader L.K. Advani, was adopted at the BJP's National Executive meeting in Palampur, Himachal Pradesh in June 1989. The resolution commits the BJP to

the BJP became actively engaged with the Hindu nationalist RSS and VHP networks in a large-scale ethno-nationalist political mobilization strategy leading up to the 1989 national election.

As part of the Ram temple movement, the VHP's grassroots network mobilized thousands of religious processions throughout the country in the form of *Ram Shilas Pujans*. A *Ram Shilas Pujan* entailed offering prayer (puja) to a sacred brick with the name Ram (Ram Shilas) inscribed on it, combined with door-to-door fundraising efforts of approximately 1.25 rupees per household.[28]

Jaffrelot notes that these "rituals of mobilization" were also in effect "rituals of confrontation."[29] As a result, the *Ram Shilas Pujan* processions led to an outbreak of communal rioting in multiple locations in the months leading up to the 1989 national election. The Congress party lost the 1989 election to the National Front coalition. Although the BJP did not win the election, its electoral gains were significant: the party won 85 parliamentary seats and increased its vote share to 11.4 percent.[30]

The short-lived National Front coalition (December 1989 to March 1991) initially had the support of both the BJP and the Communist Party. However, this was before the National Front government made the highly controversial announcement in August 1990, that it would implement recommendations put forward a decade earlier by the Mandal Commission to expand the number of reserved seats for socio-economically

---

the *Hindutva* ideology and to supporting the Vishna Hindu Parishad's (VHP) movement to build a temple to the Hindu Deity, Ram, at Ayodhya. Ramakrishnan, Venkitesh, "The Hindutva Road," *Frontline*, 21(25), December 4-17, 2004. Bharatiya Janata Website, www.bjp.org.

[28] Chandhoke, Neera, "The Tragedy of Ayodhya," *Frontline*, 17(3), June 24-July 7, 2000. Jaffrelot, p. 373.

[29] Jaffrelot, pgs. 373 & 395. Jaffrelot in turn notes that he borrows this expression from N. Bhattarya.

[30] *Statistical Report on General Elections, 1989, to the Ninth Lok Sabha, Volume 1*, New Delhi: Election Commission of India, http://eci.nic.in/eci_main/statisticalreports/LS_1989/Vol_I_LS_89.pdf.

disadvantaged individuals in educational institutions and public sector jobs by twenty-seven percent.[31] The government's decision to implement Mandal sparked widespread violent protests across the country and dozens of protest-suicides by upper caste college students.[32]

A month after the Mandal decision, BJP leader, L.K. Advani, announced that he would undertake a *Rath Yatra* (a pilgrimage by chariot) on September 25, 1990 to mobilize support for constructing the Ram temple. The plan was for the religious procession to arrive in Ayodhya and inaugurate a *Kar Seva* (religious services). Advani drove across several Indian states in a van decorated as a chariot but was arrested on October 23 in the state of Bihar. Violence between Hindus and Muslims followed in the wake of Advani's *Rath Yatra*.[33] In response to Advani's arrest, the BJP withdrew its support from the National Front coalition, forcing national elections.

Less than a year after Advani's *Rath Yatra*, the BJP nearly doubled its voted share in the 1991 national election compared to the 1989 election, winning 20 percent of the vote and 120 Lok Sabha seats.[34] The Congress party, winning 35 percent of the vote, was able to form a stable government for a full five-year term. However, the Congress-led government's tenure was beset by a major economic crisis, corruption scandals, and bitter

---

[31] The Mandal Commission was created in 1979 to determine criteria for socially and educationally disadvantaged groups. Led by Bindheshwari Prasad Mandal, the Mandal Commission Report recommended expanding the number of reserved seats in public sector posts and educational institutions by twenty-seven percent for Other Backward Classes (OBCs). This proposed reservation for OBCs was in addition to reservations constitutionally recognized for Scheduled Castes (SCs) and Scheduled Tribes (STs). In effect, the recommendations by the Mandal Commission would raise the total number of reserved seats for SCs, STs and OBCs to forty-nine percent. See Ramaiah, A., "Identifying Other Backward Classes," *Economic and Political Weekly*, 27(23), June 6, 1992.

[32] Frankel, p. 689.

[33] Jaffrelot, pgs. 416-420.

[34] *Statistical Report on General Elections, 1991, to the Tenth Lok Sabha, Volume 1*, New Delhi: Election Commission of India, http://eci.nic.in/eci_main/StatisticalReports/LS_1991/VOL_I_91.pdf.

criticism that it did not take appropriate action to prevent the destruction of the Babri Mosque in Ayodhya, described below.

Facing an immediate economic crisis spurred by public debt pressure and critically low foreign exchange reserves, the Congress-led government in 1991 instituted comprehensive economic reforms to liberalize the economy. Despite earlier efforts, in particular by Rajiv Gandhi, to promote economic reforms, Prime Minister Narasimha Rao, with his Finance Minister, Dr. Manmohan Singh, was able to implement an integrated set of economic policies to transform the Indian economy on a path toward greater openness and sustained economic growth.[35]

The following year, in November 1992, BJP leader, L.K. Advani, announced that he would resume the *Rath Yatra*, which had not been completed due to his arrest in October 1990, in order to inaugurate religious services in Ayodhya. In taking this decision, the BJP effectively endorsed the VHP's goal of relaunching the *Kar Seva* in Ayodhya on December 6, 1992.[36] With L.K. Advani present, on December 6, 1992, thousands of *kar sevaks* broke through security into the disputed Ayodhya site and proceeded to demolish the Babri mosque.[37] Communal riots broke out throughout the country, with some of the worst violence in the cities of Bombay and Surat.

---

[35] As Prime Minister, Rajiv Gandhi promoted economic policies to reduce state control of Indian companies while reducing some tariffs. However, the reforms during the Prime Minister Rao's government were much more comprehensive. These economic reforms instituted a broad based transformation of India's planned economy, including dismantling much of the "License Raj" system of regulations for setting up a business, tax concessions, devaluing the rupee, removing import quotas, and reducing restrictions on foreign investment. Frankel, pgs. 587 & 591.

[36] Frankel, p. 713.

[37] Prime Minister Rao did not preemptively impose President's Rule until the evening of December 6, 1992. Jaffrelot quotes BJP leader, Atal Bihari Vajpayee, expressing the following day that the demolition of the Babri mosque was the "worst calculation" ever made by his party. Jaffrelot, pgs. 457 & 464.

In addition to criticism that the national government did not take effective actions to prevent the destruction of the Babri mosque, the remainder of Rao's government was deeply marred by major corruption scandals. The BJP also criticized the government's private sector policies initiated in the 1991 economic reforms, triggering a national debate about the nature and implementation of economic reforms. The BJP at the time signaled its commitment to *swadeshi* (economic self-reliance) to protect and promote Indian business in solidarity with the RSS's nationalist position on the economy. Once in power, however, BJP leadership under Atal Bihari Vajpayee would become more vocal in advocating economic reforms that promoted privatization and opening the economy to foreign direct investment.[38]

The BJP's 1996 national election manifesto promoted *swadeshi* (economic self-reliance), *suraksha* (security), *shuchita* (probity) and *samrasata* (social harmony), and highlighted *Hindutva* as, "the rainbow, which will bridge our present to our glorious past and pave the way for an equally glorious future."[39] The party won the greatest number of Lok Sabha seats in the 1996 election, increasing its share to 161. However, it could not maintain a stable majority, and as a result, the BJP's tenure was limited to 13 days.

After a series of short-lived coalition governments collapsed, new national elections were called for in 1998. The BJP continued to assert the principle of *Hindutva* and its commitment to building the Ram temple."[40] The 1998 BJP party manifesto also contrasted what it deemed the "phony liberalization," under the

---

[38] Frankel, p. 731.
[39] Bharatiya Janata Party, *1996 Election Manifesto*, 1996.
[40] *1998 Bharatiya Janata Party Election Manifesto*, available at the BJP website, www.bjp.org. The manifesto goes on to state, "The BJP is committed to facilitate the construction of a magnificent Shri Ram Mandir at Ram Janmasthan in Ayodhya where a makeshift temple already exists. Shri Ram lies at the core of Indian consciousness. The BJP will explore all consensual, legal and constitutional means to facilitate the construction of Shri Ram Mandir at Ayodhya," page 4.

Congress party, in which foreign companies flourish while Indian companies flounder, with its preferred *swadeshi* approach to economic policy making which emphasizes internal liberalization before globalization."[41] In the 1998 election, the BJP repeated its performance from 1996 and again won the greatest number of Lok Sabha seats, while increasing its vote share to 25.6 percent. The BJP-led National Democratic Alliance coalition ruled for 13 months.

In the run-up to the 1999 national election, the BJP campaigned on producing one year of economic growth, its handling of the Kargil Conflict, in which India forcefully repelled Pakistani militants who had infiltrated and occupied positions within the Indian-controlled section of Kashmir during the summer of 1999, and emphasizing the party's national homegrown political leadership under Atal Bihari Vajpayee, compared to the Congress party's "foreign" leadership under Sonia Gandhi, the Italian-born wife of Prime Minister Rajiv Gandhi.[42]

Although the common agenda for the BJP-led National Democratic Alliance (NDA) for the 1999 national election did not refer to the Ram temple issue as it had in the BJP's own 1998 election manifesto, it is important to note that the BJP itself did not reverse or back away from its 1989 Palampur Resolution, in which the party explicitly declared it would support the movement to build a Ram temple at Ayodhya. This time the BJP and its NDA coalition won a majority of Lok Sabha parliamentary seats and maintained a government for a full five-year term from 1999 to 2004.

Five years later, during the 2004 national elections, the BJP launched its "India Shining" campaign, using the slogan, "the feel good factor," and highlighting

---

[41] Ibid., p. 12.
[42] *1999 National Democratic Alliance (NDA) Election Manifesto*, www.bjp.org.

economic growth, during its tenure.⁴³⁴⁴ While the BJP did not actively emphasize the Ram temple issue or *Hindutva* in its campaign strategy, the party continued to affirm its positions on these issues in its "Vision Document 2004," located on the party's official website."⁴⁵

This time, the Congress party took the BJP head on and was deeply critical of the BJP's positions with regard to issues of cultural nationalism and social harmony. The 2004 Congress election manifesto charged that the BJP engages in a form of "inconsistent double-speak" with its support for the construction of the Hindu Ram Temple and the party's links with Hindu nationalist organizations on the one hand, and its talk of preserving secularism on the other. Perhaps most seriously, the Congress party charged the BJP with deliberately inciting communal carnage with regard to the massive Hindu-Muslim rioting that engulfed Gujarat in 2002.⁴⁶ Although the BJP was expected to win the 2004 election, its coalition lost 62 Lok Sabha seats, while the Congress-led UPA gained 89 seats and was able to create a stable majority.

After five years of Congress rule, the BJP's 2009 election platform espoused an agenda for change, focusing on the goals of good governance, development, and

---

⁴³ The Indian economy grew at 8 percent in 2003 and in 2004, though it was more sluggish the preceding three years, from 2000 to 2003, with GDP rates of 4.0, 5.2 and 3.7 percent. See World Bank, Development Indicators for India.

⁴⁴ Tripathi, Purnima, "Reworking Strategies," *Frontline*, 21(3), Jan. 31-Feb. 13, 2004.

⁴⁵ See, *2004 BJP Vision Document – 2004*, www.bjp.org. The party's Vision Document 2004 states, "We believe that Cultural Nationalism for which Indianness, Bharatiya and Hindutva are synonyms -- is the basis of our national identity." The vision document also states the party's reaffirmation to, "its commitment to the construction of a Ram temple in Ayodhya."

⁴⁶ The 2004 Congress Party election manifesto claims, "The BJP's "cultural nationalism is a device for dividing Indians emotionally. The Congress unites the Indian nation through consensus; the BJP divides the Indian nation through confrontation.... the BJP-led NDA government has damaged social harmony by deliberately inciting and sponsoring a communal carnage in Gujarat; by glorifying violence against missionaries; [and] by encouraging viciously communal and fascist organizations like the VHP/Bajrang Dal to spread hate," http://www.aicc.org.in.

security.[47] However, the party's formal issue agenda was significantly subsumed by political controversy during the campaign, by the remarks made by BJP political candidate, Varun Gandhi, grandson of Indira Gandhi.[48] During a campaign rally, Varun Gandhi was reported to claim that he would cut off the hand of any Muslim who threatened a Hindu.[49] India's powerful Election Commission of India urged the BJP to drop Varun Gandhi as a political candidate, but the party did not do so. The Election Commission initiated criminal charges against Varun Gandhi for inciting communal tensions.[50]

In refusing to take a strong stand against Varun Gandhi's threatening rhetoric, the BJP's action, or lack thereof, made it difficult to delink the party from its long-standing connection with ethno-nationalist political mobilization and ideology. The 2009 election results were decisive: the Congress-led UPA coalition added 44 seats to create a stable majority coalition for a second five-year term.

In summary, this chapter highlights the rise of the Bharatiya Janata Party in the 1990s to become the second most popular party in India to provide the historical political context for studying the nature of voter support for this ethnic party. As this chapter shows, a key aspect of the rise of the BJP in electoral politics in India is the party's use of an ethno-political mobilization strategy emphasizing issues such as constructing the Ram temple and a vision of Indian national unity expressed through the concept of *Hindutva*. In the following chapter, I discuss the role of the BJP's

---

[47] *2009 BJP Election Manifesto*, www.bjp.org.
[48] Varun Gandhi is the grandson of Indira Gandhi and the cousin of Rahul and Priyanka Gandhi. While the Gandhi family is primarily associated with the Congress Party, Varun Gandhi is affiliated with the BJP.
[49] "Case filed against Varun for inflammatory speech," *India Today*, March 17, 2009.
[50] Ibid. The BJP stated that Varun Gandhi should apologize for his remarks, but the party did not drop him as a candidate.

ethno-political mobilization strategy as one important factor influencing voter perceptions of ethnic group conflict.

Chapter 3: Ethnic Politics and Urban Voting Behavior in India

This chapter begins with an overview of the main themes in the scholarship on Indian electoral politics and voting behavior, followed by an analysis of the relevant literature on ethnic politics and voting behavior, retrospective voting, and voter-party linkage mechanisms. I then introduce the theory, Ethnically Mediated Retrospective Voting (ERV), and discuss its testable implications for explaining variation in urban voter support for the BJP over space and time.

Indian Electoral Politics and Voting Behavior

In the historical context of a politically dominant Congress system, scholarship on Indian electoral politics has often highlighted 1) the patronage-based nature of party politics, and 2) ethnic identity variables, such as caste or religion, to explain vote choice.[51] Scholars writing about Indian electoral politics in the 1950s and 1960s referred

---

[51] Weiner, Myron, ed. *State Politics in India.* Princeton: Princeton University Press, 1968. Weiner, Myron and John Osgood Field, eds. *Electoral Politics in the Indian States: Party Systems and Cleavages.* New Delhi: Manohar Book Service and Massachusetts Institute of Technology: 1975. Eldersveld, S.J., and Bashiruddin Ahmed, *Citizens and Politics: Mass Political Behavior in India.* Chicago: University of Chicago, 1978. Chhibber, Pradeep and John Petrocik, "The Puzzle of Indian Politics: Social Cleavages and the Indian Party System", *British Journal of Political Science*, 19(2), 1989. Malik, Yogendra and V.B. Singh, *Hindu Nationalists in India: The Rise of the Bharatiya Janata Party*. Boulder: Westview Press, 1994. Gould, Harold and Sumit Ganguly, eds. *India Votes - Alliance Politics and Minority Governments in the Ninth and Tenth General Elections*. Boulder: Westview Press, 1993. Hansen, Thomas Blom and Christophe Jaffrelot, eds. *The BJP and the Compulsion of Politics in India*. Oxford: Oxford University Press, 1998. Jaffrelot, Christophe, *The Hindu Nationalist Movement and Indian Politics*. New York: Columbia University Press and London: Hurst, 1996. Jaffrelot, Christophe, *India's Silent Revolution: The Rise of the Lower Castes in North India*. New York: Columbia University Press and London: Hurst, 2003. Shastri, Sandeep, K. C. Suri and Yogendra Yadav, eds. *Electoral Politics in Indian States: Lok Sabha Elections in 2004 and Beyond*. Delhi: Oxford University Press, 2009. Heath, Anthony and Roger Jeffery, eds. *Diversity and Change in Modern India: Economic, Social and Political Approaches*. London: Oxford University Press, 2010.

to the "machine model," in which politicians provide material rewards in exchange for votes, to describe the way in which political parties operate in the states of India. In the context of ethnic group concentration and ethnic group demands for autonomy and/or secession, some scholars suggested at the time that the machine model of politics was useful to reconcile competing ethnic interests and hold Indian states together.[52]

Kanchan Chandra characterizes India as a form of patronage democracy, which she defines as one in which 1) the state rather than the private sector monopolizes access to jobs and services, and 2) where elected officials have significant power in the allocation of jobs and services at the disposal of the state.[53] A primary motivation for voting in a patronage democracy is to secure access to state benefits (i.e., jobs, resources, services, etc).

In a similar vein, writing about historical voter-party linkages in India, Steve Wilkinson writes that nearly a decade before Indian independence in 1938, Congress leader Jawaharlal Nehru indicated his concerns to Mahatma Gandhi that the party under his leadership had succumbed to "Tammany Hall" politics.[54] The Congress party's singular control of the state administration and resources provided it with "enormous pools of patronage," writes Wilkinson, such that *clientelistic politics based on ethnic identifiers like religion or caste, underscored party-voter relations.*[55]

Yet, Ralph Meyer in the late 1980s hypothesized that many Indians vote retrospectively and that economic factors are an important factor in vote choice. At the

---

[52] Weiner, Myron, *The Politics of Scarcity*. Chicago: University of Chicago Press, 1962.
[53] Chandra, Kanchan, *Why Ethnic Parties Succeed: A Comparative Study of the Bahujan Samaj Party*, Doctoral Dissertation Harvard, 2000. P. 57.
[54] Wilkinson, Steven, "Explaining Changing Patterns of Party-Voter Linkages in India," in *Patrons, Clients and Policies – Patterns of Democratic Accountability and Political Competition*, Eds. Herbert Kitschelt and Steven Wilkinson. Cambridge: Cambridge University Press, 2007.
[55] Ibid., p. 110.

time, Meyer noted the lack of individual public opinion data in India to test this argument. Instead, using aggregate data, he compared changes in agricultural production and per capita net national product with electoral support for the incumbent party, and found that voters are politically sensitive to shifts in agricultural production. [56][57]

More recently, Rahul Verma argues that ethnic identifiers, such as caste and religion, alone are not adequate determinants of national electoral outcomes. Rather, using recent survey data from the Indian National Election Study, Verma highlights that voters assess government performance and work done at multiple levels (i.e., national, state and constituency), and that their decision to either punish or reward government performance based on this aggregate assessment of work done is the best predictor of the 2004 election outcomes.[58]

In investigating why many Dalit[59] voters did not vote for the incumbent Bahujan Samaj Party (BSP), an ethnic party that has typically done well with the Dalit community, in the 2012 State Assembly elections in Uttar Pradesh, Sanjay Kumar and Oliver Heath recently found that voter assessment of the party's ability to deliver on programmatic concerns, particularly related to development and corruption, was a

---

[56] Meyer, C. Ralph, "How Do Indians Vote?," *Asian Survey,* 29(12), 1989. Meyer, C. Ralph and David Malcolm, "Effects of Economic Change and New Party Formation," *Asian Survey* 33(3), 1993.

[57] Additionally, other notable scholars in the 1970s and 1980s analyzed and explained electoral success through the lens of policy and performance. For example, Myron Weiner highlighted the governments "excesses," referring to the national emergency and unpopular policies such as the sterilization program, as important factors in the defeat of the incumbent Congress party in the 1977 national elections. Weiner, Myron, *India at the Polls: The Parliamentary Elections of 1977.* Washington DC: American Enterprise Institute for Public Policy Research, 1977.

[58] Verma Rahul, "What Determines Electoral Outcomes in India? Caste, Class or Voters' Satisfaction with Government Performance," *Asian Survey,* 52(2), 2012.

[59] Dalit is the term used for untouchables. The Indian government recognizes them as scheduled castes, meaning those individuals who have been historically disadvantaged.

significant factor in explaining reduced Dalit voter support for the BSP.[60] In addition, the authors found that, while older Dalits were still more likely to vote for the BSP, Dalits with higher incomes, more education, and/or were living in urban areas, were significantly less likely to vote for the BSP.[61] The authors conclude that, while the Dalit identity continues to be an important factor in vote choice in Uttar Pradesh, performance assessment on programmatic issues relating to development and corruption were also key factors in explaining why many Dalits failed to support the BSP, suggesting evidence of a "public policy-oriented performance failure."[62]

Thus, while the study of Indian electoral politics and voting behavior has often focused on the patronage nature of electoral politics and on ethnic factors to explain voting behavior, recent access to empirical data of voting behavior has spurred research to examine the nature and degree to which voter assessment of party performance on programmatic concerns are also a factor in vote choice.

These differing views on how to understand and explain electoral politics and voting behavior in India, (i.e., predominantly through a focus on ethnic identity or a focus on performance on programmatic issues), broadly mirror the competing explanations for explaining the upsurge in voter support for the BJP in the 1990s, leading to their election to a full term in the 1999 election.

As noted in the introduction, one predominant explanation for the BJP's electoral success focuses on religious/ethnic factors, and posits that Hindus felt threatened by the changes taking place in the social and political order, and thus were attracted to the BJP's

---

[60] Heath, Oliver and Sanjay Kumar, "Why Did Dalits Desert the Bahujan Samaj Party in Uttar Pradesh," *Economic and Political Weekly*, July 14, 2012, p. 41.
[61] Ibid, pgs. 44 & 48.
[62] Ibid, p. 47.

discourse of a unifying Hindu nationalist vision particularly through its advocacy of *Hindutva*.[63] But this explanation has difficulty explaining why some voters voted for BJP for principally programmatic reasons.

Two other explanations have focused on non-ethnic factors to explain electoral support for the BJP. A second explanation argues against a focus primarily on religious/ethnic factors such as *Hindutva*, and highlights the role of economic factors, arguing that BJP supporters wanted a reduced role for the state in the economy.[64] However, this predominantly economic perspective has difficulty explaining why some voters identify ethnic identity factors, such as *Hindutva* or support for building the Ram temple, as a primary reason for voting for the BJP.

A third explanation focuses on issues of governance and corruption, and argues that electoral support for the BJP, in particular from the emerging upper middle class, was driven primarily by voters' attempts to support better governance, less corruption and for a more effective, coherent party.[65] However, this explanation too does not account for voters who identify ethnic interests as a primary factor in their support for the BJP. All of these three explanations of electoral support for the BJP have been applied in particular to explain middle class support for the BJP.

---

[63] Hansen, Thomas Blom, *The Saffron Wave: Democracy and Hindu Nationalism in Modern India*. Princeton: Princeton University Press, 1999. Fernandes, Leela and Patrick Heller, "Hegemonic Aspirations – New Middle Class Politics and India's Democracy in Comparative Perspective, *Critical Asian Studies* 38 (4), 2006.

[64] Chhibber, Pradeep, "Who Voted for the Bharatiya Janata Party?," *British Journal of Political Science* 27(4), 1997. Chhibber, Pradeep, *Democracy Without Associations: Transformation of the Party System and Social Cleavages in India*. Ann Arbor: University of Michigan Press, 1999.

[65] Jaffrelot, Christophe, *The Hindu Nationalist Movement in India*. New York: Columbia University Press, 1996. Jaffrelot's book provides a comprehensive account of the nature of the BJP's ethno-nationalist political mobilization strategy in the 1980s and 1990s. But he also notes that there was political support for the BJP, particularly from the upper middle classes, who stressed the benefits of economic liberalization and were attracted to the party for reasons other than ethnic issues, particularly concerns about political corruption and governance, pgs. 431-433.

Each of these theoretical explanations highlights either ethnic factors or programmatic factors to explain the upsurge in voter for support for the BJP in the 1990s and its election to a full term in the 1999 national election.

However, these theories are unable to explain why some voters vote for the BJP based primarily on ethnic appeals, such as the party's support for the construction of the Ram temple, while other voters vote for the BJP based primarily on programmatic appeals, such as concerns about economic development, or account for variation in the propensity of voters to emphasize either ethnic or programmatic appeals when voting for an ethnic party.

A noted exception is recent research by Tariq Thachil, who has sought to provide a comprehensive theoretical explanation for understanding variation in low-income voter support for the BJP. Thachil has recently offered a theory positing a services strategy mechanism as a distinct form of party-voter linkage, to explain poor voters' electoral support for the BJP.[66]

Thus, we are left without a theoretical framework for understanding the way in which ethnic and programmatic interests influence voter support for an ethnic party, and the conditions under which each of these factors increase in salience in voters' political choices.[67]

---

[66] Thachil, Tariq, "The Saffron Wave Meets The Silent Revolution: Why The Poor Vote For Hindu Nationalism In India." PhD Dissertation, Cornell University, 2009. Tariq Thachil, "Embedded Mobilization: Nonstate Service Provision as Electoral Strategy in India," *World Politics*, 63(3), 2011.

[67] In discussing the most recent 2009 national election outcome, Tariq Thachil posits the inadequacy of referring to identity politics or programmatic politics in absolute terms to explain Indian voting behavior. Rather, he suggests the need to look at the role of both caste-based politics and programmatic issues in analyzing Indian voting behavior. See Thachil, Tariq, "Do Policies Matter in Indian Elections?" *India In Transition*, April 26, 2010, at the Center for the Advanced Study of India website, http://casi.ssc.upenn.edu/iit/thachil.

Before turning to the literature on ethnic politics, retrospective voting, and voter-party linkages, I would like to address the reason why I chose to focus this research project on urban voting behavior in examining voter support for the BJP.

In a developing country context, economic development and urbanization are deeply interlinked, as urban areas often represent the focal point of socio-economic changes related to economic growth and development.[68]

As noted earlier, scholars have characterized India as a form of patronage democracy, in which a primary motivation for voting is to secure access to state benefits. Yet, over the past two decades, as the country has undergone major socio-economic structural change, India is also an example of a rapidly developing maturing democracy in which multiple ethnic parties compete for votes.

During this time, the urban population in India has continued to grow, increasing from 25.7 percent in 1991, to 31.1 percent of the total population in 2011.[69] In addition, India's urban population currently generates 60 percent of the country's GDP. One policy study estimates that by the year 2030, forty percent of Indians will live in urban areas, and will generate 70 percent of the country's GDP.[70]

---

[68] Davis James and J. Vernon Henderson, "Evidence on the political economy of the urbanization process," *Journal of Urban Economics*, 53(1), 2003.

[69] The Census of India defines an urban area as satisfying the following three criteria: i) a minimum population of 5,000; ii) at least 75 per cent of the male working population engaged in non-agricultural pursuits; and iii) a density of population of at least 400 person/sq. km. (1,000 person/sq. mile). See http://censusindia.gov.in/Metadata/Metada.htm.

[70] See, "India's urban awakening: Building inclusive cities, sustaining economic growth," *McKinsey Global Institute*, April 2010. According to the 2011 Census, India's urban population added 91 million people over the past ten years, growing from 286 million to 377 million people, representing an increase from 27.7 percent to 31.1 percent of the population. During the ten-year timeframe from 2001 to 2011, the annual urban growth rate was 2.76 percent, compared to the rural growth rate of 1.15 percent. Bhagat, R.B., "Emerging Pattern of Urbanisation in India," *Economic & Political Weekly*, August 20, 2011.

In spite of these dramatic socio-economic structural changes taking place, little research exists on the factors affecting urban voting behavior in India.[71] In this context, a research project focusing on voting behavior in India's expanding urban areas provides a unique lens for studying ethnic politics and voting behavior in a rapidly developing country context, and the ways in which ethnic and programmatic factors influence voter support for an ethnic party.

Review of Literature

ERV theory seeks to provide a theoretical framework for understanding voter support for an ethnic party such as the BJP, which takes into account both ethnic and programmatic factors in a developing country context. ERV theory is informed by three strands of literature: 1) ethnic politics and voting behavior, 2) retrospective voting, and 3) voter-party-linkage mechanisms. This section discusses the way in which each strand of literature provides critical insight in developing ERV.

Ethnic politics and voting behavior

Scholars hold differing views on the impact of ethnicity on electoral politics. In the book, *Ethnic Groups in Conflict*, Donald Horowitz notes that the main features of an ethnic party system can be summarized as the following: stable parties, unstable

---

[71] An earlier generation of scholars of Indian politics did examine aspects of urban politics focusing primarily on city politics and urban voting trends. One collection of articles on Indian city politics is included in the series, "Urban Politics in a Plural Society," *The Journal of Asian Studies*, 20(03), 1961. A second collection of articles on Indian urban politics is included in the series "Symposium on Indian Urban Politics," *Asian Survey*, 13(4), 1973. Rodney Jones focuses on the politics of Indore, Madhya Pradesh. See Jones, Rodney. *Urban Politics in India: Area, Power and Policy in a Penetrated System.* Berkeley: University of California Press, 1974. Myron Weiner and John Osgood Field examined urban voting trends in India from 1952 to 1972. See Weiner Myron and John Osgood Field, "India's Urban Constituencies," *Comparative Politics*, 8(2), 1976. However, this literature does not specifically focus on urban voting behavior and the factors affecting urban voters' political choices in India.

politics.[72] Because there is little relief from the ethnic character of politics, and because ethnicity is largely an ascriptive affiliation, "the ultimate issue in every election is, starkly put, ethnic inclusion or exclusion."[73] In particular, early scholarship on ethnic politics and conflict highlighted the mechanism of ethnic outbidding, in which ethnic parties make increasingly more extreme ethnic appeals that lead to political instability.[74] Sri Lanka presents an example of the way in which ethnic outbidding led to decades of ethnic violence and civil war.[75]

While some scholars have identified ethnic parties with political instability, more recent empirical research has identified the benefits and stabilizing influence of ethnic political participation in developing countries and maturing democracies.[76] In her book, *Why Ethnic Parties Succeed*, Kanchan Chandra theorizes that ethnic parties in a developing country such as India succeed in obtaining the support of members of their targeted ethnic group because in India's patronage-democracy characterized by severe information constraints, voters are inclined to favor co-ethnics at the polls by supporting the party with the greatest number of co-ethnics.[77] Within this structural context of a patronage democratic system characterized by severe information constraints, it is

---

[72] Horowitz, Donald, *Ethnic Groups in Conflict*. Berkeley: University of California Press, 1985, p. 101.
[73] Ibid, p. 348.
[74] Rabushka, Alvin and Kenneth Shepsle, *Politics in plural societies: A theory of democratic instability*. Columbus: Charles Merrill, 1972.
[75] DeVotta Neil, "From ethnic outbidding to ethnic conflict: the institutional bases for Sri Lanka's separatist war," *Nations and Nationalism* 11(1), 2005.
[76] For a formal model explaining the possibility of cooperation between ethnic groups, see Fearon and Laitin, "Explaining interethnic cooperation," *American Political Science Review*, 90(4), 1996
[77] Chandra, Kanchan, *Why Ethnic Parties Succeed: Patronage and Ethnic Head Counts in India*. Cambridge: Cambridge University Press, 2004.

strategically more efficient to exchange votes for patronage goods based on ethnically based "bloc voting."[78]

Comparative empirical research by Birnir shows that in new democracies, ethnic identity functions as a 'stable but flexible information shortcut for politics choices," and similar to Chandra's findings, ethnic identity is used strategically by voters as a means of achieving ethnic group objectives.[79] Birnir's research identifying nonviolent ethnic political participation in Bulgaria, Romania, and Spain, shows that ethnic groups can engage and compete peacefully in electoral politics.

The models by Chandra and Birnir provide new theoretical insights into ethnic political participation and the mechanisms linking ethnic identity and interests with vote choice. Birnir's model in particular can account for variation in an ethnic voter's political choices, (i.e. whether she votes for an ethnic party or a non-ethnic party), based on the representative capabilities of the ethnic and non-ethnic parties, and by ethnic issue salience.[80] Accordingly, her model shows that an ethnic voter could vote for a non-ethnic party in power if 1) she ascertains that the non-ethnic party has included the salient ethnic policy issue into its platform, or 2) the ethnic issue has decreased in importance, or no longer has political salience for the voter.[81] *Birnir's model provides a useful theoretical mechanism for explaining the way in which ethnicity is used strategically by voters, which in turn can account for variation in ethnic voters' political choices.*

---

[78] Chandra, 2000, pgs. 11-13.

[79] Birnir, Jóhanna Kristín, *Ethnicity and Electoral Politics*. Cambridge: Cambridge University Press, 2007, p. 9. Birnir uses the term ethnicity to refer to characteristics that are either impossible to change, such as color of skin, or very difficult to change, such as primary language. p. 4.

[80] Ibid, p. 51.

[81] Ibid, p. 52.

Many scholars of comparative politics have focused on why some social cleavages rather than others become politically salient. Lipset and Rokkan focus on the impact of historical conflict and change in influencing which social cleavages became politically salient over time and the basis for stable party systems to emerge in Western Europe.[82] Laitin identifies the impact of colonial rule to explain why religious divisions are not politicized while tribal divisions remain politically salient in Yoruba, Nigeria.[83] More recently, Posner identifies group size as a key factor to explain why certain ethnic group identities are politically salient in Malawi, but not in Zambia.[84]

Scholars of ethnic politics have also examined what institutional factors influence variation in the political salience of ethnic identity. In *Institutions and Ethnic Politics in Africa*, Daniel Posner's research on ethnic politics in Zambia shows that formal political institutions can have a profound impact on which ethnic cleavage becomes salient in voter's political choices.[85] More recently, using an experimental research design, Thad Dunning and Lauren Harrison show that an informal cultural institution called cousinage in Mali functions to decrease the salience of ethnic identity on vote choice in Mali.[86] This research shows how institutional context, both formal and informal, can impact the political salience of ethnicity on vote choice.

---

[82] Lipset, Seymour Martin and Stein Rokkan, *Party Systems and Voter Alignments: Cross-National Perspectives*. New York: The Free Press, 1967.

[83] Laitin, David, *Hegemony and Culture*. Chicago: University of Chicago Press, 1986.

[84] Posner, Daniel, "The Political Salience of Cultural Difference: Why Chewas and Tumbukas are Allies in Zambia and Adversaries in Malawi," *American Political Science Review*, 98(4), 2004.

[85] Posner, Daniel, *Institutions and Ethnic Politics in Africa*. Cambridge: Cambridge University Press, 2005.

[86] Dunning, Thad and Lauren Harrison, "Cross-Cutting Cleavages and Ethnic Voting: An Experimental Study of Cousinage in Mali," *American Political Science Review*, 104(01), 2010.

Yet, a question remains: how do we explain variation in the salience of ethnic identity and interests in voter's political choices over space and time across a similar institutional context? In the context of this research project, as noted in the introduction, we find variation in the propensity of voters to emphasize ethnic appeals over space and time. *What conditions influence variation in the political salience of ethnic group identity and interests over space and time?*

In the study of American voting behavior, scholarship on ethnic politics in the 1960s revealed the persistence of the role of ethnic voting in American politics.[87] In response to Robert Dahl's assimilation theory in *Who Governs,* which predicted that ethnic voting would decline as immigrants assimilated socially and economically, Wolfinger found that ethnic voting persisted despite changes in social assimilation.[88] Although the debate about the causes and persistence of ethnic voting subsided in the 1970s, more recent debates framed around the politics of race and religion indicate the important role social group identity continues to play in understanding American politics.[89]

Recent scholarship on social group identity and urban voting behavior in America has sought to explain under what conditions social group identity is salient to voter's political choices. In her recent book, *The Urban Voter*, Kaufmann examines changes in voting behavior in New York and Los Angeles, and shows that *the relative levels of perceived intergroup conflict are correlated with variation in the political salience of*

---

[87] Wolfinger, Raymond, "The Development and Persistence of Ethnic Voting," *American Political Science Review,* 59(4), 1965. Parenti, Michael, "Ethnic Politics and the Persistence of Ethnic Identification," *American Political Science Review,* 61(3) 1967.

[88] Dahl, Robert, *Who Governs?* New Haven: Yale University Press, 1961.

[89] Kaufmann, Karen, *The Urban Voter: Group Conflict and Mayoral Voting Behavior in American Cities.* Ann Arbor: The University of Michigan Press, 2004, pgs. 24 & 25.

group identity.[90] Higher levels of perceived intergroup conflict are associated with an increase in the political salience of social group identification, whereas in low levels of social group conflict, voting behavior is more apt to reflect considerations such as party identification and/or retrospective evaluations of an incumbent's performance.[91]

Informed by group conflict theory, Kaufmann's model is able to account for variation in the political salience of social group identity through its proposition that group identity and group cohesiveness are dynamic, and that intergroup conflict is conditioned by the perception of competition over symbolic and material resources between groups.[92] Group-based competition over symbolic or material resources in turn induces social conflict, which increases the political salience of social group identity and group distinctive voting.

Drawing from sociological research, which highlights the role that changes in the perception of group threat and competition play in influencing the level of group identification and group cohesiveness, Kaufmann's model defines conflict as salient group-based resentment resulting from heightened perceptions of intergroup competition. Kaufmann explains, "Under conditions where the candidates, the campaign rhetoric or the external political environment emphasizes competition over scarce, desirable resources, group members will likely exhibit higher levels of in-group identification and will in essence become more cohesive in the face of external competition to the values and valued resources of the group."[93]

---

[90] Ibid, p. 3.
[91] Ibid, p. 152.
[92] Ibid, p. 32.
[93] Ibid, pgs. 32& 33. See Bobo, Lawrence and Vincent Hutchings, "Perceptions of Racial Group Competition: Extending Blumer's Theory of Group Position to a Multiracial Context," *American*

Kaufmann discusses several important contextual factors which can influence the perception of group conflict at a given point in time, namely, 1) institutional factors, such as electoral rules and local form of government, 2) party program and campaign strategy, such as whether or not a party or candidate focuses on a particular group-specific agenda and 3) external factors, such as socio-political history or the local economy.[94]

In the context of India, the constitutionally created Election Commission of India (ECI) directly controls the election process for all national and state level elections, which includes establishing uniform electoral rules across all states. Thus, one feature of conducting a comparative analysis of political behavior across Indian states is a degree of institutional similarity relating to electoral rules as a result of the Indian election commission's powerful role overseeing the entire election process.

While Indian states share common electoral laws, the party systems of individual states do vary, ranging from two-party systems to multiparty systems.[95] In *Votes and Violence*, Steven Wilkinson identifies the conditions under which politicians protect minorities and act to prevent violence, and the conditions under which they do not act to prevent ethnic violence.[96] His research finds that the nature of party competition and the effective number of parties competing for votes at the town and state level play a pivotal role in determining the electoral incentives for preventing or allowing ethnic violence. While Wilkinson focuses primarily on the institutional elements of party system variation in India in explaining why Hindu-Muslim violence takes place, his model also

---

Sociological Review, 61(6), 1996. Bobo and Hutchings discuss a framework for understanding the formation of perceived group threat and competition.

[94] Ibid, pgs. 40 & 50.

[95] Chhibber, Pradeep and Irfan Nooruddin, "Do Party Systems Count? The Number of Parties and Government Performance in the Indian States," *Comparative Political Studies*, 37(02), 2004.

[96] Wilkinson, Steven, *Votes and Violence: Electoral Competition and Ethnic Riots in India*. Cambridge: Cambridge University Press, 2004.

underscores the functional role that social conflict plays in influencing the salience of social identity in voters' electoral choices.[98]

In the context of this dissertation project, the state party systems of Delhi and Gujarat are similar in that both states have two-party systems in which the Congress party and the BJP are the predominant parties competing for votes. While the state party systems are held constant for this dissertation, in the following discussion about party program, I identify the role of the BJP's ethno-political mobilization strategy as an important factor influencing perceptions of ethnic group conflict over time.

The BJP's political party program and campaign strategy related to Hindu-Muslim relations in India have varied over time. As discussed in Chapter Two, in the late 1980s and 1990s, the BJP engaged in a decade long ethno-political mobilization strategy focusing on support for building the Ram temple and advocating a vision of Indian unity through the concept of *Hindutva*. By 2009, the BJP's party program had formally shifted its focus to issues such as promoting good governance, development and security. However, the events surrounding Varun Gandhi's alleged claim that he would cut off the hand of any Muslim who threatened a Hindu, and the party's inaction to drop him as a political candidate, indicated that the BJP at the national level had somewhat, though not entirely, curtailed its relationship of allowing ethno-political mobilization relating to Hindu-Muslim relations. This variation in the BJP's party program involving ethno-political mobilization relating to Hindu-Muslim relations is an important contextual factor influencing perceptions of ethnic group conflict.

---

[98] Ibid, p. 4.

Socio-political factors related to historical Hindu-Muslim relations have also varied across space and time in India. In 1999, all of India experienced the threat of the Kargil war as Pakistan invaded India, putting stress on already fragile Hindu-Muslim relations. Ten years later, the country continued to experience incidents of terror, but not outright violent conflict or war with Pakistan. The socio-political context relating to Hindu-Muslim relations also varies considerably over space. For example, Delhi has had a history of low to medium conflict between Hindus and Muslims, whereas Gujarat has experienced several major episodes of violent ethnic conflict between Muslims and Hindus over the past forty years. This variation in the context of Hindu-Muslim relations across space and time is another important contextual factor influencing perceptions of ethnic group conflict.

Kaufmann's finding that voters' perceptions of intergroup conflict influence the political salience of social group interests, combined with Birnir's finding that ethnic identity is used strategically by voters as a means of achieving ethnic group objectives, suggests a potential mechanism to test, which links changes in the perceived level of ethnic group conflict to changes in the political salience of ethnic group identity and interests, as a means of explaining fluctuation in electoral support for an ethnic party, and variation in urban voter support for the BJP.

For example, during a high level of perceived ethnic group conflict, this mechanism would predict that voter support for an ethnic party, such as the BJP, would be influenced by a general heightened political salience of ethnic group identity and interests, such as a party's stated goal to support a particular ethnic group objective like building a Hindu temple. Yet, if conditions change and the perception of ethnic group conflict is reduced over time, we would expect ethnic group objectives to decrease in salience in voter's political choices.

Retrospective Voting and Voter-Party Linkages

An important question remains: How do we explain a voter who votes for an ethnic party for non-ethnic identity reasons and instead votes based on programmatic interests, such as economic growth, corruption, or employment? In the context of contemporary American politics, we might explain such voting behavior through a theory of retrospective voting. Accordingly, we could test the degree to which party choice is reflective of a voter's evaluation of party performance on policy outcomes and an assessment of future party performance.

Theories of retrospective voting view voters as having policy interests and a policy results orientation, and interprets swing voters as voters who change their votes based on rational political decisions.[99] While Key posits that voters focus on policy outcomes, Fiorina argues that citizens both monitor party promises and party performance on outcomes related to their particular policy interests, and also make an assessment of future incumbent and opposition party performance on policy outcomes, with vote choice representing a running tally of a voter's evaluation. Over time, retrospective voting predicts that these evaluations by voters of party performance on policy outcomes are reflected in party identification. Thus, this theory accounts for changes in party choice depending on the individual's assessment of party promises and performance on policy outcomes and future party performance. Retrospective voting has

---

[99] Fiorina, Morris, *Retrospective Voting in American National Elections*. New Haven: Yale University Press, 1981. Key, V.O., Jr., *The Responsible Electorate: Rationality in Presidential Voting, 1936-1960*. Cambridge: Belknap Press of Harvard University Press, 1966.

been applied and tested to voting behavior in countries including the United States, Canada, and Nordic countries.[100]

In the historical context of a socially based patronage democracy like India, how do we situate retrospective programmatic voting? Scholars studying voter-party linkages have posited that, just as certain conditions are favorable to patronage-based voting, other conditions can open up the door for programmatic appeals by voters.

From a comparative perspective, I believe we can gain some useful insight about changes in voting behavior and voter-party linkages by looking at how scholars have characterized the nature of American politics and voting behavior in the late 19th and early 20th centuries. In writing about the history of voter registration and voter turnout, Frances Fox Piven and Richard Cloward describe nineteenth-century politics in America as being organized by clientelist methods through party machines, and marked by ethnic and religious divisions.[101] In *City Politics*, Edward Banfield and James Wilson characterize a machine as a "party organization that depends crucially upon inducements that are both specific and material."[102] Cities such as Chicago and Philadelphia were the strongholds of party machines, while immigrants who were unfamiliar with American politics and institutions and lower-income groups were often their targets.[103]

Some scholars have compared the political characteristics of this era in American politics with contemporary conditions in many developing countries. Piven and Cloward

---

[100] Uslaner, Eric, "Looking Forward and Backward: Prospective and Retrospective Voting in the 1980 Federal Elections in Canada," *British Journal of Political Science*, 19(4), 1989. Söderlund, Peter, "Retrospective Voting and Electoral Volatility: A Nordic Perspective," *Scandinavian Political Studies*, 31(2), 2008.

[101] Piven, Frances Fox and Richard Cloward, *Why Americans Still Don't Vote and Why Politicians Want It That Way*. Boston: Beacon Press, 2000, pgs. 49-51.

[102] Banfield, Edward and James Q. Wilson, *City Politics*. Boston: Harvard University Press, 1963, p. 115.

[103] Piven and Cloward, p. 53; Banfield and Wilson, p. 118.

write, "And as in other developing countries, it was clientelist party organization that emerged to solve the problems of coordination and political integration. Clientelism appears to thrive in situations where formal enfranchisement precedes industrialization and the self-organization of the working class that industrialization makes possible."[104] Writing about the causes of corruption in developing countries, James Scott also draws parallels with the social and institutional context that fostered clientelism in 19th century American politics (i.e., strong influence of ethnic or social identity and weak formal political institutions) to the conditions in India and some Western African states.[105]

Scholars have pointed to the socio-economic changes brought about by industrial capitalism and the political reforms undertaken during the Progressive Era, as factors influencing the decline of the political machine in American politics. As incomes rose, more people moved above the poverty line, and public welfare programs extended, voters increasingly no longer depended on the material benefits provided by the machine, and *patronage increasingly became an insufficient method of organizing and a less effective linkage between parties and voters.*[106]

I have included this short background about late 19th and early 20th century American politics and the influence of party patronage and ethnic or religious identity during this era because I believe it provides an historical example of the way in which

---

[104] Piven and Cloward, p. 52.

[105] Scott, James, "Corruption, Machine Politics and Political Change," *The American Political Science Review*, 63(4), 1969, p. 1145.

[106] Burham, Walter Dean, "Party Systems and the Political Process," in *The American Party Systems: States of Political Development Second Edition*," Eds. William Nisbet Chambers and Walter Dean Burnham. New York: Oxford University Press, 1975. See also, Piven and Cloward, p. 69; Banfield and Wilson, pgs. 118 and 123. Banfield and Wilson write, "As one moves out from the river [the river wards being where the poorest live] and the railroad yards first into lower-middle class districts, then into middle-class ones, and finally (usually in the suburbs beyond the city proper) into upper-middle class territory, fewer and fewer precincts are manned and the ties to the machine become fewer and weaker until they cease to exist," p. 118.

some scholars have viewed the impact of structural socio-economic changes on political development (i.e. the move away from machine party politics) and on the linkages connecting parties to voters.

As the nature of American politics evolved and changed in the 20th century, scholars developed new theories to explain voting behavior beyond the machine, developing new schools of thought, most prominently the social-psychological approach, and the economic or rational choice approach, to the study of American voting behavior.

Recent scholarship in comparative politics has sought to conceptualize the different types of voter-party linkage mechanisms in democracies, and to provide the theoretical underpinnings for explaining linkage formation and change.[107] In *Linkages Between Citizens and Politicians in Democratic Polities*, Herbert Kitschelt outlines the conceptual differences between three types of voter-party linkage mechanisms (charismatic, clientelistic and programmatic) and presents several theoretical approaches for explaining voter-party linkage formation and change.[108]

Kitschelt, in particular, focuses on providing analytical distinctions between clientelistic (or patronage-based) and programmatic linkages, which are distinguished by different modes of political exchange (direct versus indirect), and the degree of policy

---

[107] It is relevant to note here that earlier modernization literature addressed a related issue of political development and the question of what social or economic changes promote different types of political organization and political participation. A classic example of this literature is Samuel Huntington's critique of modernization theory in *Political Order in Changing Societies*. New Haven: Yale University Press, 1968. While Huntington associates the early stages of modernization with corruption, he associates the latter stages of modernization with the potential for stronger political parties and partisanship. Huntington's analysis gives a macro-level account of the distinctions between economic and social development, and political development, and the importance of the latter on the nature of political organization and political participation, but it does not provide the micro-level foundations for explaining how voters in the context of a patronage democracy in transition would have the incentive to vote based on partisan or programmatic issues.

[108] Kitschelt, Herbert, "Linkages between Citizens and Politicians in Democratic Polities," *Comparative Political Studies*, 33(6-7), 2000.

preference identification and ranking (program formation). Among several theoretical approaches outlined in the article to explain voter-party linkage formation and change, *two approaches in particular, which focus on socioeconomic development and political economy, are particularly useful in situating programmatic voting in a developing country context, by highlighting the factors that create the conditions for programmatic appeals by voters.*

The socioeconomic development approach highlights factors such as changes in citizen income and education levels as key factors in explaining voter-party linkage formation and change. The micrologic of this approach is that poor citizens discount future rewards and must rely on clientelistic or patronage-based exchanges, whereas increasing levels of affluence put citizens in a position to be able to demand indirect collective goods. The political economy approach highlights structural changes such as trade exposure and the size of the public sector economy to explain linkage formation and change. The micrologic of this approach is that the size of the public sector economy impacts politicians' ability to employ public sector resources to build clientelistic linkages.

Together, these two approaches, socioeconomic development and political economy, can be useful in explaining how, as economic reforms and rapid economic growth in a developing country context create the conditions for rising incomes and a new range of economic opportunities not limited to the public sector, more citizens are in a position to make programmatic appeals and to vote based on a retrospective assessment of party programmatic performance.

Recent empirical studies suggest the relevance of these theoretical approaches in understanding changes in voter-party linkages in developing countries. In an empirical study of patronage and partisanship in the context of Argentine electoral politics, Calvo and Murillo find that low income/skilled workers are more sensitive to patronage spending than higher income/skilled workers, and that patronage in particular benefits parties with low-skilled constituencies. The authors posit that the changes produced from economic development on voter demand, including changing income and skill levels and distribution, and new employment alternatives, in turn affects the propensity of citizens to accept patronage in return for votes.[109]

Research on changes in political party behavior in Brazil identifies major state and market reforms of the 1990s as the key catalyst for explaining a shift away from patronage-based electoral strategies and toward a greater use of programmatic-based electoral strategies.[110] Hagopian et al. argue that the structural changes resulting from Brazil's state and market reforms have reduced the efficiency of patronage based electoral strategies (such as reducing the level of access to government spending for patronage), in turn, making programmatic elements of party competition more attractive. While the paper focuses on the changes taking place in the behavior of politicians, it does not explore the impact of Brazil's state and market reforms on voting behavior, and the possible changes in voters' evaluation and demands on political parties.

Of particular relevance for this study, in *Explaining Changing Patterns of Party-Voter Linkages in India*, Steven Wilkinson makes a similar argument based on changes in

---

[109] Calvo, Ernesto, and Maria Victoria Murillo, "Who Delivers? Partisan Clients in the Argentine Electoral Market," *American Journal of Political Science*, 48(4), October 2004.

[110] Hagopian, Frances, Carlos Gervasoni and Juan Andrews Moraes, "From Patronage to Program – The Emergence of Party-Oriented Legislators in Brazil," *Comparative Political Studies*, 42(3), 2009.

India's political economy and economic development, positing that India's economic reforms and rapid economic development have led to higher income and education levels, and growth and diversity in the private sector, which has opened up the door for the possibility of a decline in the usefulness of patronage, such as less reliance on state jobs or subsidies, and an increase in programmatic demands by voters.[111]

Wilkinson posits that demands for reform of clientelist politics and an increase in demand for programmatic party competition is not equal across India, and ranks Indian states according to the likelihood of demand for political reform based on economic, social and media indicators. *According to his analysis, the states of Delhi and Gujarat are among the states with the highest likelihood for political change away from clientelistic politics and toward programmatic appeals by voters, because these states have experienced high levels of economic growth, and have a comparatively high level of literacy and a large mass media audience.*[112]

The political economy and socioeconomic development theoretical approaches to explaining voter-party linkage formation and change outlined by Kitschelt and the recent empirical studies of the factors affecting voter-party linkage formation and change in developing counties such as Argentina, Brazil and India, *suggest a means of situating and contextualizing retrospective programmatic voting in India.*

These theoretical approaches to explaining voter-party linkage mechanisms and the factors affecting programmatic linkage formation suggest a second mechanism to

---

[111] Wilkinson, Steven, "Explaining Changing Patterns of Party-Voter Linkages in India," in *Patrons, Clients and Policies – Patterns of Democratic Accountability and Political Competition,*" Eds. Herbert Kitschelt and Steven Wilkinson. Cambridge: Cambridge University Press, 2007, p. 133.

[112] Wilkinson uses three indicators to rank Indian states by the likelihood that they will be open to political reform away from clientelistic politics and toward programmatic politics: 1: per capita net state domestic product, 2) literacy, and 3) media penetration, p. 139.

test, which links the changes resulting from economic growth and economic reforms to creating the conditions for an increasing number of voters to make retrospective programmatic appeals, as a means of explaining programmatic electoral support for ethnic parties, and variation in urban voter support for the BJP.

This second mechanism could potentially explain why a voter might vote for an ethnic party for non-ethnic reasons and instead vote based on retrospective programmatic interests such as employment, inflation or economic growth. For example, this mechanism could explain how a voter in one election votes for the BJP largely in support of the party's programmatic positions on the economy (or some other set of programmatic issues), and in a subsequent election, she may choose to continue to vote for the BJP, or she may punish the party and vote for another party, based on a retrospective evaluation of party performance on policy outcomes and an assessment of future party performance.

Ethnically Mediated Retrospective Voting Theory (ERV)

Drawing from theoretical ideas highlighted in this chapter on ethnicity and electoral politics, retrospective voting behavior, and voter-party linkage mechanisms, I present *Ethnically Mediated Retrospective Voting (ERV)*, a theoretical framework for understanding the way in which ethnic and programmatic interests influence voter support for an ethnic party, and explaining variation in urban voter support for the BJP.

ERV theory proposes two mechanisms which aim to explain the conditions under which 1) ethnic group identity and interests, and 2) retrospective programmatic interests, function to explain the BJP's rise to power and continued dominance from 1999 to 2009 in Gujarat, compared with the rise and fall of BJP dominance in Delhi over the same timeframe.

As noted in the introduction, ERV is a theory of retrospective voting which is adapted to explain voting behavior and voter support for an ethnic party in a developing country context, that seeks to account for the impact of 1) changes in the perceived level of ethnic group conflict, and 2) changes brought about by rapid economic growth and reform, on voters' political choices.

Before outlining ERV theory, it is useful to first define some key terms and clarify assumptions used in the following discussion and throughout the remainder of the dissertation. *Ethnicity and ethnic identity* are defined as a subset of identity categories in which eligibility for membership is determined by attributes associated with descent or descent-based attributes.[113] Drawing from constructivist arguments, ethnic identity and ethnic identification are conceived as fluid and may change over time.[114] Drawing from Kaufmann and group conflict theory, *ethnic group conflict* is defined as group-based resentment or friction resulting from perceptions of heightened group threat or competition between or among groups.[115] This definition views ethnic group conflict as a dynamic condition, which may change over time depending on contextual factors.

As noted in the introduction, an *ethnic party* is defined as a party that overtly represents itself as a champion of an ethnic group to the exclusion of others.[116] In India, key ethnic identities include Hindu versus Muslim, or upper-caste versus lower-caste.

---

[113] Chandra, Kanchan, "What is Ethnicity and Does it Matter?," *Annual Review of Political Science*, 9, 2006. Chandra reviews existing definitions of ethnic identity and highlights that descent is an important aspect of these earlier definitions.
[114] Birnir, 2007, p. 4.
[115] Kaufmann, pgs. 32 & 39.
[116] Chandra, 2004, p. 3.

The Bharatiya Janata Party is considered an ethnic party in the context of this dissertation research project. *Ethnic voting* refers to voting for a party that is identified with a voter's ethnic group or an ethnic group objective.[117]

Drawing from the literatures on American voting behavior and on voter-party linkage mechanisms, I use the term, *retrospective programmatic voting*, to mean voting based on an assessment of incumbent performance as well as an assessment of future incumbent and opposition party performance on programmatic issues of concern. It is similar to Fiorina's definition of retrospective voting, but emphasizes the programmatic element of political exchange (i.e., indirect, based on a package of policy positions, etc.).[118]

Informed by Kitschelt's research on voter-party linkage formation and change (i.e. the socioeconomic development and political economy approaches), I use the phrase, *the political economy of development*, to refer to the structural changes associated with economic reform (such as changes in economic openness and the size of the public sector) and economic development (such as changes in citizen income and level of affluence, etc.) in a developing country context.[119]

---

[117] Horowitz, *Ethnic Groups in Conflict*, pgs. 319-320. Horowitz identifies two definitions of ethnic voting. In the first definition, members of an ethnic group identify with a particular party. In the second definition, members of an ethnic group vote for a candidate belonging to the same ethnic group. For this dissertation I use ethnic voting to mean the former definition.

[118] One may reasonably ask why not just use the term, retrospective voting. In the literature on American voting behavior, retrospective voting refers to making an assessment of party performance on policy outcomes. In the Comparative Politics literature, programmatic politics and voter-party linkages refers to politics that are not based on patronage or ethnic group identity. Taking into consideration the different connotations of both terms, retrospective voting and programmatic politics, I use the term retrospective programmatic voting to mean voting that is neither based on patronage voter-party linkages, nor based on an assessment of performance on ethnic policy issues, but rather based on an assessment of performance on programmatic issues, which could include issues such as development, corruption, inflation, etc.

[119] Kitschelt, pgs. 856 & 862.

In addition to the above definitions, I make the assumption that *an Indian voter makes a vote choice in a way that best serves her particular objectives.* I assume that voters have political preferences that can be ordered, however, I do not assume that voters value the same sorts of things. This assumption has been characterized as instrumental rationality or a thin-rational account of human behavior.[120]

In presenting ERV theory, I will first describe each mechanism individually, and then show how these two mechanisms together create testable scenarios for explaining voting behavior and voter support for an ethnic party such as the BJP over space and time. The first mechanism posits that an increase in the perceived level of ethnic group conflict in turn creates the conditions for an increase in the political salience of ethnic group identity and interests. The second mechanism posits that changes resulting from economic reform and economic growth create the conditions for increasing retrospective programmatic demands by voters.

I start with the assumption that in many poor countries, voters often sell their votes in exchange for access to state-provided material goods and services, such that the party-voter relationship is often based on an expectation of votes in return for patronage. As discussed earlier, electoral politics in India have been characterized by patronage democratic linkages between parties and voters that has favored ethnic bloc voting.

ERV first posits that under conditions of heightened levels of perceived ethnic group conflict, ethnic group identity and interests increase in salience for voters' political choices.

---

[120] Green, Donald and Ian Shapiro, *Pathologies of Rational Choice Theory: A Critique of Applications in Political Science.* New Haven: Yale University Press, 1994.

This first mechanism is based on Kaufmann's idea that changes in the level of perceived ethnic group conflict have a corresponding influence on the political salience of ethnic group identity and interests.[121] As noted above, ethnic group conflict is understood as group-based resentment or friction resulting from perceptions of heightened group threat or competition between and among groups. Contextual factors, such as institutional environment, party program and campaign strategy, and socio-political history, can influence perceptions of ethnic conflict, which in turn increases in-group identification and cohesiveness. Drawing from Birnir, ethnic group identification is viewed as both fluid and as something that can be used strategically by voters as a means of achieving ethnic group objectives.[122] The following schemata outlines this mechanism, which links changes in the perceived level of ethnic group conflict with shifts in the political salience of ethnic group identity and interests on vote choice.

Figure 3.1 Ethnic Group Conflict and Shifts in the Political Salience of Ethnic Group Identity and Interests[123]

Factors influencing ethnic group conflict:	→	Changes in the perception of group threat or competition	→	Changes in the political salience of ethnic group identity and interests on vote choice
-Institutional factors		Change in in-group identification and group cohesiveness		-Ethnic identity (Hindu or Muslim) takes on greater/lesser degree of political importance
-External Factors: socio-political context				
-Party program, campaign strategy				-Ethnic interests (Ram Temple) take on greater/lesser degree of political importance

---

[121] Kaufmann, p. 39.

[122] Birnir, pgs. 9 & 50.

[123] It is important to note that this mechanism does not imply that in conditions of low ethnic conflict, the political salience of ethnic group identity and interests will completely disappear. Rather, the mechanism provides a means of explaining relative changes in the political salience of ethnic group identity and interests.

Based on this mechanism, I posit that changes in the perceived level of ethnic group conflict in Delhi and Gujarat correspond to shifts in the political salience of ethnic group identity and interests on urban voting behavior.

> *Hypothesis 1: All things being equal, urban electoral support for the BJP hinges upon changes in the perceived level of ethnic group conflict and the corresponding shifts in the political salience of ethnic group identity and interests on vote choice.*

H1 hypothesizes that variation in urban voter support for the BJP during the 1999-2009 timeframe can be explained by changes in the perceived level of ethnic group conflict between Hindus and Muslims, leading to corresponding shifts in the political salience of ethnic group identity and interests on voting behavior. In particular, voters in Delhi and Gujarat have had different experiences with regard to ethnic group conflict over the 1999 to 2009 timeframe. Both Delhi and Gujarat have experienced some common contextual factors, such as the BJP's ethno-political mobilization strategy focusing on a particular group specific agenda (i.e., Ram temple and *Hindutva*), and the Kargil War with Pakistan in 1999, which in turn heightened the perception of group threat in both locations, particularly during the 1999 election. However, other contextual factors, such as historical Hindu-Muslim relations in each state have varied considerably. Gujarat, and Ahmedabad in particular, has experienced several major episodes of large-scale violent ethnic group conflict over the past four decades, whereas Delhi has experienced low to medium levels of conflict between Hindus and Muslims. This variation in the context of Hindu-Muslim relations at the state level has influenced whether or not the perception of group threat has remained heightened or decreased over time. H1 posits that this variation in the perception of ethnic group conflict between Hindus and Muslims over time and space can explain the differences in the political salience of ethnic group identity and interests, and in turn, variation in electoral support for the BJP.

Second, ERV posits that under conditions of economic reform and rapid economic development, voters are inclined to approach political choices based on a retrospective assessment of party performance pertaining to programmatic issues.

This second mechanism is based on Kitschelt's idea that structural changes associated with a strong political economy of development support programmatic voter-party linkage formation and retrospective programmatic demands. This claim posits that economic development and economic reforms create the conditions for new opportunities and expectations by voters, which in turn creates the possibility for an increasing number of voters to make retrospective programmatic demands on government and political leaders. The following schemata outlines this mechanism, which links rapid economic development and economic reforms with an increase in retrospective programmatic demands by voters.

Figure 3.2 Political Economy of Development and Shifts in Retrospective Programmatic Demands by Voters

Economic Reforms and Economic Development	⟶	New opportunities to increase skills, income and education Growing size of private sector, Expansion of different types of Employment opportunities	⟶	Changes in voter demands on government and political leaders Voters are able to consider future indirect needs and rewards, and engage in programmatic assessment of party performance (i.e., consider public policies, public goods provisions, etc.)

Based on this mechanism, I posit that rapid economic reform and development in Delhi and Gujarat have created the conditions in which increasing numbers of voters are able to consider future indirect needs and rewards, and in turn to make retrospective programmatic demands when choosing government and political leaders.

> *Hypothesis 2: All things being equal, urban electoral support for the BJP hinges upon changes in the political economy of development and the corresponding shift in retrospective demands on party performance pertaining to programmatic issues and policies.*

H2 hypothesizes that variation in urban voter support for the BJP during the 1999-2009 timeframe can be explained by changes in the political economy of development, leading to shifts in retrospective programmatic demands by voters. In particular, Delhi and Gujarat have each experienced a high political economy of development in recent years. Delhi experienced high levels of economic growth during the entire 1999-2009 timeframe, while Gujarat experienced low economic growth in 1999, and increasingly higher levels of growth in the following years. H2 posits that the changes associated with a strong political economy of development can explain changes in retrospective programmatic demands by voters, and in turn variation in electoral support for the BJP. For voters living in conditions with an increasingly strong political economy of development, H2 predicts that retrospective programmatic interests are increasingly influential factors explaining voter support for the BJP.

How does ERV help us better understand voter support for an ethnic party such as the BJP? While political patronage in return for votes will likely continue in India into the future, in positing the conditions which increase the political salience of ethnic group identity and interests, ERV offers a mechanism for understanding variation in voter support for an ethnic party, based on shifts in the perceived level of ethnic group conflict.

Additionally, in providing a mechanism to explain programmatic voter-party linkage formation, which posits the conditions in which an increasing number of voters are able to make retrospective programmatic demands in a developing country context, ERV also offers a means to understand how voters may view and evaluate an ethnic party not only in terms of its promises to a particular ethnic group, but also in terms of the party's ability to deliver on non-ethnic (i.e., programmatic) issues, such as inflation, economic growth, public works, or corruption. Figure 3.3 illustrates the emerging voter-party linkages in India posited by ERV.

Figure 3.3 ERV: Theorizing Emerging Linkages between Voters and Parties in India

Historical Linkage between Voters and Parties in India	Mechanisms of Change	Emerging Linkages between Voters and Parties in India
1) *Socially-based Patronage voting* (voting in exchange for access to state resources along ethnic lines)	1) *Political Economy of Dev't* (creates new set of political and economic expectations)	1) Programmatic demands by voters: Retrospective programmatic voting
	2) *Shifts in Ethnic conflict* (creates changes in salience of ethnicity on vote choice)	2) Shifts in political salience of ethnic group identity and interests: Ethnic group identity voting

The left side of the table represents the historical voter-party linkage mechanism in which votes are given in exchange for access to state resources often along ethnic lines. The middle column represents ERV's mechanisms linking changes in the political economy of development with a new set of political and economic expectations such as demanding indirect collective (i.e. programmatic) goods rather than direct (i.e. patronage) goods, and shifts in ethnic conflict with changes in the political salience of ethnic group identity and interests. The right column postulates emerging linkages between voters and parties, suggesting a strengthening of retrospective programmatic voter-party linkages in India, particularly in areas experiencing a sustained high level of economic reform and development. The potential for voting based on ethnic group identity and interests does not go away, but is increasingly linked to shifts in the perceived level of ethnic group conflict.

Alternative Hypothesis

> *Hypothesis 3: All things being equal, urban electoral support for the BJP hinges upon changes in the level of religiosity of voters.*

Social cleavage theory is one predominant means of explaining voting patterns and party systems. Chhibber notes that Indian electoral politics have been studied through the lens of social cleavages, particularly caste or religion, to explain vote choice. This hypothesis tests the relevance of the cleavage related a voter's religious beliefs and degree of religiosity to explain urban voter support for the BJP.

ERV's Testable Implications

To illustrate ERV's theoretical propositions, the following table identifies four different predicted scenarios of patterns of voting behavior resulting from the combination of these two mechanisms. The vertical axis identifies and characterizes conditions based on the H1 mechanism (i.e. different levels of ethnic group conflict); the horizontal axis identifies and characterizes conditions based on the H2 mechanism (i.e. different levels of political economy of development). Each cell posits different generalized scenarios of the relative influence of ethnic and programmatic interests in explaining overall voter support for an ethnic party such as the BJP.

Table 3.1 ERV's predicted generalized scenarios of voting behavior and voter support for an ethnic party in different social and economic conditions

ERV Mechanisms: H1, H2	H2. Political Economy of Development: High	H2. Political Economy of Development: Low
H1. Ethnic Conflict: High	Scenario 1 i. Retrospective programmatic voting high ii. Political salience of ethnic group identity and interests on vote choice is high	Scenario 2 i. Limited retrospective programmatic voting ii. Political salience of ethnic group identity and interests on vote choice is high
H1. Ethnic Conflict: Low	Scenario 3 i. Retrospective programmatic voting high ii. Political salience of ethnic group identity and interests on vote choice is low	Scenario 4 i. Limited retrospective programmatic voting ii. Patronage-based voting high

Though the four scenarios of patterns of voting behavior are generalized ideal types, the above table is useful for positing the ways in which ERV's two mechanisms together predict the relative influence of ethnic and programmatic interests in explaining overall voter support for an ethnic party such as the BJP under different socio-economic conditions. To begin with, in conditions with little economic reform and low economic growth, and a low level of ethnic conflict, represented by scenario 4 in the lower right hand corner, many voters are expected to discount future rewards and rely more heavily on direct patronage-based exchanges. These conditions are reflective of the assumption that in many poor countries, many voters often sell their votes in exchange for access to state provided material goods and services. Patronage-based voting may have an ethnic component.

While some scholars such as Ralph Meyer and Myron Weiner have considered the role of retrospective voting and government policy in explaining electoral outcomes in India, scenario 4 represents the assumption by many scholars of Indian politics that electoral politics in India has historically been characterized by patronage-based democratic linkages between parties and voters (i.e., represented in the left-hand side of Figure 3.3). Kanchan Chandra's research on patronage and ethnic parties in India best addresses the predicted pattern of voting behavior in this scenario, and provides the most in-depth theoretical work explaining the historical patronage-based nature of Indian politics, and why voters may vote for an ethnic party in the context of a patronage democracy. In this scenario, voting behavior and voter support for an ethnic party is largely driven by the aim of securing access to state benefits.

Under conditions where the perceived level of ethnic conflict is high but the political economy of development is low, represented by scenario 2 in the upper right hand corner, ERV predicts an increase in the political salience of ethnic group identity and interests to explain voting behavior and voter support for an ethnic party, while retrospective programmatic interests are limited. In this scenario, the effect of H1 (i.e. a heightened political salience of ethnic group identity and interests) is posited to have a relatively greater influence than the effect of H2 (i.e. retrospective programmatic interests) on voting behavior and explaining voter support for an ethnic party. Under socio-economic conditions represented by scenario 2, we would expect that voting behavior and explaining voter support for the BJP would be strongly influenced by a heightened political salience of ethnic group identity and interests, while retrospective programmatic interests would be a less influential factor.

Alternatively, under conditions where the perceived level of ethnic conflict is low but the political economy of development is high, represented by scenario 3 in the lower left hand corner, ERV predicts that an increasing number of voters can make retrospective programmatic demands on government and political leaders to explain voting behavior and voter support for an ethnic party, while the political salience of ethnic group identity and interests is a less influential factor. In this scenario, the effect of H2 (i.e. retrospective programmatic interests) is posited to have a relatively greater influence than the effect of H1 (i.e. a heightened political salience of ethnic group identity and interests) on voting behavior and explaining voter support for an ethnic party. Under socio-economic conditions represented by scenario 3, with a low degree of ethnic conflict and a high political economy of development, we would expect that retrospective programmatic interests would play a strong role in explaining voting behavior and voter support for the BJP, while ethnic group identity and interests would be a less influential factor.

Finally, under conditions of a high level of political economy of development, and a high level of ethnic group conflict, represented by scenario 1 in the upper left hand corner, we would expect to find both retrospective programmatic interests and ethnic group identity and interests to be strong factors in explaining voting behavior and voter support for an ethnic party. In the previous two scenarios, one mechanism is posited to have a relatively greater influence than the other mechanism in explaining overall voter support for an ethnic party. However, in this scenario, both mechanisms are posited to have strong roles in explaining overall voter support for an ethnic party.

Scenarios 1, 2 and 3 hypothesize the ways in which the combination of ERV's two mechanisms under different socio-economic conditions predict different patterns in the relative influence of ethnic group identity and interests and retrospective programmatic interests on voting behavior and explaining overall voter support for an ethnic party. As these scenarios are ideal types representing the way in which different constellations of ethnic group interests and retrospective programmatic interests factor into explaining *overall* electoral support for an ethnic party, a key question to consider is if the combination of these mechanisms influences *individual* voters' political choices in different ways.

As noted earlier, I assume in this dissertation that an Indian voter makes a vote choice in a way that best serves her particular objectives. I assume that voters have political preferences that can be ordered, but I do not assume that voters value the same sorts of things. Thus, we may ask if some voters' political choices are generally more influenced by the risks (i.e., perception of group threat or competition) associated from the perception of ethnic group conflict than the rewards associated from economic reforms and development, while other voters are in general more influenced by the rewards of economic reforms and development than the threats associated from ethnic group conflict. *In other words, could differences in an individual voter's assessment of ethnic group conflict and economic reforms and development have a subsequent role in the relative influence of ethnic group identity and interests or retrospective programmatic interests on vote choice and explaining individual voter support for an ethnic party?* The following table posits four hypothesized types of individual voting behavior, which represent the impact of differences in a voter's perception of the in-group threat from ethnic group conflict and the rewards from economic reforms and development on vote choice.

Table 3.2 Scenarios of Individual Voting Behavior: based on differences in the way in which ERV's mechanisms impact individual vote choice

Individual Voting Behavior Type	Ethnic Conflict Perceived Group Threat	Economic Reforms and Development Perceived Reward	Impact on Vote Choice/Support for Ethnic Party
Type 1	Low	High	Predominantly influenced by programmatic interests
Type 2	High	Low	Predominantly influenced by ethnic identity interests
Type 3	High	High	When ethnic conflict heightened, ethnic interests override programmatic interests; when economic reforms and dev't increases, programmatic interests override ethnic interests
Type 4	Low	Low	Influenced by reward from patronage, or other interests

While table 3.1 posits four generalized scenarios of patterns of voting behavior, mapping the combination of ERV's two mechanisms under different socio-economic conditions with changes in the relative degree of influence of ethnic and programmatic interests in explaining overall voter support for an ethnic party, table 3.2 posits 4 types of individual voting behavior based on the different ways in which ERV's mechanisms impact individual vote choice. These four hypothesized types of individual voting behavior posit differences in an individual voter's assessment of the perceived risks and rewards from ethnic group conflict and from economic reforms and development, which in turn impact the relative influence of ethnic group identity and interests and retrospective programmatic interests on vote choice at the individual level and the reasons for voting for an ethnic party.

The first type of individual voting behavior, type 1, is characterized by a voter who perceives a high level of reward from the opportunities arising from economic reforms and development, and generally perceives a lower level of in-group threat from ethnic group conflict. For this type of voter, changes in the perception of group threat or competition is generally less likely to impact the individual's sense of in-group identification and result in the increase in the political salience of ethnic group identity. Rather, this voter is generally more influenced by the opportunities posed by economic reforms and development, and thus vote choice and the evaluation of an ethnic party is predominantly influenced by retrospective programmatic interests under scenarios of low ethnic conflict as well as high ethnic conflict.

Alternatively, the second type of individual voting behavior, type 2, is characterized by a voter who perceives a generally high level of risk of group threat or competition from ethnic conflict, and a comparatively lower level of reward arising from economic reforms and development. For this type of voter, the perception of group threat or competition is high, increasing an individual's sense of in-group identification and resulting in a general heightened political salience of ethnic group identity and interests.

As a result, this voter is quite sensitive to the perceived threat from ethnic group conflict (i.e., under scenarios with a high level of perceived ethnic conflict as well as a low level of perceived ethnic conflict), and thus vote choice and the evaluation of an ethnic party is predominantly influenced by a heighted political salience of ethnic group identity and interests.

The third type of individual voting behavior is characterized by a voter who perceives both a high level of risk from ethnic group conflict, *and* a high level of reward from economic reforms and development. For this voter, who is influenced by both the perceived risks of group threat or competition from ethnic conflict and the perceived opportunities posed by economic reforms and development, we can hypothesize that changes in socio-economic conditions in turn change the relative importance of ethnic group identity and interests and retrospective programmatic interests on vote choice and the factors affecting support for an ethnic party.

In conditions of a heightened level of perceived ethnic group conflict, such as in scenario 2 in table 3.1, the political salience of ethnic interests for this voter is likely to swamp out retrospective programmatic interests in explaining vote choice and voter support for an ethnic party. By contrast, in conditions of a high political economy of development such as in scenario 3 in table 3.1, retrospective programmatic interests are likely to swamp out ethnic group identity and interests in explaining vote choice and voter support for an ethnic party.

We can ask, what happens to this voter in conditions of a high level of ethnic conflict and a high political economy of development, represented in scenario 1 in table 3.1. Since this voter is influenced by both the perceived risks of ethnic group conflict and the rewards of economic reforms and development, I posit that it depends on what conditions changed that resulted in scenario 1, which in turn impacts the relative degree of influence of ethnic interests and programmatic interests on vote choice.

Thus, if a heightened level of perceived ethnic group conflict led to a change in conditions from scenario 3 to scenario 1, I posit that the political salience of ethnic group identity and interests is likely to swamp out retrospective programmatic interests in explaining vote choice and voter support for an ethnic party. However, if an increasingly high political economy of development led to a change in conditions from scenario 2 to scenario 1, I posit that retrospective programmatic interests are likely to swamp out ethnic interests in explaining vote choice and voter support for an ethnic party.

For this third type of voting behavior, the interaction of ERV's mechanisms under different socio-economic conditions changes the relative influence of ethnic group identity and interests and retrospective programmatic interests on individual vote choice, which in turn helps to explain in part relative changes in the overall level of influence of ethnic and programmatic interests in explaining voter support for an ethnic party.

Lastly, the fourth type of individual voting behavior is characterized by a voter who perceives both a low level of reward from economic reforms and development, as well as a low level of risk from ethnic group conflict. For this voter, I hypothesize that either patronage-based interests or some other type of interest influences vote choice and the decision to vote for an ethnic party.

In testing ERV as a means of explaining variation in urban voter support for the BJP, it is important to examine not only the impact of ERV's mechanisms on overall support for the BJP, but also the impact of these mechanisms on individual voting behavior. In the following chapter discussing research design and methodology, I put forward a research plan for examining the way in which ethnic and programmatic interests influence voter support for the BJP at the societal level, and also how these factors influence voting behavior and voter support for the BJP for the individual voter.

To test the implications of ERV theory for explaining variation in urban voter support for the BJP over space and time, I have created below a table which categorizes the social and economic conditions in Delhi and Gujarat by 1) the level of political economy of development, and 2) ethnic conflict relating to Hindu-Muslim relations, during the 1999, 2004 and 2009 national elections. Since no previous categorization exists for assigning levels of ethnic group conflict and the political economy of development for Indian states, I then discuss the rationale behind the metrics used for categorizing these two conditions in Delhi and Gujarat in the 1999, 2004 and 2009 elections.

Table 3.3 Levels of political economy of development and ethnic conflict in Delhi and Gujarat, 1999, 2004 and 2009 elections

National Election Year	Level of Political Economy of Development	Level of Ethnic Conflict
Delhi: 1999	High	Medium
Delhi: 2004	Very high	Medium-Low
Delhi: 2009	Very high	Low
Gujarat: 1999	Low	Very high
Gujarat: 2004	High	High
Gujarat: 2009	High	Medium

Source: Author's categories

Informed by Kitschelt's socioeconomic development approach and political economy approach to explaining programmatic voter-party linkage formation, I use three measures to categorize the level of political economy of development.[124] The socioeconomic development approach identifies rising levels of affluence as an important factor for explaining programmatic voter-party linkage formation. Based on this proposition, I use measures of state domestic product and state poverty levels as indicators of socioeconomic development.

The political economy approach highlights the size of the public sector and trade exposure (i.e. economic openness) as important factors influencing programmatic voter-party linkage formation. Economic openness is often measured from trade flows, FDI inflows and financial capital inflows. Though state level data of the size of the public sector and state trade flows are unavailable, some studies of statewide variation in FDI inflows over time in India do exist. Therefore, I use FDI inflows as a measure of economic openness. These three measures, 1) state domestic product, 2) state poverty levels, and 3) state wide variation in FDI inflows, provide an overall picture of changes in socioeconomic development and economic openness at the state level, which are used to categorize the level of political economy of development for each state during the 1999, 2004 and 2009 elections.

I use two measures to categorize the level of ethnic group conflict for each state: 1) the historical political context of ethnic relations, including riots resulting from Hindu-Muslim violence during the ten-year timeframe and 2) voter survey data from the 1999 and 2004 Indian National Election Studies about the perception of changes in relations between Hindus and Muslims. I draw in part from the Varshney Wilkinson Dataset on Hindu-Muslim Violence in India to assess the political context

---

[124] Kitschelt, pgs. 856 & 862.

of the degree of ethnic riots over time in each state.[125] Additionally, voter survey data from the Indian NES provides unique insight into voter perceptions about Hindu-Muslims relations, and whether these relations have improved or deteriorated. Using this combination of empirical data on ethnic conflict and data on voter perceptions of ethnic relations, I categorize the level of ethnic group conflict for each state during the 1999, 2004 and 2009 elections.

Political Economy of Development in Delhi

Delhi's economy is one of the largest in the country, and has experienced increasingly high levels of economic growth and openness from 1999 to 2009.[126] During this timeframe, Delhi's annual economic growth rates, measured in changes in the state domestic product, were robust and continued to increase, from 11.9 percent in 1999-2000, to 14.5 percent in 2004-2005, and 16.8 percent in 2008-2009.[127] From January 2000 to March 2009, Foreign Direct Investment (FDI) annual inflows into India grew by 1500 percent, increasing from US $2,155 million to US $33,613 million. Over this time, Delhi received 14 percent of the country's total FDI, the second highest amount after Mumbai.[128]

---

[125] "Varshney Wilkinson Dataset on Hindu-Muslim Violence in India, Version 2," Ashutosh Varshney and Steven Wilkinson, October 8, 1004, available at www.icpsr.umich.edu.

[126] According to the Planning Commission of India, as of 2011-2012, Delhi's contribution to the Gross Domestic Product is 313,934 in crores (1 crore equals ten million) rupees, approximately equal to a $ US 56 billion economy.

[127] Gross and net State Domestic Product is available from *The Reserve Bank of India's Handbook of Statistics on Indian Economy* published annually. Growth rates listed here are based on the annual change in net State Domestic Product using current prices: 1999-2000: 11.9 percent, 2004-2005: 14.5 percent, and 2008-2009: 16.8 percent. See Table 4, Net State Domestic Product at Factor Cost – State Wise at current prices,
http://www.rbi.org.in/scripts/AnnualPublications.aspx?head=Handbook%20of%20Statistics%20on%20Indian%20Economy.

[128] Foreign Direct Investment (FDI) is defined as cross-border investment made by a resident in one economy with the objective of establishing a lasting interest in an enterprise that resides in another

During this time, Delhi's services (tertiary) sector became the predominant sector in the economy, in conjunction with a decrease in the manufacturing (secondary) and the agriculture (primary) sectors. The following table lists changes in the sectoral composition of Delhi's Gross State Domestic Product over time.[129]

Table 3.4 Sectoral Composition of Delhi Economy: 1993-2009

Sector	1993-1994	1999-2000	2004-2005	2008-2009
Primary	3.85	1.40	1.09	.7
Secondary	25.20	18.32	18.45	16.78
Tertiary	70.95	80.28	80.46	82.52

Figures listed in percentage contribution to Gross State Domestic Product, at current prices

As Delhi's economy has expanded and opened, poverty levels have declined. Poverty levels in Delhi, which were 26 percent in 1983-1984, witnessed a significant decline to 14.6 percent in 1993-1995, and then to 10.2 percent in 2004-2005.[130]

These statistics suggest that as Delhi's economy has undergone a significant degree of expansion and opening from 1999 to 2009, the economic livelihood of its residents have improved with lower levels of poverty. *The overall picture in Delhi is a place in which the political economy of development has moved from a high to a very high category of political economy of development from 1999 to 2009.*

---

country. India's FDI inflows have increased from U.S. 2,155 million in 1999-2000, to U.S. 6,051 million in 2004-2005, to U.S. 33,613 million in 2008-2009. See "FDI in India and its Growth Linkages," http://dipp.nic.in/English/Publications/Reports/FDI_NCAER.pdf.

[129] Data on Delhi's sectoral composition is available from the following reports: 1) "Government of NCT of Delhi Estimates of State Domestic Product 2011-2012," *Directorate of Economics and Statistics*, and 2) "Economic Survey of Delhi 2005-2006," *Delhi Planning Department*. The primary sector is defined as comprising agriculture and livestock, forestry and logging, fishing, mining and quarrying. The secondary sector is defined as including manufacturing, electricity, gas and water supply, and construction. The tertiary sector is defined as comprised of the following: trade, hotels and restaurants; railways, transport by other means, storage, communication, banking and insurance, real estate, ownership of dwellings and businesses, legal services, public administration and other services.

[130] *Reserve Bank of India's Handbook of Statistics on Indian Economy*, Table 162: Number and Percentage of Population Below Poverty Line. The 2004-2005 poverty level is the most recent available.

Ethnic Conflict in Delhi

Unlike other parts of India, which have experienced major episodes of Hindu-Muslim violence, Delhi has generally maintained moderate to low levels of Hindu-Muslim conflict.[131] In recent history, from 1950 to 1995, Delhi experienced 33 Hindu-Muslim relating riots, and 93 deaths resulting from Hindu-Muslim violence.[132]

In 1999, Hindu-Muslim relations in Delhi and throughout the country were strained by the Kargil War with Pakistan, and by the BJP's decade long political mobilization strategy emphasizing the cultural nationalist notion of *Hindutva* and its advocacy of building the Hindu Ram temple. However, Delhi itself did not experience major ethnic violence.

Looking at voters' perceptions of Hindu-Muslim relations in Delhi during this time, we find that in the 1999 election survey, thirty percent of election survey respondents indicated that Hindu-Muslim relations had *not* improved, while forty-nine percent of survey respondents indicate that relations had improved. This political context of a heightened level of Hindu-Muslim tensions combined with a lack of local level ethnic violence suggests *a medium level of ethnic conflict in Delhi in 1999.*

Five years later in 2004, voters' perceptions of Hindu-Muslim relations in Delhi are more positive: while 14 percent of respondents indicated that Hindu-Muslim relations had deteriorated, thirty percent of respondents indicated that conditions had

---

[131] Although Delhi has experienced fewer incidents of violent Hindu-Muslim conflict compared to other locations in India, it is important to note that the area experienced severe anti-Sikh rioting beginning on October 31, 1984 after Prime Minister Indira Gandhi was assassinated by her Sikh bodyguards. I address this incident in chapter 5.
[132] Data on deaths resulting from Hindu-Muslim violence from, "Varshney Wilkinson Dataset on Hindu-Muslim Violence in India." See Varshney, Ashutosh. *Ethnic Conflict and Civic Life - Hindus and Muslims in India.* New Haven: Yale University Press, 2002, p. 105.

stayed the same, and forty-four percent indicated that conditions had improved. Delhi continued to experience negligible levels of Hindu-Muslim ethnic violence, *suggesting a medium-low level of ethnic conflict in Delhi in 2004.*[133]

Delhi continued to experience little Hindu-Muslim conflict in 2009, absent ethnic riots or violence. During the 2005-2009 timeframe, Delhi witnessed less than .2 deaths per million which were related to communal violence, statistically equal to less than 4 deaths from ethnic violence.[134] Although we do not have survey data on voter perceptions of Hindu-Muslim relations in 2009, the absence of ethnic riots or violence, *suggests a low level of ethnic conflict in Delhi in 2009.*

Political Economy of Development in Gujarat

Gujarat, like Delhi, is one of India's strongest economic regions, representing the sixth largest contributor to the country's gross domestic product.[135] For the past ten years, Gujarat has also been the fourth largest state recipient of foreign direct investment, receiving about six percent of the total FDI inflows into the country.[136]

---

[133] The 1999 and 2004 NES include a question regarding voter's assessment of Hindu-Muslim relations: 1) 1999 NES: Do you think Hindu-Muslim brotherhood has gone up, and 2) 2004 NES: Have conditions regarding Hindu-Muslim brotherhood improved or deteriorated, 1999 and 2004 NES survey questionnaires. In both surveys, a small percentage of respondents indicated "no opinion" for this question.

[134] Kumar, Rohit, "Communal Violence in India: 2011," Vital Stats Report available at *PRS Legislative Research* website, www.prsindia.org. The report indicates that from 2005-2009, Delhi witnessed less than .2 deaths per million, statistically equal to 3.3 deaths (based on a population of 16.7 million).

[135] See, Gross State Domestic Product at current prices data table, Government of India, Planning Commission, dated March 15, 2012, at http://planningcommission.nic.in/data/datatable/0904/tab_104.pdf. According to the Planning Commission of India, as of 2011-2012, Gujarat's contribution to the Gross Domestic Product is 513,173 in crores (1 crore equals ten million) rupees, approximately equal to $US 93 billion.

[136] The three highest recipients of FDI inflows are Mumbai (34.2 percent), Delhi (14.2 percent), and Karnataka (6.5) percent. See "FDI in India and its Growth Linkages," http://dipp.nic.in/English/Publications/Reports/FDI_NCAER.pdf.

Over the 1999-2009 timeframe, while Delhi's tertiary (services) sector became the predominant sector in the economy, Gujarat's economy has remained economically diversified, with a strong presence in various industries, including textiles, pharmaceuticals, cement, chemicals, petrochemicals, and fertilizer. The following table lists changes in the sectoral composition of Gujarat's Gross State Domestic Product over time.[137] The table shows that Gujarat's secondary (manufacturing) and tertiary (services) sectors each currently contribute about forty percent to the state's economic output, while its primary (agricultural) sector contributes the remaining twenty percent to the state economy.

Table 3.5 Sectoral Composition of Gujarat Economy: 1993-2009

Sector	1993-1994	1999-2000	2004-2005	2008-2009
Primary	25.5	18.6	18.4	19.8
Secondary	35.7	39.2	38.8	40.8
Tertiary	38.8	42.2	42.8	39.4

Figures listed in percentage contribution to Gross State Domestic Product, at current prices

During the 1990s, Gujarat was one of the few states to experience consistently high levels of economic growth in the eight percent range.[138] However, in 1999, after years of strong economic performance, Gujarat experienced a major economic downturn. In 1999-2000, the Gujarat economy contracted to less than one percent economic growth.[139] Production of commodities, metals and agricultural inputs,

---

[137] "Socio-Economic Review Gujarat State 2009-2010," Directorate of Economics and Statistics, Government of Gujarat, Gandhinagar, February 2010.

[138] Montel, Ahluwalia, "State Level Performance Under Economic Reforms in India," paper presented at the Centre for Research on Economic Development and Policy Reform Conference on Indian Economic Prospects: Advancing Policy Reform at Stanford University, May 2000. The state of Maharashtra is the only other state to maintain an average economic growth rate of 8 percent during this time.

[139] *The Reserve Bank of India's Handbook of Statistics on Indian Economy,* Table 4, Net State Domestic Product at Factor Cost – State Wise at current prices.

including sugar, salt, iron, steel and cement, all declined during this time.[140] This significantly contracted economy, coinciding with the 1999 national election, *suggests a time of low political economy of development for Gujarat.*

Five years later, during the 2004 national election, the economic landscape of Gujarat had greatly improved. In 2003, Gujarat's Chief Minister, Narendra Modi, initiated a new global investor's summit called "Vibrant Gujarat," in the effort to attract foreign investment to the state.[141] The state economy was now growing at a strong 8.9 percent.[142]

As Gujarat's economy expanded and opened, its poverty levels declined significantly. The state poverty level, which was nearly one-third (32.79 percent) of its population in 1983-84, and a quarter (24.2 percent) of its population in 1993-95, was reduced to 12.5 percent by 2004-2005.[143]

Thus, by 2004, the combination of a strong economic rebound, a major effort to induce outside foreign investment, and a pattern of decreasing poverty *suggests a high level of political economy of development in Gujarat.*

From 2004 to 2009, Gujarat continued to experience high levels of economic growth, reaching 11.8 percent during 2008-2009.[144] The Gujarat government under Chief Minister Modi continued to seek foreign investment through its biennial "Vibrant Gujarat" investor's summit.

---

[140] "Slowdown in the State? Blame it on the Global Recession," *Times of India*, August 18, 2001.
[141] See Vibrant Gujarat website at www.vibrantgujarat.com.
[142] *The Reserve Bank of India's Handbook of Statistics on Indian Economy*, Table 4, Net State Domestic Product at Factor Cost – State Wise at current prices.
[143] *Reserve Bank of India's Handbook of Statistics on Indian Economy*, Table 162: Number and Percentage of Population Below Poverty Line. The 2004-2005 poverty level is the most recent available.
[144] *The Reserve Bank of India's Handbook of Statistics on Indian Economy*, Table 4, Net State Domestic Product at Factor Cost – State Wise at current prices.

During the 2009 national election, Narendra Modi highlighted both the state's high level of economic growth, and his government's successful efforts to bring employment opportunities to the state, such as securing the relocation of the Nano car manufacturing plant to Gujarat, touted as the world's least expensive car aimed at India's emerging middle class.[145]

The 2009 economic conditions in Gujarat, characterized by double-digit growth, and a continued opening of the state's economy by actively pursuing global investment, *suggests a continuing high level of political economy of development in Gujarat.*

Ethnic conflict in Gujarat

Gujarat, and in particular its largest city Ahmedabad, has experienced over the past four decades some of the most deadly episodes of Hindu-Muslim conflict in India. From 1950 to 1995, Gujarat experienced 243 Hindu-Muslim riots.[146] As will be described in more detail in chapter 6, Gujarat has experienced several instances of large scale ethnic rioting in 1969, 1985-86, 1990, 1992, 1999, and most recently, in 2002. The political and social context of Gujarat can be described as *displaying a culture with multiple severe episodes of ethnic conflict.*

In the lead up to the 1999 election, Hindu-Muslim relations in Gujarat were significantly strained. The BJP's Hindu nationalist mobilization strategy during the 1990s was keenly felt in Gujarat. In 1990, BJP leader L.K. Advani began his famous mobilization effort to liberate the Hindu Ram temple from the city of Somnath in Gujarat,

---

[145] "In Gujarat, BJP rides the Nano," *The Indian Express,* April 8, 2009.
[146] Varshney Wilkinson Dataset on Hindu-Muslim Violence in India.

which caused ethnic rioting in the state. In 1992, when the Babri mosque was torn down at the disputed Ayodhya site, major rioting again broke out this time in the city of Surat in Southern Gujarat.

In late 1998, human rights groups reported instances of violence against Christians in Southern Gujarat. In the summer of 1999, Hindu-Muslim riots broke out in Ahmedabad during the Kargil War with Pakistan. In the 1999 national election survey, nearly forty percent of respondents from Gujarat responded that Hindu-Muslim relations had not improved, while twenty-seven percent of respondents indicated that relations had improved.[147] This political context of high level of ethnic tensions and local level ethnic violence *suggests a very high level of ethnic conflict in Gujarat in 1999.*[148]

While the state experienced one of the worst episodes of Hindu-Muslim rioting and violence in 2002 during the same year as the state assembly elections, the lead up to the 2004 national election was notably absent of ethnic conflict. One scholar of Gujarati politics called the 2004 national election the first somewhat "conventional" election that the BJP contested in the state, absent ethnic rioting and with less direct influence of Hindu nationalist organizations in the election.[149]

However, voter's perceptions of Hindu-Muslim relations in Gujarat in 2004 were still quite weak: forty-one percent of survey respondents said that Hindu-Muslim relations had deteriorated, twenty percent of respondents indicated that relations had stayed the same, and only twenty-six percent of respondents indicated that relations

---

[147] Response from 1999 NES survey question: "Do you think Hindu-Muslim brotherhood has gone up?"
[148] Patel, Priyavadan, "Gujarat – Anti-incumbency Begins," *Economic & Political Weekly*, December 18, 2004. Patel characterizes the period from February 1998 to December 2002 as a time marked by "the dominance of hardline Hindutva" by the BJP in Gujarat using ethno-political mobilization and polarization for electoral gains.
[149] Ibid, p. 5475.

had improved.[150] This political context of a continued heightened level of Hindu-Muslim tension despite little ethnic violence *suggests a high level of ethnic conflict in Gujarat in 2004.*

In the run-up to the 2009 national election, Gujarat did not experience episodes of major ethnic violence. Although we do not have national election survey data on voter perceptions of Hindu-Muslim relations for 2009, as part of my own data collection for the in-depth case studies, I asked voters in the survey administered in Ahmedabad if they agreed or disagreed with the opinion that it was time for Gujarat to move forward with regard to the violence in 2002. Although the sample size is small, about one quarter (24 percent) of voters interviewed responded that they disagreed that it was possible to move forward from the 2002 riots. Despite a lack of ethnic violence, the continued presence of ethnic tensions *suggests a medium level of ethnic conflict in Gujarat in 2009.* [151]

ERV's predictions to explain urban voter support for the BJP

Based on the above categorizations of the level of political economy of development and the level of ethnic conflict in Delhi and Gujarat, ERV predicts the following scenarios of voting behavior and the influence of ethnic and programmatic interests in explaining overall voter support for an ethnic party such as the BJP.

---

[150] Response from the 2004 NES survey question: "Have conditions regarding Hindu-Muslim brotherhood improved or deteriorated?"

[151] The survey questionnaire asked Ahmedabad voters the following question: You may have heard the recent remarks by Darul Uloom vice-chancellor, Maulana Ghulam Mohammed Vastenvi, who said that eight years has passed since the violence in 2002 and that it was time for Gujarat to move forward. Do you agree or disagree with this opinion/sentiment?

ERV's predictions for Delhi and New Delhi

1. In 1999, with Delhi experiencing a medium level of ethnic conflict and a high level of political economy of development, ERV predicts that voter support for the BJP is the result of both a heightened political salience of ethnic group identity and interests and strong retrospective programmatic interests by voters, best represented by scenario 1.

2. In 2004, as the political economy of development continued to strengthen while ethnic conflict decreased markedly in Delhi, ERV predicts an increasing influence of retrospective programmatic interests combined with a decrease in the political salience of ethnic group identity and interests to explain voter support for the BJP in the 2004 elections, best represented by scenario 3.

3. In 2009, with economic growth in the double digits and continued very low levels of ethnic polarization in Delhi, ERV again predicts an increasing influence of retrospective programmatic interests combined with continued decrease in the political salience of ethnic group identity and interests to explain voter support for the BJP in the 2009 election, best represented by scenario 3.

In summary, ERV predicts that variation in voter support for the BJP in Delhi over the 1999 to 2009 timeframe can be explained by shifts in voting behavior approximately represented by a shift from scenario 1 to scenario 3.

ERV's predictions for Gujarat and Ahmedabad

1. By comparison, in Gujarat in 1999, with a very high level of ethnic conflict and a low political economy of development, ERV predicts that voter support for the BJP in the 1999 election is strongly influenced by ethnic group identity and interests and less influenced by retrospective programmatic interests, best represented by scenario 2.

2. In 2004, with an increasingly robust political economy of development and a high level of ethnic conflict in Gujarat, ERV predicts a stronger influence of retrospective programmatic interests combined with a strong, though less extreme, influence in the political salience of ethnic group identity and interests, to explain voter support for the BJP in the 2004 election, best represented by scenario 1.

3. In 2009, with Gujarat experiencing a high political economy of development and a moderate level of ethnic conflict, ERV predicts a continued strong influence in retrospective programmatic interests combined with a slightly more moderate influence of ethnic group identity and interests to explain voter support for the BJP in the 2009 election, best represented by scenario 1.

In summary, ERV predicts that variation in voter support for the BJP in Gujarat over the 1999 to 2009 timeframe can be explained by shifts in voting behavior approximately represented by a shift from scenario 2 to scenario 1.

Chapter 4: Research Design and Methodology

This chapter presents the research design and methodology for testing ERV theory as a means of explaining variation in voter support for the Bharatiya Janata Party in the 1999, 2004 and 2009 national elections in two highly urbanized locations. This dissertation research project employs a mixed-methods research design strategy combining statistical analysis and case studies.[152] The research design and methodology employed for this study is based on the goal of making inferences about voting behavior and explaining urban voter support for an ethnic party in a rapidly developing country context.

The chapter begins by providing a brief backdrop of the recent evolution in thinking about research design and methodology in comparative politics and the study of Indian politics, to contextualize the use of a mixed-methods research design for this project, followed by a detailed description of the design, methods, and data used for this study.

In choosing to implement a mixed-methods research design, it is informative to recall that the field of comparative politics once experienced a vigorous debate over the merits of qualitative versus quantitative research methodology. In 1994, Gary King, Robert Keohane and Sidney Verba published *Designing Social Inquiry*, (DSI) which sought to bring a unified logic – the goal of making inferences from the particular to

---

[152] The dissertation research was approved by the University of Maryland's Institutional Review Board (IRB), on September 9, 2010. IRB Protocol 10-0497.

something more generalizable that is not directly observed – to both qualitative and quantitative research methods in social science.[153] DSI ushered in multiple waves of debate and research about the process of designing and conducting research, which has arguably forced researchers to be more rigorous in their thinking about research design and methodology.

Shortly after the publication of DSI, scholars explored and identified the merits and challenges of using multiple research methodologies to study particular research areas, such as the study of democratic peace.[154] In 2000, David Laitin, in *Comparative Politics: The State of the Subdiscipline*, suggested that a new consensus in comparative politics had emerged which both accepts and promotes the use of statistical, formal and narrative (case study) research methods.[155]

Recent research on the range of research methods used in comparative politics suggests a growing place for the use of research using mixed-methodology. For example, Gerardo Munck and Richard Snyder analyzed published articles from three leading

---

[153] King, Gary, Robert Keohane and Sidney Verba, *Designing Social Inquiry: Scientific Inference in Qualitative Research*. Princeton: Princeton University Press, 2004, p. 8. Following the publication of DSI in 1994, the American Political Science Association's Comparative Politics Newsletter became a forum for debate over several years about the direction of the Comparative Politics field, the similarities and differences between qualitative and quantitative research approaches, and also whether or not it is possible for social sciences to be scientific. See *Comparative Politics Newsletter*, 7(1), Winter 1996. For the viewpoint that it is a misguided endeavor for social sciences to focus on generating scientific knowledge or developing theory, see Bent Flyvbjerg, *Making Social Science Matter – why social inquiry fails and how it can succeed again*. Cambridge: Cambridge University Press, 2001. My research design is based on the goal of making inferences about voting behavior and understanding voter support for an ethnic party in a rapidly developing country context.

[154] Bennett, Andrew and Alexander George, "An Alliance of Statistical and Case Study Methods: Research on the Interdemocratic Peace," in the *Comparative Politics Newsletter*, Vol. 9. No. 1. Winter 1998. See also, Sidney Tarrow, "Bridging the Quantitative-Qualitative Divide," in Brady, Henry and David Collier, Eds. *Rethinking Social Inquiry – Diverse Tools, Shared Standards*. Oxford: Rowman & Littlefield Publishers, 2004.

[155] Laitin, David, "Comparative Politics: The State of the Subdiscipline," first presented at the Annual Meeting of the American Political Science Association, Washington, DC, 2000.

comparative politics journals and found that over forty percent of the articles employed some type of a mixed-methods research design.[156]

While comparative politics has developed a place for the use of multiple research methods, it is relevant to note that the discipline of Political Science in India for a long time did not place heavy emphasis on the use of quantitative research methods, and particularly survey methods. Indian Political Scientist, Yogendra Yadav, explains that in the historically left-wing orientation of political science in India, the empirical study of politics in India was viewed with deep suspicion as a cultural importation of a type of research practice from the West.[157]

In this context, the systematic study and data collection of citizens' attitudes and voting behavior in India was not emphasized. However, Yadav notes, a new perception has recently taken hold that it is possible to engage in the study of voting behavior in India and to use survey methods which are locally shaped and guided, marking a shift in the practice of political science in India.[158] Consequently, since the mid-1990s, Indian Political Science scholars have begun to systematically collect data on voting behavior using survey methods. Drawing in part from this new collection of election study survey data, *this dissertation research project seeks to be part of a new body of empirical research and comparative analytical studies of Indian politics through an exploration of voting behavior and voter support for an ethnic party in India.*

---

[156] Munck, Gerardo and Richard Snyder, "Debating the Direction of Comparative Politics: An Analysis of Leading Journals," *Comparative Political Studies*, Vol. 40, No. 1, January 2007. Munck and Snyder analyze articles from three leading comparative politics journals from 1989 to 2004. They find that over 40 percent of the articles employ a mixed-methods research design (19 percent employed mixed methods that were predominantly more qualitative, and 23.6 percent employed mixed methods that were predominantly more quantitative).

[157] Yadav, Yogendra, "Whither Survey Research? Reflections of on the State of Survey Research on Politics in Most of the World," Malcolm Adiseshiah Memorial Lecture, 2008, p. 11.

[158] Ibid, p. 4.

Nested Analysis Research Design

This dissertation study uses a mixed-method strategy of data collection and analysis referred to as "nested analysis."[159] Nested analysis is a mixed-methods research design strategy that integrates statistical analyses of a large sample of cases, large-N analysis, with an in-depth investigation of one or more cases, small-N-analysis.[160] I will provide a brief overview of nested analysis research design, and then describe how it will be employed to carry out data collection and analysis for this research project.

Evan Lieberman notes that nested analysis usually begins with large-N analysis. What is needed at the beginning are initial hypotheses and access to data in order to test a baseline theory. Nested analysis then integrates large-N analysis with case study analysis, by leveraging the information from the former to inform decisions about the latter. A key benefit of small-N case study analysis, within the context of this design strategy, is that it takes the information gained from the large-N analysis, and focuses the research on exploring in more detail specific mechanisms linking independent variables to outcomes.

Nested analysis is both an appropriate and useful research method for this research project. Indian Political Science scholars have been collecting voting behavior survey data that can be used for the large-N analysis, and the country's open political culture allows for the possibility of conducting in-depth case studies of individual voters to examine in greater detail the effects of individual factors on vote choice. Combining the two methods, statistical analysis of a large sample of voters' preferences with case studies of individual voters, aims to both corroborate and deepen the research findings.

---

[159] Lieberman, Evan, "Nested Analysis as a Mixed-Method Strategy for Comparative Research," *American Political Science Review*, 99(3), 2005. This description of nested analysis draws from Lieberman's article, which provides both a conceptual and practical overview of how to use this type of research design.
[160] Ibid., p. 436.

Large-N Analysis

The large-N analysis component of this project entails logistic regression analysis of voting behavior in three Indian national elections, 1999, 2004 and 2009, in order to test ERV's ability to explain the way in which ethnic and programmatic interests influence voting behavior and voter support for the BJP at the societal level. As noted in the introduction, the 1999 national election marked the rise to power of the BJP at the national level and its ability to maintain a coalition government that lasted a full five-year term, while the 2009 national election marks a significant retrenchment of voter support for the BJP.

Using a most-similar research design, the large-N analysis focuses on comparing voting behavior in these three national elections in the states of Delhi and Gujarat.[161] As discussed in the theory chapter, the states of Delhi and Gujarat share several commonalities. First, both states have relatively large urban populations compared to the rest of India.[162] Economically, both states have experienced increasingly higher levels of economic growth over time. Politically, Gujarat and Delhi have been dominated by a two-party system comprised of Congress and the BJP, with little influence from other regional political parties.

However, during the 1999-2009 timeframe, Delhi did not experience episodes of major violent ethnic conflict, whereas Gujarat did. In 1999, Gujarat witnessed violent attacks against Christians mostly in the south, and Hindu-Muslim riots in Ahmedabad. In

---

[161] Most-similar design is also known as the method of differences, after J.S. Mill, in which chosen cases are similar in all respects except the variable(s) of interest. See Gerring, John. *Case Study Research – Principles and Practices.* Cambridge: Cambridge University Press, 2007, p. 131.
[162] According to the 2001 Census, Delhi's urban population is 92 percent, and Gujarat's urban population is 44 percent. http://www.censusindia.gov.in/Census_Data_2001.

February 2002, Ahmedabad and many other cities experienced major Hindu-Muslim riots for several months.

The large-N analysis examines what factors influence electoral support for the BJP in Delhi and Gujarat over time. The dependent variable for the large-N analysis is vote choice, a binary, or dichotomous, dependent variable, coded 0 for individuals who voted for the Congress Party, and 1 for individuals who voted for the BJP. Because of its dichotomous nature, the research employs logistic regression to test for the effects of two categories of indicators, ethnic group identity and interests, and retrospective programmatic voting interests, on the likelihood of voting for the BJP.[163]

To test ERV theory and its two hypothesized mechanisms for explaining changes in voter support for the BJP over space and time, I created a typology of two categories of indicators representing 1) ethnic group identity and interests, and 2) retrospective programmatic interests. The following tables provide a description of the two types of indicators used for the large-N analysis.

---

[163] The logit model is a probability model that can be used with a dichotomous dependent variable, and tests the probability of event Y occurring (i.e. a voter voting/not voting for the BJP), given changes in values for X. A logit model is a more appropriate model to use with a dichotomous dependent variables than an Ordinary Least Squares (OLS) model, which assumes that the change in a dependent variable, Y, is the same for all values of an independent variable, X. The logit model allows for a non-linear relationship between a dependent and independent variables, such that, at different values of X, the effect of X on Y may be different.

Table 4.1: Ethnic Group Identity and Interest Indicators

Variable Name	Type	Description	Data Source
1. Religion	Dummy	Indicates voter's religion, and whether or not they are Hindu	NES 1999: B10 NES 2004: B7 NES 2009: Z8
2. Caste	Dummy	Indicates voter's caste, and whether or not they are upper caste	NES 1999: B9A NES 2004: B6A NES 2009: Z7A
3. Class	Dummy	Indicates voter's economic class	Composite NES data draw from income and household items
4. Religiosity	Ordinal	Measures voter's level of personal religious practice	NES 1999: B1,B1A NES 2004: Q34 NES 2009: Q30
5. Social Harmony	Ordinal	Measures voter's opinion of social harmony/Hindu-Muslim harmony	NES 1999: 16D NES 2004: Q20E
6. Hindu Ram Temple Views	Ordinal	Measures voter's opinion about building the Ram Temple	NES 1999: 22G NES 2004: 24D NES 2009: A3 a,b

The table above lists indicators measuring ethnic group identity (i.e., religion, caste) and ethnic group interests (i.e., perceptions of Hindu-Muslim relations, views about building the Hindu Ram Temple). In addition, I have also included in this typology an indicator for class. A complete list of the NES survey data questions used to develop these indicators is included in Appendix A.

Recall that the BJP is typically associated with being a party which represents the interests of upper castes and Hindu voters. To test the influence of these ethnic factors, I created two dummy variables, *Religion* and *Caste*. *Religion* is coded 0 for non-Hindu and coded 1 for Hindu. *Caste* is coded 0 for non-upper caste and 1 for upper caste. These indicators measure two different attributes of a voter, which are related but not necessarily correlated (i.e., caste in the context of this dissertation refers to the subset of attributes of being a Hindu).

In addition to being associated with the interests of upper caste and Hindu voters, the BJP is also associated with the interests of higher income voters. I have created a dummy variable, *Class*, coded 0 for non-rich and 1 for rich, to test for the effects of class on vote choice. Though an individual's class and caste measure two different attributes, they can be correlated (i.e., higher caste individuals have been associated with greater access to education and employment opportunities leading to higher income). However, this relationship is changing as non-upper caste individuals gain greater access to education and employment opportunities.

The indicator, *Social Harmony*, measure's a voter's assessment of how well the government has acted to improve Hindu-Muslim relations. Because the voter response categories are different in the 1999 and 2004 NES surveys (see Appendix A), this indicator has two values (Hindu-Muslim relations have deteriorated, Hindu-Muslim relations have improved) for the 1999 analysis, and three values (deteriorated, the same, improved) for the 2004 analysis.

The indicator, *Hindu Ram Temple Views*, measures a voter's opinion about whether or not a temple dedicated to the Hindu Deity, Lord Ram, should be built at the site where the Babri Mosque was torn down in Ayodhya. Because, the voter responses categories are different in the 1999, 2004, and 2009 NES (see Appendix A), the indicator has two values for the 1999 analysis (i.e., agree the temple should be built, disagree the temple should not be built) and four values for the 2004 analysis (i.e., fully agree temple should be built, somewhat agree, somewhat disagree and fully disagree). The related question in the 2009 NES survey has completely different response categories from the 1999 and 2004 NES survey question. The indicator has five values for the 2009 analysis (i.e., only a temple should be built, only a mosque should be built, neither should be built, both should be built, no opinion).

These indicators are employed to test H1: *All things being equal, urban electoral support for the BJP hinges upon changes in the perceived level of ethnic group conflict and the corresponding shifts in the political salience of ethnic group identity and interests on vote choice,* as a means of examining the conditions under which ethnic group identity and interests increase in salience on vote choice.

Finally, to test for the effects of religiosity in explaining electoral support for the BJP, I have included an indicator, *Religiosity*, which provides a measure of a voter's personal religious practices. Because the voter response categories are different in the 1999, 2004 and 2009 NES surveys (see Appendix A), *Religiosity* has two values for the 1999 analysis (yes practice, no do not practice) and four values for the 2004 and 2009 analysis (never practice, practice on festivals, practice weekly and practice daily).

Table 4.2 Retrospective Programmatic Interest Indicators

Variable Name	Type	Description	Data Source
1. Personal Financial Conditions	Ordinal	Measures voter assessment of changes in household economic conditions	NES 2004: Q31 NES 2009: E2
2. Employment	Ordinal	Measures voter assessment of changes in employment opportunities	NES 2004: Q20C
3. Price Levels	Ordinal	Measures voter assessment of changes in price levels	NES 1999: 16A
4. Development	Ordinal	Measures voter assessment of changes in development conditions	NES 2004: Q20F NES 2009: C13 and E5
5. National Security or Terrorism	Ordinal	Measures voters assessment of changes in national security threat or concerns about terrorism	NES 1999: 16C NES 2004: Q20B NES 2009: B5A
6. Law and Order	Ordinal	Measures voter assessment of changes law and order conditions and personal safety	NES 1999: 16F
7. Corruption	Ordinal	Measures voter assessment of changes in levels of corruption	NES 1999: 16B NES 2004: Q20A
8. Central Government Performance	Ordinal	Measures overall voter level of satisfaction of performance of central government	NES 1999: 6 NES 2004: Q12 NES 2009: Q20

The table above lists indicators measuring a voter's retrospective assessment of the status of several programmatic factors (i.e., changes in price levels, personal financial conditions, economic development, etc.) during the current political administration. These indicators for retrospective programmatic voting are all ordinal in nature. Similar to the ethnic indicators described above, the voter response categories for these indicators are often different in the 1999, 2004 and 2009 NES surveys.

Personal Financial Conditions measures a voter's assessment of changes in household economic conditions during the current political administration. The indicator has three values for the 2004 analysis (i.e., worse, same, improved) and five values for the 2009 analysis (i.e., much worse, worse, same, better, much better). *Employment* measures a voter's assessment of changes in employment opportunities during the current political administration. The indicator has three values for the 2004 analysis (i.e., worse, same, improved). *Price Levels* measures a voter's assessment of changes in price levels during the current political administration. The indicator has two values for the 1999 analysis (i.e., agree prices have gone up, disagree prices have not gone up). *Development* measures a voter's assessment of changes in the overall development conditions in India during the current political administration. The indicator has three values for the 2004 analysis (i.e., worse, same, improved), and five values for the 2009 analysis (i.e., much worse, worse, same, better, much better).

National Security/Terrorism measures a voter's assessment of changes in the overall national security conditions in India during the current political administration. The indicator has two values for the 1999 analysis (i.e., agree national security worsened, disagree national security improved), and three values for the 2004 analysis (i.e., worsened, the same, improved). The related question in the 2009 NES survey has different response categories, specifically addressing voter assessment of government responses to Mumbai terrorist attacks. The indicator has four values for the 2009 analysis (i.e., fully dissatisfied with government response, somewhat dissatisfied, somewhat satisfied, fully satisfied). *Law and Order* measures a voter's assessment of changes in personal safety during the current political administration. The indicator has two values for the 1999 analysis (agree people and belongings are safer, disagree people and belongings are not safer). *Corruption* measures a voter's assessment of changes in levels of corruption during the current political administration. The indicator has two values for the 1999 analysis (i.e., agree levels of corruption have improved, disagree corruption has worsened), and three values for the 2004 analysis (i.e., worse, the same, improved).

Central government performance measures a voter's overall assessment of the performance of the central government during the current political administration. The indicator has three values for the 1999 analysis (i.e., not at all satisfied, somewhat satisfied, very satisfied), and five values for the 2004 and 2009 analysis (i.e., fully dissatisfied, somewhat dissatisfied, somewhat satisfied, and fully satisfied).

These indicators are employed to test H2: *All things being equal, urban electoral support for the BJP hinges upon changes in the political economy of development and the corresponding shift in retrospective demands on party performance pertaining to programmatic issues and policies,* as a means of examining the conditions under which retrospective programmatic interests increase in salience on vote choice.

As noted earlier, a primary goal of the large-N analysis is to test ERV as a means of explaining variation in urban voter support for the BJP at the societal level. Recall that table 3.1 in the previous chapter presents four generalized types of patterns of voting behavior by illustrating how ERV's two mechanisms predict the relative the degree of influence of ethnic and programmatic interests on voting behavior under different socio-economic conditions. These indicators of ethnic group identity and interests and retrospective programmatic interests described above will be used to analyze the factors affecting voting behavior in Gujarat and Delhi in the 1999, 2004 and 2009 elections, which in turn will allow us to examine the relative influence of ethnic and programmatic interests on voting behavior under different socio-economic conditions.

The data used for the large-N analysis comes from the Indian National Election Study (NES) post-poll surveys for the 1999, 2004 and 2009 elections. The Indian National Election Study (NES) survey is considered the largest and most comprehensive social science survey of India's national elections. The NES is designed to provide insight into voters' political preferences and to determine the reasons for the electorate's vote choice, using in-depth questionnaires and a sample frame based on probability sampling (elements of the sample are selected using a probability mechanism, allowing for statistical analysis and inference to the overall population). Respondents for the NES are randomly selected from electoral rolls of polling stations, a tradition that has been used throughout the NES series.

The Indian NES has been carried out in India since 1967 by CSDS, a social science research institution based in New Delhi, India. Scholars at the CSDS refer to three generations of NES studies: the first generation is from 1967-1971, which is quite limited in scope; the second generation is from 1996-1999, and the third generation, which includes the 2004 and 2009 national elections. Each generation has seen an increase in the overall number of people surveyed.[164] A large portion of the data analysis for this dissertation took place during seven months I spent as a dissertation research fellow at CSDS from October 2010 thru April 2011.

Data Limitations: It must be noted that there are some particular limitations with the Indian NES data used in the large-N analysis. First, some of the questions asked are not always consistent over the years. So that, for example, questions about a voter's assessment of personal financial conditions are asked in the 2004 NES and the 2009 NES surveys, but not in the 1999 NES survey. This non-uniformity often hinders the ability to make direct comparisons of the effect of a particular indicator over all three national elections. Second, as noted in the discussion about the indicators used for the large-N analysis, the voter response categories for a similar question are not always the same across the NES surveys. Despite these aspects of non-uniformity of the data across time, the Indian NES surveys are the most comprehensive data on voter preferences in India. By employing indicators of ethnic and programmatic interests, I have sought to preserve as much comparability as possible. Lastly, though the overall NES country sample sizes are large from 1999 to 2009, the sample size in some cases for particular Indian states is small. For example, the sample size for Delhi in 1999 is under 100, but over 1000 in 2004 and 2009. For this reason, I have focused the large-N analysis to the state level, Delhi and Gujarat, rather than to the city level (New Delhi, and Ahmedabad), in which the sample sizes would be even smaller. Additionally, the sample size for the Delhi 1999 analysis is

---

[164] Total achieved sample size for Indian National Election Studies (NES): 1999: 9,418; 2004: 27,189; 2009: 36,169. Data from "National Election Study 2009: A Methodological Note," *Economic and Political Weekly*, September 26, 2009.

too small to employ a logistic regression. Instead I use cross tabs and examine differences in sample proportions for the Delhi 1999 analysis. In conclusion, in spite of some of the non-uniform aspects of the data across NES surveys, it is a critical component in allowing us to examine the relative influence of ethnic interests and programmatic interests on voter support for the BJP in different socio-economic contexts across time and space.

Case Study Analysis

The second component of research for this project entails in-depth case studies of urban voters and their voting behavior in the cities of New Delhi, Delhi and Ahmedabad, Gujarat, two of the largest cities in India. Focusing on case studies of urban voters in these two large cities aims to create a structured, focused comparison of individual urban voting behavior which complements the large-N analysis of voting behavior in the highly urbanized states of Delhi and Gujarat. [165]

Similar to Delhi and Gujarat, the cities of New Delhi and Ahmedabad share several commonalities. Both New Delhi and Ahmedabad rank in the top ten most populated cities in India, ranking number two and five respectively. Politically, the landscape in New Delhi and Ahmedabad has been defined by a two-party system

---

[165] George, Alexander and Andrew Bennett, *Case Studies and Theory Development in the Social Sciences.* Cambridge: MIT Press, 2005. George and Bennett define a case as "an instance of a class of events," and describe a research strategy for designing structured and focused case studies which are guided by 1) a well-defined class of events or cases, 2) a clear research objective, 3) employing variables of theoretical interest, and, borrowing from survey research design, 4) asking a set of standardized questions for each case which is guided by the research objective. These components taken together orient case studies toward an "orderly, cumulative development of knowledge and theory" about a particular class of events.

between Congress and the BJP. However, Ahmedabad experienced major Hindu-Muslim violent conflict during the 1999-2009 timeframe, whereas New Delhi did not.

The principle research objective for the small-N component of this research is to test ERV theory's mechanisms as a means of explaining variation in urban voter support for the BJP on individual voting behavior, by examining the ways in which ethnic and programmatic interests influence voting behavior and voter support for the BJP for the individual voter. Like the large-N analysis, the dependent variable for the case study analysis is vote choice.

I first created a standardized survey questionnaire in order to conduct in-depth interviews of urban voters in both cities about their vote choices and political preferences in the 1999, 2004 and 2009 national elections. The survey questionnaire for the case studies is similar in design to the surveys used as part of the Indian National Election Surveys, however, it is designed to engage voters about changes in their political choices and preferences over a ten-year time frame covering the 1999, 2004, and 2009 national elections.[166] The text of the survey questionnaire is included in Appendix C.

A key aspect of the questionnaire is that it asks voters questions about their political preferences over the 1999 to 2009 time frame covering three national elections, which raises concerns about memory bias. Memory or recall bias in the context of a survey occurs when a respondent's answer is either enhanced or impaired by his/her memory.

---

[166] The survey questionnaire was written in English and Hindi, or English and Gujarati, and the questions were pretested with Indian voters to ensure that the structure of the questionnaire and the wording of the individual questions were understandable to interviewees.

Collaborative research between survey methodologists and cognitive scientists have studied the impact of the passage over time on reporting performance in surveys, and have found that using memory cues in surveys can enhance memory and recall.[167] Therefore, to assist the survey respondent's memory recall, the survey questionnaire was structured chronologically, beginning with questions about the 1999 national election and ending with questions about the 2009 national election. In addition, the survey includes a short introduction about the nature and structure of the survey, and also uses memory cues for each section of the survey.[168]

The survey questionnaire includes questions focused on gaining information about what factors or issues were important to a voter in each of the 1999, 2004 and 2009 national elections. Specifically, the survey includes some questions that were asked three times – once for each national election.[169] This structure, though somewhat redundant, was used in part to detect whether or not a voter's priorities had changed over time, and also as a means of checking the consistency of a respondent's answers.

---

[167] Tourangeau, Roger, "Remembering What Happened: Memory Error and Survey Reports," (chapter 3), and Menon, Geeta and Eric Yorkston, "The Use of Memory and Contextual Cues in the Formation of Behavioral Frequency Judgments," (chapter 5), in *The Science of Self-report: Implications for Research and Practice*, Eds. Stone, Arthur, Christine Bachrach, Jared Jobe, Howard Kurtzman, Virginia Cain, Eds. London: Lawrence Erbaum Associates, 2000.
Jobe, Jared, Roger Tourangeau and Albert Smith, "Contributions of Survey Research to the Understanding of Memory," *Applied Cognitive Psychology*, Vol. 7, 567-584, 1993. Jared Jobe et al. discuss the various ways in which researchers have sought to improve memory cues in the course of conducting a survey, including 1) increasing question length, 2) asking additional questions related to a main question, and 3) ordering the questions in different ways, p. 572.

[168] For example, each section of the survey begins with a fact-based memory cue, such as the following: "I will begin by asking you some questions about the 1999 Lok Sabha Election. Recall that the BJP-led National Democratic Alliance government was in power briefly in 1998, leading up to the 1999 national elections."

[169] This survey question is asked three times: "I would like to ask you, in the 1999 (2004 and 2009) election: 1) Were any of the following issues important to you in your vote choice. (yes, no, no opinion). 2) What would you say was the most important issue in 1999 (2004, 2009): a) reduction corruption, b) national security, c) employment or prices, d) development of country, e) party leadership, f) Mandir/Masjid temple dispute, g) other issues not listed here."

To explore the impact of ethnic group identity and interests on vote choice over time, respondents were asked, "1) Over the past ten years, have ethnic issues become more or less important to you in your vote choice (more, less, the same); and 2) Why have ethnic issues increased/decreased/stayed the same with regard to your vote choice?"[170] The survey includes two questions related to ethnic group interests. The first question asks respondents if the dispute involving the Hindu Ram Temple was a factor in their vote choice. The second question asks voters their views about *Hindutva* in the 1999 election and the 2009 election.

The survey includes some open-ended questions, such as asking respondents to identify the issues or concerns that have increased in importance with regard to their vote choice over the ten-year time frame. This question is included as a means of identifying changes in the importance of ethnic and programmatic factors on vote choice over time, and also as means of checking for the internal consistency of the voter's previous responses.

George and Bennett note that one of the more common critiques of case studies is selection bias, in particular, selecting cases on the dependent variable (i.e., cases which share a particular outcome).[171] For this analysis, it is important to note that in choosing these individual cases, *it was not known in advance how a particular voter voted, or the reasons why a voter voted for a particular party.*

In choosing a data collection method for the case studies of urban voters, I used a *purposive sampling design*, in which cases of individual voters were selected based

---

[170] An initial version of the survey indicated that voters had a difficult time answering the question, "Are there certain factors that increase the importance of ethnicity in your vote choice." However, the question became more accessible to respondents when it was broken down into these two parts.
[171] George and Bennett, p. 23.

on a combination of several socio-economic indicators (i.e., religion, caste, class/income, and nature of employment).[172]

The table 4.3 below lists the variation in socio-economic characteristics of the individual voters interviewed in New Delhi. The same design was used to identify voters in Ahmedabad.

Table 4.3: New Delhi Cases

Respondent	M/F	Age	Caste/Religion	Class	Occupational Status	Sector
24	M	40s	Upper Caste/Brahmin	Rich	Partner, International Consulting Firm	Private
33	F	40s	Kashmiri Pandit/Brahmin	Rich	Senior Executive, Large Multinational Bank	Private
25	M	30s	Upper Caste/Brahmin	Rich	Partner, International Consulting Firm	Private
18	M	50s	Punjabi Khatri	Rich	President/CEO, Event Management Company	Private
13	F	30s	Upper Caste/Punjabi	Upper-middle Class	Highly Skilled Business Professional (Chief Finance Officer, FMCG company)	Private
35	F	30s	Punjabi Khatri	Upper-middle Class	Highly Skilled Business Professional (Director of Human Resources)	Private
30	M	40s	Kashmiri Pandit/Brahmin	Upper-middle Class	Highly Skilled Business Professional (Director, Steel Company)	Private
26	M	60s	Minority/Muslim	Upper-Middle Class	Highly Skilled Business Professional (Senior Executive, Indian company)	Private
29	F	30s	Brahmin	middle class	Mid-Level Business Profrressional (Administrative Secretary)	Private
32	F	50s	Minority/Christian	middle class	Mid-Level Business Profrressional (Teacher at Private School)	Private
8	M	50s	Lower Caste	Working Class	Security Guard	Private
19	F	40s	Brahmin	Upper-middle class	Highly skilled Senior Gov't (Doctor)	Public
20	F	30s	OBC	Upper-middle class	Highly skilled Senior Gov't (Doctor)	Public
14	M	30s	Scheduled Caste	Upper-middle class	Highly skilled Senior Gov't (Doctor)	Public
16	M	50s	Scheduled Caste	Upper-middle class	Highly skilled Senior Gov't (Medical School Department Head)	Public
34	F	50s	Hindu Jatt or Gurjar	Middle Class	Mid-Level Gov't (Section Officer, Delhi University)	Public
22	M	50s	Hindu Rajput	Middle Class	Mid-Level Gov't (Lab Technician)	Public
21	M	50s	Hindu Rajput	Middle Class	Mid-Level Gov't (Classroom Technician)	Public
15	M	30s	Hindu Rajput	Middle Class	Mid-Level Gov't (Clerk)	Public
17	M	40s	Lower Caste	Working Class	Low Skilled Administrative Govt (Office Assistant)	Public
27	F	30s	Lower Caste	Working Class	Low Skilled Administrative Govt (Cleaning)	Public
28	M	30s	Lower Caste	Working Class	Low Skilled Administrative Govt (Cleaning)	Public
23	M	50s	Minority/Muslim	Working Class	Low Skilled Administrative Govt (File clerk)	Public
2	M	20s	Punjabi	Middle Class	Small clothing shop	Unorganized
5	M	30s	Muslim/Minority	Lower Middle Class	Owns small furniture shop	Unorganized
1	M	40s	Punjabi	Working Class	Owns small magazine stand	unorganized
3	M	60s	Kayastha=Brahmin/Kshatriya	Working Class	Small stand sells backpacks	Unorganized
7	F	30s	Brahmin	Working Class	Small stand where sells food	Unorganized
31	M	60s	Brahmin	Working Class	Tailor	Unorganized
6	M	70s	Lower Caste	Poor	Very small ironing stand	Unorganized
9	M	30s	SC/Lower Caste	Poor	Mehndi stand	Unorganized
11	F	50s	Lower caste	poor	Construction/bricks	Unorganized
4	F	40s	Muslim/Minority	Poor	Very small tobacco stand	Unorganized
12	F	40s	Muslim/Minority	Poor	Not employed	Unorganized
10	M	40s	Muslim/Minority	Poor	Vegetable seller	Unorganized

---

[172] For the case study sample, I used the following categories to label an individual's family income/class in rupees/day: 1) 0-125 Rs/day: poor; 2) 125-625 Rs/day: working class; 3) 625-3,500 Rs/day: middle class; 3,500-25,000 Rs/day: upper middle class; 25,000-up: rich. The rupee recently has fluctuated between 46-56 Rs per US dollar. The income categories include a higher upper range than the income categories used in the NES survey data. While the NES data must take account of average income levels across all Indian states in rural and urban areas, the case studies focus on two of the most prosperous cities in India.

It is important to note that a purposive sampling design does not provide a representative sample of the population of voters. The choice of a purposive sampling design was guided by two primary considerations. First, the Indian National Election Study survey data used in the large-N analysis provides a random sample to identify general patterns of the effects of different indicators on vote choice. This kind of randomly sampled survey data, which covers the entirety of India, is entirely unique and expensive to carry out.

Second, a primary goal of the case study analysis is to test ERV as a means of explaining urban voter support for the BJP for the individual voter. Recall that table 3.2 posits four types of individual voting behavior based on the different ways in which ERV's mechanisms impact individual vote choice through differences in an individual voter's assessment of the perceived risks from ethnic group conflict and the perceived rewards from economic reforms and development. This in turn impacts the relative influence of ethnic group identity and interests and retrospective programmatic interests on vote choice at the individual level and the reasons for voting for an ethnic party.

Through the use of purposive sampling, I want to explore whether or not voters with certain combinations of socio-economic characteristics, (i.e., religion, caste, class/income, and employment sector) show similar patterns of individual voting behavior with regard to the reasons why a voter votes for the BJP. In particular, I want to explore if voters with certain socio-economic characteristics are more inclined to base their votes on 1) retrospective programmatic interests, 2) ethnic group identity and interests, 3) both retrospective programmatic interests and ethnic group identity and interests, or 4) something entirely different. Using this purposive sampling design, I conducted research on a total of 72 case studies, including 35 in-depth voter interviews in New Delhi, and 37 in-depth voter interviews in Ahmedabad.

In addition to the large-N analysis of Indian NES survey data for Delhi and Gujarat, and the small-N analysis of case studies of urban voters in New Delhi and Ahmedabad, I also conducted a dozen expert interviews to gain additional insight about the BJP and local knowledge about the politics of Delhi and Gujarat. These interviews focus on individuals with unique knowledge or perspective pertaining to the dissertation topic, and include Indian political scientists, Congress and BJP politicians, journalists and political analysts.

Finally, my research also draws from 1) official government documents, 2) BJP and Congress party documents, 3) Indian newspaper and magazine articles, and 4) the academic literature on Indian politics.

Chapter 5: Ethnic Politics and Voting Behavior in Delhi and New Delhi

The National Capital Territory of Delhi, or "Delhi," is India's second largest metropolis and home to the nation's capital, New Delhi. Delhi is the most urbanized state (city-state) in India with one of the highest levels of economic growth.[173] One recent study predicts that over the next twenty years, Delhi's population will grow from its current population of 16.7 million to 26 million, while its per capita income is projected to increase four-fold.[174]

The highly urbanized character of Delhi, combined with the nature of its politics, which have been dominated by India's two national political parties, Congress and the Bharatiya Janata Party, make Delhi an ideal location for this project focusing on the factors affecting voter support for an ethnic party, and specifically explaining urban voter support for the BJP over time.

Yet little research exists about the voting behavior of Delhi's 16.7 million voters,[175] the factors affecting their vote choice, or patterns of voting behavior in the area over time. Once a Congress party stronghold in the 1980s, the BJP came to dominate

---

[173] Delhi was 93 percent urban in 2001, *Census of India 2001*. Gross and net State Domestic Product is available from *The Reserve Bank of India's Handbook of Statistics on Indian Economy* published annually. Growth rates listed here and throughout the remainder of the chapter are based on the annual change in net State Domestic Product using current prices: 1999-2000: 11.9 percent, 2004-2005: 14.5 percent, and 2008-2009: 16.8 percent.

[174] Sankhe, Shirish et al., "India's Urban Awakening: Building Inclusive Cities Sustaining Economic Growth," *McKinsey Global Institute*, April 2010. This would give the Delhi metropolitan area a population similar to many countries (i.e., Australia: 21 million; Taiwan: 23 million, Syria: 21 million).

[175] 2011 Census of India population tables for the National Capital Territory of India, http://www.censusindia.gov.in/2011-prov-results/prov_data_products_delhi.html.

Delhi politics in the 1990s, followed by a steep decline in BJP electoral support and a reemergence of Congress dominance. What explains this major shift in urban voter support for the BJP in Delhi from the 1999 election to the 2009 election?

This chapter presents an empirical analysis of voting behavior in Delhi and an in-depth analysis of voting behavior in the Capital, New Delhi, and tests Ethnically Mediated Retrospective Voting (ERV) theory as a means of explaining variation in urban electoral support for the BJP over the 1999, 2004, and 2009 national elections.[176] The chapter is comprised of three main sections: 1) an overview of the politics of Delhi, 2) an analysis of Indian National Election Study (NES) survey data of Delhi voters for the 1999, 2004 and 2009 national elections, and 3) an examination of case studies of individual voters and voting behavior in New Delhi.

Delhi

The area of modern Delhi has had a long history as a seat of power and governance in the Indian subcontinent going back centuries.[177] In 1639, the Emperor Shah Jahan established the walled city of Shahjahanabad as the capital of the later Mughal Empire, where it remained until the Empire's defeat by the British in 1857. Under the British, the Indian capital was initially relocated to Calcutta, but then it was

---

[176] India's general (national) elections are held every five years or if parliament is dissolved. Voters directly elect members to the Lok Sabha, India's lower house of parliament. Thus, the 15th Lok Sabha, refers to the Indian national elections in 2009. Since 1967, Delhi has contested 7 seats in the Lok Sabha.

[177] Before the Mughal Empire, Delhi was the site of the Delhi Sultanate, a series of Muslim Kingdoms that ruled from the 11th century until it fell to the Mughal Emperor Babur in 1526.

transitioned back to Delhi in 1911[178]. Over the next two decades, British architect Sir Edwin Lutyens developed the new capital of British India, New Delhi, located southwest of Shahjahanabad. In 1947, New Delhi was named the capital of the newly independent government of India. Since independence, the status of Delhi has evolved from a state, to a union territory, to most recently, the constitutionally mandated National Capital Territory of Delhi, or NCT.[179][180] *New Delhi is both the capital of the central Government of India and the NCT (Delhi).*

Delhi has a diverse social demographic makeup, which has been influenced recently by two distinct waves of migration. Following the partition of India and Pakistan in 1947, large numbers of Punjabis fled from the newly created state of Pakistan and settled in refugee camps in Delhi. This initial influx of Punjabis established an active trading and business community, which has led to a strong Punjabi cultural and political influence in the city.[181] In the 1980s, another wave of migrants came to Delhi, in

---

[178] On December 12, 1911, at the annual coronation of King George V and Queen Mary as the ruling sovereigns of India, George V transferred the seat of the Government of India from Calcutta to Delhi, with the goal of reducing the influence of any one Provincial Government upon the workings of the Central Government. The following year, the city of Delhi was formally separated from the Punjab and constituted as a separate province. See Vajpeyi, S.C. and S.P. Verma, "Administrative Set-Up of Delhi," in *Landmarks in Delhi Administration Post-Independence Era 1947-1997.* Eds. S.C. Vajpeyi and S.P. Verma. New Delhi: Gyan Publishing House, 1998, pgs. 40-41.

[179] In 1956, as part of the States Reorganization Act, Delhi lost its status as a "Part C State" and became a Union Territory, losing its Legislative Assembly and coming under the direct administration of the President of India. Four decades later, in 1991, the Indian Constitution was amended by the Sixty-Ninth Amendment Act, which changed the official status of the Union Territory of Delhi to the National Capital Territory (NCT) of Delhi, and reinstated Delhi's Legislative Assembly, which is elected by the citizens of Delhi and is enabled to make laws for the NCT. The NCT is comprised of nine districts, including New Delhi, which is its seat of government. See Vajpeyi and Verma, pgs. 52-58.

[180] The text of the Constitution (Sixty Ninth Amendment) Act of 1991 is available at http://delhiassembly.nic.in/constitution.htm.

[181] Raj, Pushkar, "Delhi: Benefitting from Two-Layered Incumbency," *Economic and Political Weekly*, December 18, 2004, p. 5502.

particular from the Northern Indian states of Uttar Pradesh, Bihar, Haryana, Punjab and Rajasthan, increasing the OBC, Dalit and Muslim populations.[182]

Unlike other parts of India, such as the state of Gujarat, which have experienced several episodes of major violent ethnic conflict, Delhi has maintained moderate to low levels of ethnic conflict, including Hindu-Muslim relations. However, three exceptions are of note. The first recent episode of major social conflict occurred on October 31, 1984, when the assassination of Prime Minister Indira Gandhi by two of her Sikh bodyguards triggered four days of widespread anti-Sikh riots throughout Delhi killing thousands of Sikhs.[183] A second episode occurred when riots broke out in Chandni Chowk between Hindus and Muslims in October and November 1990 following L.K. Advani's *Rath Yatra* through Delhi.[184] A third episode occurred following the destruction of the Babri mosque in Ayodhya on December 6, 1992, when riots between Hindus and Muslims broke out in Delhi's Seelampur district.[185]

---

[182] Ibid, p. 5502. Pushkar cites data from a survey of voters during the 2003 assembly elections in Delhi indicating that, of the voters who said that they had migrated to Delhi in the 1980s, 27 percent said they were from Uttar Pradesh, 7 percent were from Bihar, 6 percent from Haryana, 4 percent from Punjab and 3 percent from Rajasthan.

[183] The assassination of Prime Minister Indira Gandhi by her Sikh bodyguards was in retaliation to her orders to carry out "Operation Blue Star," a military operation conducted in June 1984 to remove Sikh militant separatists operating from the Golden Temple holy site in Amritsar, Punjab. The anti-Sikh riots began within hours of her assassination. Rajiv Gandhi was famously quoted as saying of the assassination of his mother, Indira Gandhi, and the subsequent anti-Sikh riots in Delhi, "When a giant tree falls, the earth below shakes," for which he was later deeply criticized. See "Leaders 'incited' anti-Sikh riots," BBC News, August 8, 2005 at http://news.bbc.co.uk/2/hi/south_asia/4130962.stm. Estimates of the number of Sikhs killed in Delhi during the 1984 riot range from 1000 to 3000.

[184] Estimates of the number of people killed in the riots range from eight to upwards of 100. "16 Get Life for 1990 Delhi Riots," Rediff India Abroad, September 8, 2006 at http://www.rediff.com/news/2006/sep/08riot.htm. Saba, Naqvi, "A Beast Asleep?" *Outlook India*, March 5, 2012.

[185] Drogin, Bob, "Deadly Religious Riots Spread to India's Capital: Rampaging youths torch homes and shops, residents flee violence stemming from razing of mosque," *Los Angeles Times*, December 12, 1992. Miller, Sam. *Delhi: Adventures in a Megacity*. New York: St. Martin's Press, 2009, p. 258. Estimates of the number of Muslims killed in Delhi during the 1992 riot range from 3 to 20 people.

Since independence, Delhi politics has been dominated by a two-party rivalry at the national and state levels between the Congress party and the Jan Sangh party, (the precursor party to the BJP), followed by the BJP. While the Congress has historically drawn its base from the poor, the lower middle class, Other Backward Classes (OBCs), and Muslims, the Jan Sangh in Delhi was associated with the interests of the Punjabi refugees, who became a dominant part of the Delhi trading community, and the Hindu upper castes.[186] When the BJP was created in 1980, it adopted the same social base of support as the Jan Sangh, and came to be known as the "Bania, Brahmin, Punjabi party" in Delhi.[187] In addition, after the anti-Sikh riots in Delhi, the BJP became a viable option for the Sikh community who previously voted for Congress.

In 1989, the BJP gained a footing in Delhi, winning a majority of the Lok Sabha parliamentary seats over the Congress party. Over five elections, (1989, 1991, 1996, 1998 and 1999) the BJP dominated Delhi politics in the national elections, until 2004, which witnessed a sharp swing toward the Congress party. A similar pattern emerges in the Delhi state assembly elections. In the first state assembly election in 1993, the BJP won two-thirds of the assembly seats. However, the 1998 assembly election witnessed a sharp swing toward the Congress party, which has maintained its power in the subsequent 2003 and 2008 assembly elections. Table 5.1 lists the party winner in Delhi of the national Lok Sabha elections and the state assembly elections from 1989 to 2009.

---

[186] Raj, "Delhi: Benefiting from Two-Layered Incumbency," p. 5503. Pushkar Raj notes that the Jan Sangh was once labeled the party of refugees, referring to its base of Punjabi refugees who migrated to Delhi after the partition of India and Pakistan. Andersen, Walter and Mahender Kumar Saini, "The Congress Split in Delhi: The Effect of Factionalism on Organizational Performance and System Level Interactions," *Asian Survey*, 11(11), November 1971.

[187] Brahmins are high caste Hindus. Banias are traders or merchants and often considered upper caste.

Table 5.1: Party Winner of Delhi Elections at the National and State Levels

Delhi National Elections	Delhi State Elections
1989: BJP	
1991: BJP	
1996: BJP	1993: BJP*
1998: BJP	1998: Congress
1999: BJP	
2004: Congress	2003: Congress
2009: Congress	2008: Congress

Source: Election Commission of India
*1993 was the first year Delhi held State assembly elections

This similar pattern of a swing away from the BJP to the Congress party in the national and state elections in Delhi is not entirely surprising given that New Delhi is both the national capital of India and the state capital of the NCT. Additionally both the central government of India and the NCT jointly administer New Delhi. Thus, the interplay of national and state level politics is an important factor to consider in understanding politics in Delhi.

We'll begin the recent story of Delhi politics with the 1998 national election. Of particular relevance to Delhi, the BJP called for constitutional reforms that would give the national capital full statehood. The national election did not lead to an absolute majority, but the BJP was temporarily able to forge a coalition government. In Delhi, the BJP won 6 out of 7 Lok Sabha seats.

Eight months later, a very different outcome emerged in Delhi's state assembly elections. During the BJP's five-year tenure as the leader of the Delhi state government, the party changed its state Chief Minister three times, while civic amenities languished, crime increased, and commodity prices soared. The Congress party's 1998 state assembly election campaign focused particularly on the BJP's deficiencies in providing public amenities (namely water, power and transport) and its inability to control prices of

113

commodities, in particular, onions. The Congress opposition, led by Delhi Congress Committee president Sheila Dixit, campaigned on the slogan that the BJP failed to provide *bijli, jal* and *pyaj*, (power, water and onions). The Congress won two-thirds of the Delhi assembly seats.[188]

As noted in Chapter Two, in the 1999 national election, the BJP campaigned on delivering one year of solid economic growth, its effective handling of the Kargil conflict with Pakistan during the summer of 1999, and emphasized the party's homegrown leadership under Atal Bihari Vajpayee. The BJP and its NDA coalition won a majority of Lok Sabha parliamentary seats. In Delhi, the BJP won all seven Lok Sabha seats.

During the 2004 national election, the BJP launched its, "India Shining" campaign, and used the slogan, the feel good factor. While the BJP drew on its national election themes, the Congress party campaigned on working for *Aam Aadmi*, or the common man, and emphasized development issues related to Delhi.[189]

Similar to its successful past state assembly election campaigns, the Congress party focused on the issues of *bijli, sadak, pani*, (power, roads, water).[190] The Congress party won six Lok Sabha seats in Delhi, while the BJP lost six seats and retained one.[191]

Although the BJP's 2009 election platform focused on issues of governance, as noted in Chapter Two, the party's issue agenda was largely subsumed by political

---

[188] Rajalakshmi, T.K., "Assembly Elections Capital Contest," *Frontline*, 15(23), November 7-20.1998. Ramakrishnan, Venkitesh, "A Fresh Polarisation in Delhi," *Frontline*, 15(23), December 5-18, 1998.
[189] Congress used the slogan, "Congress ka haath, aam aadmi ke saath," meaning, "The hand of Congress is with the common man." Indian National Congress Website, www.aicc.org.in/new/.
[190] Raj, "Delhi: Benefiting from Two-Layered Incumbency," p. 5502.
[191] Ibid, p. 5502.

controversy, with alleged anti-Muslim remarks made by BJP political candidate, Varun Gandhi.[192][193]

Drawing from its successful 2004 national election campaign, the Congress Party again focused its 2009 campaign on the theme of *Aam Aadmi*, the common man, emphasizing inclusive growth and development for all.[194] In Delhi, Congress again highlighted its development agenda focusing on local issues of *bijli, sadak and pani*. This time, the BJP lost all of its seats in Delhi to the Congress Party.[195]

Table 5.2 summarizes the national election results for the Congress and BJP parties in Delhi for the 1999, 2004 and 2009 national elections. The table shows the significant percentage decline in overall BJP vote share during the 1999-2009 timeframe.

Table 5.2 Delhi National Election Results, 1999-2009

Lok Sabha National Elections	1999	2004	2009
Congress percentage of vote share	41.9	54.8	57.1
Congress M.P. seats won	0	6	7
BJP percentage of vote share	51.7	40.6	35.2
BJP M.P. seats won	7	1	0

Source: Election Commission of India.

Delhi: Indian National Election Survey Analysis, 1999, 2004 and 2009

This section presents an analysis of voting behavior in Delhi in three Indian national elections, 1999, 2004, and 2009, using survey data from the Indian National Election Studies (NES). As discussed in Chapter Four, I created a typology of independent variables – one group representing indicators of ethnic group identity and interests, and a second group representing indicators of retrospective programmatic

---

[192] Varun Gandhi is the grandson of Indira Gandhi and the cousin of Rahul and Priyanka Gandhi.
[193] *2009 BJP Election Manifesto*, www.bjp.org.
[194] *2009 Congress Election Manifesto*, www.aicc.org.in.
[195] Mohanty, Biswajit, "Delhi Elections – The 'Local' Matters," *Economic and Political Weekly*, September 26, 2009, pgs. 175-176.

interests – to test ERV's ability to explain the way in which ethnic and programmatic interests influence voting behavior and voter support for the BJP at the societal level over space (i.e. Delhi and Gujarat) and time (i.e. 1999, 2004 and 2009). A complete description of these two groups of indicators is provided in Chapter Four. The dependent variable for this analysis is vote choice; a binary, or dichotomous, dependent variable coded 0 for individuals who voted for the Congress Party, and 1 for individuals who voted for the BJP.

Delhi, 1999 Election

Under conditions of a high political economy of development, with Delhi's state domestic product reaching 11.9 percent, and a medium level of Hindu-Muslim ethnic conflict, influenced by the recent Kargil War and the BJP's ethno-nationalist political mobilization strategy, the BJP won all seven of Delhi's Lok Sabha seats in the 1999 national election.

Post-poll national election surveys were conducted after the 1999 Lok Sabha election both nationally and in Delhi. Due to the sample size constraints of the 1999 NES data for Delhi (n=63), regression analysis is not appropriate.[196] Therefore, the analysis focuses on first testing if there is a statistically significant relationship between individual indicators and vote choice using cross tabs and chi-square analysis, and then examining if there are statistical and substantive differences in sample proportions for these indicators for BJP voters (for example, the percentage of Hindus

---

[196] The sample size for Delhi is 97, however 33 respondents did not provide information on who they voted for and one respondent voted for an independent candidate. Since this research is interested in the factors affecting vote choice for the BJP and maintaining a tight comparison between BJP voters and Congress voters, I removed these from the sample, reducing the sample size to 63.

who voted for the BJP versus the percentage of non-Hindus who voted for the BJP). A full list of the descriptive statistics for the Delhi 1999 election analysis is listed in table 1, Appendix B.

The results of the chi-square test indicate that both indicators of ethnic group identity and interests and retrospective programmatic interests are statistically significant with vote choice. In particular, ethnic group identity and interest indicators for 1) caste 2) social harmony related to Hindu/Muslim relations, and 3) class, are all statistically significant on vote choice. Retrospective programmatic interests for 1) prices, 2) corruption, 3) national security, and 4) law & order, are also statistically significant with vote choice.[197] However, indicators for 1) religiosity, 2) religion, 3) Ram Temple views, and 4) age, are not statistically significant on vote choice.

The following table provides a summary of the differences in sample proportions for BJP voters for indicators of ethnic group identity and interests and retrospective programmatic interests.[198] Column two "Yes" presents the proportion of voters with a particular characteristic (i.e., upper caste, Hindu, rich), or who answered in the affirmative to a particular question and voted for the BJP, while column three "No" presents the proportion of voters who do not have the particular characteristic, or who answered in the negative to a particular question and voted for the BJP. The percentage can be derived by multiplying each proportion by 100.

---

[197] The P-values for the chi-square analysis are the following: Caste: 0, Class: .04, Religion: .13, Religiosity: .6, Hindu Ram Temple views: .57, Social Harmony: .005, Price Levels: .04, Corruption: .01, National Security: 0, Law & Order: 0.

[198] Differences in sample proportions were calculated using a two-sample test of proportion (prtest) for each indicator in Stata.

Table 5.3 Differences of sample proportions for Ethnic and Retrospective Programmatic Indicators for BJP voters, Delhi 1999 election

Indicator	Yes	No	Difference in proportions
Caste (Uppercaste)	.68	.24	-.44**
Class (Rich)	.61	.33	-.28*
Religion (Hindu)	.43	0	-.43
Religiosity	.42	.33	-.09
Hindu Ram Temple views	.37	.29	-.08
Social Harmony (Improved)	.56	.18	-.38**
Price Levels (Increased)	.31	.61	.30*
Corruption (Down)	.59	.23	-.36**
National Security (Deteriorated)	.16	.62	.46**
Law & Order	.64	.17	-.47**

Source: Indian NES Survey (1999)
Significance: * = at 5%; ** = at 1%
N = 63

The difference of proportions test summarized above suggests both statistical and substantive effects for most of the indicators tested for BJP voters. If we first look at indicators of ethnic group identity and interests, we find a statistical and substantive difference for BJP voters in terms of caste: 68 percent of upper caste voters voted for the BJP, whereas only 24 percent of non-upper caste voters voted for the BJP, a difference of 44 percent. *Thus, in the 1999 election in Delhi, it appears that being upper caste is a distinguishing feature of BJP voters.* Although, *religion*, measuring whether or not a voter is Hindu, is not statistically significant, its large difference suggests substantive significance: while 43 percent of Hindus voted for the BJP, no non-Hindus voted for the BJP.[199] *These results suggest that ethnic identity related to being upper caste and being Hindu were distinguishing features of BJP voters in this election.*

The ethnic indicator, *social harmony*, relating to improvements in Hindu-Muslim relations, is both statistically and substantively significant, indicating that while 56

---

[199] Only three respondents from the sample of 63 indicated that they were non-Hindu. All three did not vote for the BJP.

percent of voters who evaluated the incumbent BJP government performance in addressing Hindu-Muslim relations favorably voted for the BJP, only 18 percent of voters who evaluated government performance on this issue unfavorably voted for the BJP.

While the results for the ethnic identity and interests indicators of *caste*, *religion*, and *social harmony*, suggest that they are distinguishing factors of BJP voters, by contrast, the indicator for *Ram temple views*, in this analysis, does not appear to be a distinguishing factor for BJP voters. This latter finding is of particular interest, because a key aspect of the BJP's electoral platform in the 1996 and 1998 Lok Sabha elections was its strong advocacy for rebuilding the Ram Temple in Ayodhya. However, in the following section examining in-depth case studies of individual voters and voting behavior in New Delhi, I find that views about the Ram Temple controversy and the desire to see the Ram Temple built *did significantly influence* electoral support for the BJP for certain voters.[200]

If we turn to examine the impact of retrospective programmatic indicators, we find both statistically significant and substantive differences on issues of *national security* and *law and order* for BJP voters. The majority of voters who assessed the incumbent BJP government performance on *national security* and *law and order* favorably voted for the BJP by 62 and 64 percent respectively, as compared to only 16 and 17 percent of voters who assessed the incumbent government on these issues unfavorably and voted for the BJP.

---

[200] The 1999 NES survey question asks the following question: "On the site where Babri Masjid was situated only Ram temple should be built (agree, no opinion, disagree)." The survey question asks a voter whether or not the Ram temple should be built." It does not specifically ask the voter if her views about the Hindu Ram Temple affected her vote choice. The survey question used for the case studies is worded differently.

The sizable difference in sample proportions for the indicators of *prices* and *corruption* are both statistically significant and suggest substantive difference of these indicators for BJP voters. Nearly 61 percent of voters who felt that prices levels had not increased during this timeframe voted for the BJP, whereas 31 percent of voters who indicated that price levels had increased during the incumbent government's tenure voted for the BJP. Additionally, the majority of voters who positively assessed the incumbent government's performance relating to corruption levels voted for the BJP by 59 percent, as compared to only 23 percent of voters who believed that corruption levels had not declined voted for the BJP. These results suggest that retrospective evaluations of government performance on several programmatic issues are distinguishing features of BJP support.

Given the unique political and administrative relationship between Delhi and New Delhi – New Delhi is both the capital of India and the capital of the NCT (Delhi), and New Delhi is jointly administered by the central government and the state government – an important question to consider is what level of government do voters indicate they are most concerned about. The following table summarizes the focus of voter concerns with regard to the level of government.[202]

Table 5.4 Delhi voter priorities in 1999: central versus state level government

	Neither	State level	Both	Central level	Other
All Voters	18.6	17.5	6.2	43.3	14.4
BJP voters	15.4	19.2	0	46.2	19.2
Congress voters	21.6	10.8	10.8	46.0	10.8

Source: Indian NES Survey (1999)
Figures above are in percentages.

---

[202] The 1999 NES survey asks the following question: "People are generally concerned about what governments do—some are more concerned about what the Central government in Delhi does, while others are more concerned with what the state government dos. How about you? Are you more concerned about what the government in Delhi does or about what the New Delhi government does?

The NES survey indicates that Delhi voters in the 1999 election were in general more focused on and concerned with the work of the central government than the state government. This pattern continues when looking at BJP voters and Congress voters. In particular, nearly half of BJP voters are more concerned with the work of the central government (46.2 percent) than with the work of the state government (19.2 percent). This data suggests that a majority of Delhi voters in the 1999 election, including BJP voters, were focused on central level government concerns.

In summary, the analysis of 1999 NES survey data indicates that ethnic group identity and interests, particularly indicators for *caste, religion, and social harmony* relating to Hindu-Muslim relations, and retrospective programmatic issues relating to *national security, law and order, corruption* and *price levels*, were both substantively important factors on voting behavior and voter support for the BJP in the 1999 national elections in Delhi. In addition, the data indicates that the majority of BJP voters were concerned with the work of the central government, suggesting that national level issues, such as the BJP's handling of the 1999 Kargil conflict, played an important role in vote choice.

In the context of Delhi's high political economy of development, and moderate levels of ethnic group conflict in 1999, influenced by the BJP's Hindu nationalist political mobilization strategy during the late 1990s and the 1999 Kargil conflict with Pakistan, ERV theory predicts this pattern of voting behavior, in which the influence of ethnic group identity and interests and retrospective programmatic interests are both strong factors in explaining voting behavior and voter support for the BJP, most closely represented by scenario 1 in table 3.1.

Delhi, 2004 Election

The 2004 national election in Delhi were a major turning point for the BJP. During this time, Delhi experienced a negligible level of Hindu-Muslim violent conflict, and voters' perceptions of Hindu-Muslim relations in Delhi had become more positive, suggesting a medium-low level of ethnic conflict. Despite an increasingly robust political economy of development, with Delhi's state domestic product increasing from 11.9 percent in 1999-2000 to 14.5 percent in 2004-2005, and a decreasing trend in poverty levels, from 14.6 percent (1993-1995) to 10.2 percent in 2004-2005, the incumbent BJP suffered an eleven-percentage point decline in overall vote share compared to its performance in the 1999 national election, shrinking from 51.7 percent to 40.6 percent of the vote share, and resulting in a loss of six out of Delhi's seven Lok Sabha seats. How do we explain this major shift away from the BJP in Delhi?

To improve survey representation at the state level, the 2004 post-poll national election survey sample size used for this analysis is almost three times larger than the 1999 national election survey sample, and the survey increased the Delhi sample size ten-fold, to 1,111.[203] Of the 1,111 survey respondents in Delhi, 287 respondents either refused to answer who they voted for (n=219) or said that they didn't know who they voted for (n=68), and 33 respondents voted for smaller regional parties. Subtracting these respondents who did not provide information about who they voted for or who voted for a small regional party, leaves a sample size of 791 respondents consisting of BJP and

---

[203] See "National Election Study 2004 Introduction," *Economic and Political Weekly*, December 18, 2004.

Congress voters. Of the 791 survey respondents, 478 voted for Congress and 313 voted for the BJP. How do we explain the significant defeat of the BJP in Delhi in 2004?

With a sample size of almost 800, in the following analysis of 2004 national election survey data in Delhi, it is possible to employ a logistic regression model to test for the effects of ethnic group identity and interests, and retrospective programmatic interests on the likelihood of voting for the BJP. A full list of the descriptive statistics for the Delhi 2004 election analysis is listed in table 3, Appendix B.

The following model includes indicators of ethnic group identity and interests: (i.e., *caste, religion, ram temple views,* and *social harmony*), and indicators of retrospective programmatic voting (i.e., *personal financial conditions, employment, development, corruption,* and *central government performance*).[204] The indicator for *central government performance* is included in the main model in column one. This indicator is removed in the second and third models, in order to better ascertain which retrospective programmatic issues are driving vote choice. The model also includes indicators for age, class and religiosity. Table 5.5 provides a summary of the regression results for all three models, with main model results listed in the first column.

Vote choice 2004 = $ß_0 + ß_1 Age_i + ß_2 Class (Rich)_i + ß_3 Caste (Upper Caste)_i + ß_4 Religion (Hindu)_i + ß_5 Religiosity_i + ß_6 RamTempleviews_i + ß_7 SocialHarmony_i + ß_8 PersonalFinance_i + ß_9 Employment_i + ß_{10} Corruption_i + ß_{11} Development_i + ß_{12} NationalSecurity_i + ß_{13} Central Government Performance_i + e_i$

---

[204] As noted in Chapter Four, due to the differences in the survey questions asked between the 1999 and 2004 Indian NES surveys, some of the indicators included in the 2004 model are different from the indicators used in the 1999 model. Specifically, survey questions about a voter's retrospective assessment about price levels and law and order are included in the 1999 NES survey, but are not included in the 2004 NES survey, whereas questions about voter's retrospective assessment about employment and development are included in the 2004 NES survey but not in the 1999 NES survey.

Table 5.5 Logit Regression Results, Delhi 2004 election

	(1)	(2)	(3)
Age	0.016*	0.016*	0.015*
	(0.007)	(0.007)	(0.007)
Class (Rich)	0.253	0.422	0.370
	(0.247)	(0.224)	(0.225)
Caste (Upper Caste)	0.475*	0.619**	0.694**
	(0.233)	(0.214)	(0.216)
Religion (Hindu)	0.595*	0.657*	0.680*
	(0.301)	(0.286)	(0.288)
Religiosity	-0.139	-0.113	-0.040
	(0.115)	(0.106)	(0.106)
Ram Temple Views	0.146	0.128	0.150
	(0.086)	(0.078)	(0.080)
Social Harmony (Hindu-Muslim)	0.202	0.328*	0.247
	(0.186)	(0.169)	(0.165)
Personal Financial Conditions	0.487**	0.520**	0.564**
	(0.172)	(0.151)	(0.153)
Employment	0.215	0.359**	0.319*
	(0.146)	(0.134)	(0.132)
Corruption	-0.167	0.159	-
	(0.161)	(0.136)	
Development	0.202	0.601**	-
	(0.186)	(0.192)	
National Security	0.667**	-	0.899**
	(0.208)		(0.172)
Central Government Performance	0.803**	-	-
	(0.121)		
Constant	-7.66**	-6.480**	-6.981**
	(0.921)	(0.802)	(0.810)
Observations	535	557	566
Pseudo R-squared	0.26	0.17	0.20

Source: Indian NES Survey (2004)
Significance: * = at 5%; ** = at 1%; standard errors are in parentheses.
Dependent Variable is vote choice, coded 0 for Congress, and 1 for the BJP

The logit coefficient estimates in the main model, column one, show that the indicators of ethnic group identity and interests relating to *caste (upper caste)* and *religion (Hindu)*, and the retrospective programmatic indicators relating to *personal financial conditions, national security,* and *central government performance* each have a positive and statistically significant impact on the likelihood of voting for the BJP, holding all else constant. We find that the retrospective programmatic indictors relating to *development, employment,* and *corruption* are not statistically significant on vote choice. The ethnic group interest indicator, *ram temple views*, is also not statistically significant on vote choice. Similar to the analysis of voting behavior in Delhi in the 1999 election, *religiosity* is also not statistically significant.

Since the indicator *central government performance* is akin to a broad job approval rating of government performance, I removed this indicator from model two and model three to better ascertain which retrospective issues are influencing vote choice. In addition, because of the moderately high correlation between indicators for *national security* and *corruption* (.50), and for *national security* and *development* (.49), I retained indicators for *corruption* and *development* in model two and removed the indicator for *national security*. In model three, I retained the indicator for *national security*, and removed indicators for *development* and *corruption*.

In model two, column two, I find that the retrospective programmatic indicators for *personal financial conditions, employment* and *development* are all positive and statistically significant on the likelihood of voting for the BJP. In addition, the ethnic group interest indicator, *social harmony*, is also statistically significant on vote choice. *Corruption* again is not statistically significant.

In model three, column three, in which *national security* is retained, I find that *national security* is positive and statistically significant on vote choice, but *social harmony* loses its statistical significance. In addition, there are no changes in the direction or the statistical significance of any of the remaining variables.

Predicted probabilities provide insight into the substantive effect of individual indicators on the likelihood of voting for the BJP.[206] Table 5.6 presents these predicted probabilities.[207]

Table 5.6 Predicted Probabilities: Delhi 2004 election

	(1)	(2)	(3)
Age	.25	.32	.30
Class (Rich)	n.s.	n.s.	n.s.
Caste (Upper Caste)	.11	.14	.16
Religion (Hindu)	.13	.15	.15
Religiosity	n.s.	n.s.	n.s.
Ram Temple views	n.s.	n.s.	n.s.
Social Harmony (Hindu-Muslim)	n.s.	.15	n.s.
Personal Financial Conditions	.22	.24	.26
Employment	n.s.	.17	.15
Corruption	n.s.	n.s.	n/a
Development	n.s.	.25	n/a
National Security	.27	n/a	.36
Central Government Performance	.50	n/a	n/a

Source: Computed from the logit coefficients.
n.s. = not statistically significant; n/a = not applicable

Predicted probabilities calculated for the main model, in column one above, indicate that ethnic group identity related to *caste (upper caste)* and *religion (Hindu)* increase the likelihood of voting for the BJP by 11 and 13 percentage points, respectively. Although conditions of ethnic conflict have reduced considerably in Delhi in 2004 compared to in 1999, ethnic factors continue to have a substantive impact on the likelihood of voting for the BJP in the 2004 election in Delhi.

Additionally, retrospective programmatic indicators relating to *personal financial conditions* and *national security* increase the likelihood of voting for the BJP by twenty-

---

[206] Logit coefficients provide information on the direction and statistical significance of different variables. Calculating predicted probabilities provides the ability to ascertain more information about the substantive effects of different indicators on the likelihood of voting for the BJP.

[207] Table 5.6 lists changes in the predicted probabilities of voting for the BJP as each indicator changes from its minimum to its maximum value, holding all other variables constant at their means, using the prchange command in Stata. See Long, J. Scott and Jeremy Freese, *Regression Models for Categorical Dependent Variables Using States Second Edition*. College Station: Stata Press, 2006, p. 169.

two, and twenty-seven percentage points, respectively. The indicator representing voter's overall assessment of *central government performance* has the greatest impact on the likelihood of voting for the BJP, increasing the likelihood of voting for the BJP by 50 percent points. Under conditions of a high political economy of development, retrospective programmatic interests appear to play a significant role in explaining voting behavior and the likelihood of voting for the BJP in the 2004 election in Delhi.

In model two, the predicted probabilities for retrospective indicators of *personal financial conditions*, *development*, and *employment* indicate significant substantive effects on the likelihood of voting for the BJP. In addition, the predicted probability for *social harmony* indicates a positive substantive effect on vote choice. In model three, the predicted probability for *national security* increases the likelihood of voting for the BJP by 35 percentage points.

These results from table 5.6 suggest that while ethnic group identity and interests continue to have substantive effects on voter support for the BJP, retrospective programmatic interests, in particular relating to *personal financial conditions*, *development*, and *national security*, appear to have strong substantive effects on the likelihood of voting for the BJP in the 2004 election in Delhi.

An additional question can be asked about the main model: since ERV's hypotheses make claims about the conditions under which ethnic group identity and interests become salient, and when retrospective programmatic interests become salient, we can ask what happens to the model if an interaction term is included which links these two factors. I generated two interaction terms, one that tests for the conditioning effects of *caste* and *development*, and a second, which tests for the conditioning effects of *caste* and *personal financial conditions*. The results are listed below in table 5.7.

Table 5.7 Logit Regression Results, Delhi 2004 election with interaction terms

	(1)	(2)
Age	0.145	0.0146
	(0.007)	(0.007)
Class (Rich)	0.261	0.218
	(0.237)	(0.240)
Caste (Upper Caste)	-0.179	-0.535
	(0.973)	(0.720)
Religion (Hindu)	0.700*	0.639*
	(0.296)	(0.297)
Religiosity	-0.123	-0.113
	(0.111)	(0.112)
Ram Temple Views	0.129	0.200
	(0.083)	(.084)
Personal Financial Conditions	0.429**	0.119
	(0.165)	(0.251)
Employment	0.287*	0.283*
	(0.141)	(0.141)
Corruption	0.046	0.052
	(0.145)	(0.145)
Development	0.311	0.495**
	(0.281)	(0.189)
Caste (Upper Caste) & Development	0.270	-
	(0.355)	
Caste (Upper Caste) & Personal Financial Conditions		0.503
		(0.321)
Central Government Performance	0.817**	0.811**
	(0.115)	(0.115)
Constant	-6.399**	-6.217**
	(1.007)	(0.9239)
Observations	555	555
Pseudo R-squared	.24	.24

Source: Indian NES Survey (2004)
Significance: * = at 5%; ** = at 1%; standard errors are in parentheses.
Dependent Variable is vote choice, coded 0 for Congress, and 1 for the BJP

I refer to, *Interaction Effects in Logistic Regression*, in the following discussion in interpreting the coefficients, focusing on column one of table 5.7.[210] Jaccard notes the

---

[210] Jaccard, James, *Interaction Effects in Logistic Regression*. Thousand Oaks: Sage Publications, 2001. See also Jaccard, James and Robert Turrisi, Interaction Effects in Multiple Regression, Second Edition. Thousand Oaks: Sage Publications, 2003.

importance of interpreting both the interaction term and the coefficients associated with the interaction term. To begin, the coefficient, *caste*, represents the odds ratio of voting for the BJP for upper caste voters versus non-upper caste voters in conditions when voters' perceptions of economic development have deteriorated.[211] This variable is not statistically significant. The coefficient, *development*, represents the ratio of the conditioning effects of development for non-upper caste voters on the odds of voting for the BJP, for a one unit increase (i.e., improvement) in voter perceptions' of economic development conditions.[212] This variable is also not statistically significant.

The variable of the interaction term, *caste&development*, represents the ratio of the conditioning effect of development on the odds ratio of voting for the BJP for upper caste voters versus voting for the BJP for non-upper caste voters, for a one unit increase (i.e., improvement) in voters' perceptions of economic development conditions.[213] The interaction term is not statistically significant. Thus, we find that the interaction effects represented by each of these three variables, *caste*, *development*, and *caste&development*, are not statistically significant. The same is true in model two, column two, in that the interaction effects represented by each of the variables, *caste, personal financial conditions*, and *caste&personalfinancialconditions* are not statistically significant.

---

[211] Jaccard notes that when a dummy variable, in this case *Caste*, is part of the product term, the coefficient is conditioned on the moderator-variable, in this case *Development*, being zero, which represents voter assessment that development conditions are not improving. In other words, the exponent of the dummy variable reflects the predicted odds ratio of voting for the BJP, comparing upper caste voters to non-upper caste voters in the case in which *Development* is equal to zero. See pgs. 20-21.

[212] Ibid, p. 31. The coefficient, *Development*, represents the conditional effects of development on the odds of voting for the BJP when *Caste* is equal to zero (i.e., non-upper caste).

[213] Ibid, p. 33. The interaction term represents a ratio of an odds ratio comparing the predicted odds of voting for the BJP when *Caste* equals 1 (i.e. upper caste voters) versus the odds of voting for the BJP when *Caste* equals 0 (i.e. non-upper caste voters), given a 1-unit increase in the conditional effect of *Development*.

We can also ask if the conditioning effect of *development* on the likelihood of voting for the BJP is statistically significant at specific point estimates for different values of the variables, *upper caste* and *development*. The following table presents the results of the marginal effects of *development* at different values of the variables, *upper caste* and *development*.[214] *Development* can take on three values, listed in the first column. *Upper Caste* can take on two values, (i.e. upper caste versus not upper caste), represented by columns three and four.

Table 5.8 Marginal effects of Development, Delhi 2004 Election

Development Variable Values	Upper Caste	Non Upper Caste
1) Development conditions have deteriorated	.31**	.35*
	(0.0561)	(0.1734)
2) Development conditions are the same	.37**	.39**
	(0.0439)	(0.134)
3) Development conditions have improved	.42**	.45**
	(0.077)	(0.096)

Source: Indian NES Survey (2004)
Significance: * = at 5%; ** = at 1%; standard errors are in parentheses.

We find that the marginal effect of *development* is statistically significant at different values of *development* and *upper caste*. For example, a positive retrospective evaluation of development conditions by upper caste voters increases the likelihood of voting for the BJP by 42 percentage points. By comparison, a positive retrospective evaluation of development conditions by non-upper caste voters increases the likelihood of voting for the BJP 45 percentages point. The results from this table indicate that the marginal effects of *Development* at different values are statistically significant, indicating a statistically significant interaction of *development* and *caste* at specific point estimates.

---

[214] Marginal effects at specific point estimates are calculated using the margins command in Stata.

Thus, while the marginal effect of *development* at different values is statistically significant at specific point estimates for *upper caste* and *development*, the results of the logistical model in table 5.7 with the interaction term indicate that the ratio of the conditioning effects of *development* on the odds ratio of voting for the BJP for upper caste voters versus voting for the BJP for non-upper caste voters, for a one unit increase in *development*, is not statistically significant.

As will be discussed in the next section examining individual case studies of New Delhi voters, I find that the relative impact of ethnic identity and interests and retrospective programmatic interests in explaining vote choice and voter support for the BJP has considerable variation among individual voters.[215]

The above analysis of 2004 Delhi survey data indicates that ethnic group identity interests and retrospective programmatic interests are significant factors influencing the likelihood of voting for the BJP. But how does this compare to 1999? Of particular interest, can we find evidence that ethnic group identity is having a greater or lesser role distinguishing voter support for the BJP in the 2004 election compared to the 1999 election?[216] Table 5.9 presents the results of the differences in sample proportions for BJP voters for indicators of caste and religion in the 1999 and 2004 election in Delhi. Column three presents the proportion of voters with a particular characteristic (i.e. upper caste, Hindu) who voted for the BJP, while column four presents the proportion of voters who do not have the characteristic and who voted for the BJP.

---

[215] Verma (2012) also created interaction terms of caste and assessment of past economic conditions using 2004 NES and 2009 NES data, and found that most of the interaction terms were statistically insignificant. See Verma, "What Determines Electoral Outcomes in India?," p. 283.

[216] It is important to note that the data examined in the 1999 election and in the 2004 election in Delhi is not panel data. Thus, making comparisons across time is limited to examining broad patterns in voting behavior.

Table 5.9 Differences of sample proportions for indicators of caste and religion for BJP voters, Delhi 1999 and 2004 elections

Year	Indicator	Yes	No	Difference in proportions
1999	Caste (upper caste)	.68	.24	-.44**
	Religion (Hindu)	.43	0	-.43
2004	Caste (upper caste)	.47	.28	-.19**
	Religion (Hindu)	.42	.28	-.14**

Source: Indian NES Survey (1999, 2004)
Significance: * = at 5%; ** = at 1%
N = 63 (1999); 791 (2004)

The results of the differences of sample proportions for caste and religion in the 1999 election and the 2004 elections indicate that the differences with respect to these ethnic indicators for BJP voters have narrowed. For example, in the 1999 election in Delhi, 68 percent of upper caste voters voted for the BJP while 24 percent of non-upper caste voters voted for the BJP. In the 2004 election, 47 percent of upper caste voters voted for the BJP while 28 percent of non-upper caste voters voted for the BJP.

In particular, if we look at the indicator for *caste (upper caste)*, we find a marked change in the percentage of upper caste voters who voted for the BJP. In the 1999 election, 68 percent of upper caste voters voted for the BJP in Delhi. Five years later, only 47 percent of upper caste voters vote for the BJP, indicating that the remaining 53 percent of upper caste voters voted for Congress. Thus, it appears that in 2004, the BJP was no longer predominantly associated with drawing upper caste voters, who instead were spread more evenly between the Congress and the BJP. *This suggests that ethnic group identity related to being upper caste had become a less distinguishing feature of BJP voters in the 2004 election compared to the 1999 election in Delhi.*

The analysis so far has shown that both ethnic group identity and interests and retrospective programmatic interests play significant factors in the likelihood of voting for the BJP in the 2004 election, but suggests that ethnic identity in particular relating to being upper caste appears to be less influential in explaining voter support for the BJP compared to the 1999 election in Delhi. In order to explain the significant change in electoral fortunes of the BJP in Delhi in the 2004 election, another aspect to consider is whether or not there have been changes in the priority of Delhi voters in terms of the importance of the work of the central government versus the work of the state level government, and how that impacts vote choice.

In the 1999 election, Delhi voters, regardless of whether they voted for the BJP or Congress, were much more concerned about the work of the central government than the work of the state government. Five years later, a different pattern emerges. The 2004 survey data shows that BJP voters continue to be much more concerned with the work of the central government, whereas Congress voters are now more focused on the work of the state government.[217] Table 5.10 identifies voters' priorities regarding the level of government in 2004.

Table 5.10 Delhi voter priorities in 2004: central versus state level government

	Neither	State level	Both	Central level	Other
All Voters	7.21	22.63	26.04	30.47	2.40
BJP voters	6.71	12.78	28.12	40.58	1.92
Congress voters	7.53	29.08	24.69	23.85	2.72

While BJP voters largely continued to focus their concerns on the work of the central government, Congress voters had become more concerned about the work of the state level government (increasing from 10.8 percent in 1999 to 29.08 percent in

---

[217] The 2004 NES survey asks the following question: "While voting some people give more importance to the work done by the state government while others give more importance to the work done by the central government. While voting in this election, what mattered to you most? (responses: Central Government in Delhi, State Government, Both, Neither, Others, Don't know)."

2004).[218] This data is suggestive that an increasing number of Delhi voters had become more focused on the work of the Congress-run state level government, which likely had a negative impact on the electoral fortunes of the BJP in the 2004 national elections.

In summary, this analysis of voting behavior in the 2004 election in Delhi indicates that, while ethnic group identity and interests continue to play a factor in voting behavior and voter support for the BJP in Delhi, a comparison of sample proportions for indicators of *caste* and *religion* in the 1999 and 2004 elections suggest that ethnic group identity, particularly being upper caste, had become a less distinguishing factor of BJP support in the 2004 election. Additionally, retrospective programmatic concerns on issues such as *development, personal financial conditions, employment* and *national security*, showed both statistical significance and strong substantive effects on the likelihood of voting for the BJP. Lastly, the findings from table 5.9 show that while BJP voters focused more on the work of the BJP-led central government, Congress voters in Delhi were more concerns about the work of the (Congress-led) state level government.

Under conditions of an increasingly strong political economy of development and a lower level of ethnic conflict compared to 1999, these findings of voting behavior in Delhi in the 2004 election, I argue, supports ERV's prediction, in which retrospective programmatic interests play a strong role in explaining voting behavior and voter support for the BJP, while the political salience of ethnic group identity is less influential, most closely represented by scenario 3 in table 3.1

---

[218] A cross tabs and chi-square analysis indicates that voter priorities regarding center versus state level government is statistically significant on vote choice. The P-value for the chi-square analysis: 0.

Delhi, 2009 Election

The 2009 national elections witnessed a continued decline in the political fortunes of the BJP in Delhi. Within a ten-year time frame, and in socio-economic conditions of a very high level of political economy of development, with state domestic product increasing to 16.8 percent in 2008-2009, and the absence of ethnic riots or violence, suggesting a low level of ethnic conflict, the BJP had gone from a party in the 1999 election which was able to win all of Delhi's seven Lok Sabha seats by capturing 51 percent of the vote share, to a party in the 2009 election that could not win a single parliamentary seat with a shrunken vote share of 35 percent.

The 2009 post-poll national election survey used for the following analysis includes 1,005 survey respondents in Delhi. Of these 1,005 survey respondents in Delhi, 358 respondents either did not provide information about which party they voted for (n=261), or indicated that they know which party they voted for (n=97). In addition, 55 respondents voted for smaller regional parties. Subtracting these respondents leaves a sample size of 592 respondents who either voted for the BJP or the Congress party. Of these 592 survey respondents, 378 voted for Congress and 214 voted for the BJP.[219] A full list of the descriptive statistics for the Delhi 2009 election analysis is listed in table 5, Appendix B.

An initial examination of the 2009 Delhi survey data reveals a slight increase in the number of Muslim respondents who voted for the BJP in the 2009 election. In the 2004 NES data for Delhi, two out of seventy Muslim survey respondents voted for the BJP, whereas in the 2009 NES data, we find that twelve out of seventy-one Muslim

---

[219] See "National Election Study 2009: A Methodological Note," *Economic and Political Weekly*, September 26, 2009.

respondents voted for the BJP. This is suggestive of a very small but increasing number of Muslim voters in Delhi who have become open to voting for the BJP despite its association with *Hindutva*.

While the sampling method used for the 2009 NES is the same as for the 2004 NES, the interview schedule used was different, which has important implications for my data analysis.[220] While the same set of survey questions was asked to all respondents in the 2004 NES, by contrast, five sets of questionnaires, including both common questions and unique questions, were randomly administered to respondents in the 2009 NES. Thus, some survey questions (i.e. class, caste, religion, religiosity, age, central government performance) were administered to all respondents, while others (including many which were asked to all respondents in 2004) were randomly administered to one-fifth of all respondents.[221]

Due to the nature of the 2009 Delhi data, which includes variables with very different sample sizes, a small logistic regression model is employed using variables with the full sample size to test for the effects of ethnic group identity interests and retrospective programmatic interests on the likelihood of voting for the BJP. Then, to better ascertain which retrospective issues are influencing vote choice, I remove the indicator, *central government performance*, and add individual indicators of retrospective programmatic voting, which have a much reduced sample size, with the results in models 2, 3 and 4.

---

[220] Ibid, p. 198. The NES uses a four-stage stratified random sampling procedure to achieve a representative sample of voters across the country. The four stages of random sampling are: parliamentary constituencies (PCS), assembly constituencies (ACS), polling stations (PSS) and respondents.

[221] As a result of this split sample interview schedule, the Delhi 2009 data includes relevant variables with a sample size of 1000, and other variables with a sample size closer to 200.

The main logit model in column one of the table below includes indicators of ethnic group identity: (i.e., caste and religion), and one indicator of retrospective programmatic voting (i.e., central government performance). The model also includes indicators for age, class and religiosity. Table 5.11 provides a summary of regression results for all four models.

Vote choice 2009 = $\beta_0 + \beta_1 Age_i + \beta_2$ Class (Rich)$_i$ + β_3Caste (Upper Caste)$_i$ + β_4Religion (Hindu)$_i$ + β_5Religiosity$_i$ + β_6Central Government Performance$_i$ + e_i

Table 5.11 Logit Regression Results, Delhi 2009 election

	(1)	(2)	(3)	(4)
Age	-0.0001	0.011	0.017	-0.001
	(0.058)	(0.012)	(0.013)	(0.014)
Class (Rich)	0.195	-0.232	0.429	-0.922
	(0.230)	(0.487)	(0.521)	(0.553)
Caste (Upper Caste)	0.813**	0.603	0.898	-0.381
	(0.225)	(0.520)	(0.575)	(0.588)
Religion (Hindu)	0.771**	2.103**	1.776*	2.287**
	(0.238)	(0.782)	(0.801)	(1.08)
Religiosity	0.068	0.041	-.0078	0.098
	(0.111)	(0.254)	(0.275)	(0.351)
Personal Financial Conditions	-	-0.117	-	-
		(0.216)		
Development	-	-	-0.494*	-
			(0.215)	
Terrorism	-	-	-	0.109
				(0.288)
Central Government Performance	-1.074**	-	-	
	(0.123)			
Constant	1.098	-3.136*	-1.782	-3.287
	(0.622)	(1.477)	(1.534)	(1.703)
Observations	555	112	103	86
Pseudo R-squared	.17	.12	.16	.12

Source: Indian NES Survey (2009)
Significance: * = at 5%; ** = at 1%; standard errors are in parentheses.
Dependent Variable is vote choice, coded 0 for Congress, and 1 for the BJP

The results of the main model in column one show that the ethnic identity indicators for *caste (upper caste)* and *religion (Hindu)* are positive and statistically significant, while the retrospective programmatic indicator for *central government performance* is negative and statistically significant on vote choice, holding all else constant. *Religiosity* is not statistically significant on vote choice.

In models two, three and four, I remove the indicator, *central government performance*, and add individual retrospective programmatic indicators, which have a reduced sample size. In column two, the retrospective programmatic indicator for *personal financial conditions* is included in the model. I find that this indicator is not statistically significant on vote choice. In column three, when the retrospective programmatic indicator for *development* is included in the model, it is negative and statistically significant on vote choice.

In the fourth model, in column four, when the *terrorism* indicator representing voter's assessment of government performance handling the 2009 Mumbai terrorism attacks is added to the model, it is not statistically significant on vote choice. Moreover, this model as a whole does not fit better than an empty model.[223] Table 5.12 below presents the predicted probabilities from the logistic regression results.

---

[223] The P-value for the likelihood ratio chi-square test statistic (LR chi2: 11.51) is .07 thus we cannot reject the null hypothesis that the model fits better than an empty model with all coefficients equal to zero.

Table 5.12 Predicted Probabilities, Delhi 2009 election

	(1)	(2)	(3)	(4)
Age	n.s.	n.s.	n.s.	n.s.
Class (Rich)	n.s.	n.s.	n.s.	n.s.
Caste (Upper Caste)	.17	n.s.	n.s.	n.s.
Religion (Hindu)	.16	.31	.26	.26
Religiosity	n.s.	n.s.	n.s.	n.s.
Personal Financial Conditions	n/a	n.s.	n/a	n/a
Development	n/a	n/a	-.40	n/a
Terrorism	n/a	n/a	n/a	n.s.
Central Government Performance	-.67	n/a	n/a	n/a

Source: Computed from the logit coefficients.
n.s. = not statistically significant; n/a = not applicable

Predicted probabilities for the main model show that ethnic identity indicators for *caste (upper caste)* and *religion (Hindu)* increase the likelihood of voting for the BJP by seventeen and fifteen percentage points respectively. *Central government performance* has the greatest negative impact on vote choice: the more satisfied one is with the incumbent Congress-led UPA government performance, the less likely one is to vote for the BJP, by 66 percentage points. *Religiosity* again is neither a statistically nor a substantively good indicator of voter support for the BJP in the 2009 election.

In column two, when the retrospective programmatic indicator *personal financial conditions* is added to the model, *religion (Hindu)* is the only indicator that has any substantive effects on the likelihood for voting for the BJP. However, in column three, when the indicator *development* is added to the model, I find a particularly strong negative substantive effect of retrospective assessments about development on vote choice: the more satisfied one is with the overall development conditions of the country during the incumbent UPA government tenure, the less likely one is to vote for the BJP by 40 percentage points. This suggests that voter concerns about and assessment of government performance on the issue of overall development conditions in India was a particularly important factor for voters, and strongly influenced whether or not a voter voted for the BJP in the 2009 election in Delhi.

Finally, when the indicator for *terrorism* is added in model four, it is neither statistically nor substantively significant, and similar to model two, *religion (Hindu)* is the only indicator that has any substantive effect on the likelihood for voting for the BJP. This is a marked change from both the 1999 and 2004 elections, in which issues of national security were important factors distinguishing voter support for the BJP. This is suggestive that issues of national security and terrorism had become less of a distinguishing factor of BJP voters in the 2009 election in Delhi.

In the analysis of voting behavior in Delhi in the 2004 election, the indicator, *ram temple views*, was not a statistically significant indicator nor did it have a strong substantively effect on vote choice. The 2009 NES survey administered a different question from the 1999 and 2004 surveys on the Ayodhya issue. The empirical results below suggest *ram temple views* did not differ markedly between Congress and BJP voters.

Table 5.13 What should be built at the Ayodhya site? (Delhi 2009)

	Neither	Mosque	Temple	Both	No opinion
All Voters	10	11	8	31	34
Congress voters	6	9	3	18	23
BJP voters	4	2	5	13	11

Source: *Indian NES Survey (2009)*
Figures above are in number of respondents.

The table presents the results from the 2009 NES survey question: What would you suggest be built on the site [at Ayodhya]?[224] We find that a larger number of

---

[224] In the 1999 and 2004 survey, a different but related question was asked: On the site where Babri Masjid was situated only Ram temple should be built (agree, no opinion, disagree). This question was asked to all survey respondents in the 2004 survey, whereas the Ayodhya-related question was

Congress voters favor a Mosque at Ayodhya than BJP voters. However, the majority of both Congress and BJP voters surveyed indicate that they have no opinion about the issue, or that they favor both a Hindu temple and a Muslim mosque to be built at the Ayodhya site. Although this is a very small sample size, it is suggestive that the ethnic group interest focusing on building the Hindu Ram temple is not a significantly distinguishing factor between Congress and BJP voters in the 2009 election in Delhi.

The analysis of voting behavior in Delhi in 2009 so far indicates that both ethnic group identity relating to *caste* and *religion*, and retrospective programmatic interests relating to *central government performance* and specifically relating to *development* are significant factors influencing the likelihood of voting for the BJP. How does the above data analysis compare to the results for the 1999 and 2004 elections with regard to the role of ethnic group identity?

Table 5.14 presents the results of the difference in sample proportions for indicators of caste and religion in the 1999, 2004 and 2009 elections for BJP voters in Delhi. Column 3 presents the proportion of voters with a particular characteristic (i.e. being upper caste) who voted for the BJP, while column 4 presents the proportion of voters who do not have the characteristic (i.e. non upper-caste) and voted for the BJP.

---

asked to only one-fifth of the respondents in the 2009 survey. The question was asked to 206 respondents in Delhi. Removing responses for "would not say" or "other" leaves a sample size of 94.

Table 5.14 *Differences of sample proportions for indicators of caste and religion for BJP voters, Delhi 1999, 2004 and 2009 elections*

Year	Indicator	Yes	No	Difference in proportions
1999	Caste (upper caste)	.68	.24	-.44**
	Religion (Hindu)	.44	0	-.43
2004	Caste (upper caste)	.47	.28	-.19**
	Religion (Hindu)	.42	.28	-.14**
2009	Caste (upper caste)	.42	.26	-.16**
	Religion (Hindu)	.40	.21	-.19**

Source: Indian NES Survey (1999, 2004, 2009)
Significance: * = at 5%; ** = at 1%
N = 63 (1999); 791 (2004); 592 (2009)

While the differences with respect to these ethnic indicators for BJP voters narrowed markedly between 1999 and 2004, the 2009 results show a slight decrease in the degree of difference in terms of being upper caste or not for BJP voters, and a slight increase in the degree of difference in terms of being Hindu versus non-Hindu for BJP voters.

If we look at the indicator for *religion (Hindu)*, although the empirical data indicates a small increase in the number of Muslims in Delhi who voted for the BJP in the 2009 election compared to the 2004 election,[225] the slight increase in the proportion of Hindus versus non-Hindus who vote for the BJP in 2009 compared to in 2004 (i.e. .14 in 2004 versus .19 in 2009) is likely explained by a decrease in the percentage of Sikh voters who voted for the BJP.[226]

If we look at the indicator for *caste (upper caste)*, we find a decreasing trend over time in the proportion of upper caste voters who vote for the BJP. In the 1999 election, 68

---

[225] In the 2004 NES sample for Delhi, two out of seventy Muslim survey respondents voted for the BJP, whereas in the 2009 NES data, twelve out of seventy-one Muslim respondents vote for the BJP.
[226] In the 2004 NES sample for Delhi, 63 percent of all Sikh voters voted for the BJP, representing 11 percent of BJP voters. However, in 2009, 31 percent of all Sikh voters voted for the BJP, representing only 3 percent of BJP voters. This shift of Sikh voters from the BJP to the Congress party contributed to a reduction in the number of non-Hindu BJP voters.

percent of upper caste voters voted for the BJP. Ten years later in the 2009 election, only 42 percent of upper caste voters vote for the BJP, thus the majority of BJP support in Delhi is no longer from upper caste voters. *This suggests that being upper caste had become a less influential characteristic distinguishing BJP voters from Congress voters in Delhi in the 2009 election, particularly compared to the 1999 national election.*

Lastly, an examination of the priority of Delhi voters in terms of the work of the central government versus the state government reveals a more similar pattern of priorities between Congress and BJP voters. While in the 2004 election, BJP voters were significantly more interested in the work at the center than were Congress voters, this pattern appears to have evened out in the 2009 election.

Table 5.15 Delhi voter priorities in 2009: central versus state level government

	Neither	State level	Both	Central level	Other
All Voters	6.08	21.96	26.18	28.04	1.86
BJP voters	8.88	23.83	23.36	24.77	1.87
Congress voters	4.50	20.90	27.78	29.89	1.85

Source: Indian NES Survey (2009)
Figures above are in percentages.

The table shows that Delhi voters from both parties place generally similar weight on the work of the state level government, while placing slightly greater weight on the work of the central government. It appears that in 2009, the differences in the priorities that existed in 2004 with regard to state versus center level government, is no longer a distinguishing feature between Congress voters and BJP voters.

The analysis of voting behavior in the 2009 election in Delhi shows that while ethnic identity interests of caste and religion are still politically salient factors, in particular being upper caste has become a less influential characteristic of voter support for the BJP over time. Additionally, we find that retrospective programmatic concerns, particularly about development, has a strong effect on the likelihood of voting for the BJP, suggesting that this issue was a particularly important factor influencing voting behavior in this election in Delhi.

Under conditions of a very high level of political economy of development and a low level of ethnic conflict, which characterized the context of the 2009 election in Delhi, ERV theory predicts relatively less influence in the political salience of ethnic group identity and a greater influence of retrospective programmatic interests in explaining voting behavior and overall voter support for an ethnic party. These empirical results, I argue, support ERV theory as a plausible means of explaining voter support for the BJP in Delhi in the 2009 election, most closely represented by scenario 3 in table 3.1.

New Delhi: Case Studies Analysis, 1999-2009

The second phase of research presents an analysis of case studies of 35 urban voters and their vote choices in the 1999, 2004 and 2009 national elections in New Delhi. As noted in Chapter Four, within the context of a nested research design, case studies provide a means to both elucidate and corroborate the findings in the large-N analysis, and in particular to examine and test ERV's hypothesized mechanisms as a means of explaining variation in urban voter support for the BJP at the level of the individual voter.

As described in Chapter Four, I use a purposive sampling design for this research component, in which cases (individual voters) were selected based on a combination of socio-economic characteristics (i.e., religion, caste, class/income, nature of employment). Table 5.16 provides a summary list of the socio-economic characteristics included in the New Delhi cases.[227]

Table 5.16 Summary of socio-economic characteristics of New Delhi case studies

Caste		Religion		Class		Sector	
Brahmin*	8	Hindu	28	Rich	4	Private	11
Punjabi Khatri*	5	Muslim	6	Upper Middle	8	Public	12
Hindu middle castes**	6	Christian	1	Middle	8	Unorganized	12
Scheduled castes***	9			Working	9		
Other	7			Poor	6		
Total	35		35		35		35

*Upper castes include Brahmins and Punjabi Khatris
**Hindu middle castes include: 3 Rajputs, 1 Kayastha, 1 Jatt/Gurgar, 1 OBC
**Scheduled castes are lower caste Hindus

The data used for the case studies analysis was collected using structured interviews of voters in New Delhi using a survey questionnaire format. In choosing these individual cases, it was not known in advance how a particular voter voted, or the reasons

---

[227] Age and gender were not purposively sampled.

why a voter voted for a particular party. These interviews were conducted in various locations throughout the city. Table 5.17 presents the details of each case study and their corresponding vote choices in the 1999, 2004 and 2009 national elections.

Table 5.17 New Delhi Cases

Case No.	M/F	Age	Caste/Religion	Class	Occupation	Sector	1999 Vote	2004 Vote	2009 Vote	Vote Type
24	M	40s	Brahmin	Rich	Partner, International Consulting Firm	Private	BJP	BJP	BJP	1
33	F	40s	Brahmin	Rich	Senior Executive, Large Multinational Bank	Private	BJP	BJP	Congress	1
25	M	30s	Brahmin	Rich	Partner, International Consulting Firm	Private	N/A	Congress	Congress	1
18	M	50s	Punjabi Khatri	Rich	President/CEO, Event Management Company	Private	BJP	Congress	Congress	1
13	F	30s	Punjabi Khatri	Upper-middle Class	Finance Officer, Multinational	Private	BJP	BJP	BJP	1
35	F	30s	Punjabi Khatri	Upper-middle Class	Director of Human Resources, Multinational	Private	BJP	N/A	Congress	1
30	M	40s	Brahmin	Upper-middle Class	Director, Indian Steel Company	Private	Congress	Congress	Congress	1
26	M	60s	Minority/Muslim	Upper-Middle Class	Senior Executive, Indian company	Private	Congress	Congress	Congress	1
29	F	30s	Brahmin	Middle Class	Administrative Secretary	Private	N/A	Congress	Congress	1
32	F	50s	Minority/Christian	Middle Class	School Teacher, Private School	Private	Congress	Congress	Congress	1
8	M	50s	Scheduled Caste	Working Class	Security Guard	Private	BJP	Congress	Congress	2
19	F	40s	Brahmin	Upper-middle class	Senior Gov't (Doctor)	Public	BJP	Congress	Congress	2
20	F	30s	OBC	Upper-middle class	Senior Gov't (Doctor)	Public	BJP	BJP	BJP	3
14	M	30s	Scheduled Caste	Upper-middle class	Senior Gov't (Doctor)	Public	Congress	Congress	Congress	4
16	M	50s	Scheduled Caste	Upper-middle class	Senior Gov't (Department Head)	Public	BJP	BJP	Congress	1
34	F	50s	Hindu Jatt/Gurjar	Middle Class	Mid-Level Gov't (Section Officer)	Public	BJP	BJP	Congress	1
22	M	50s	Hindu Rajput	Middle Class	Mid-Level Gov't (Lab Technician)	Public	BJP	BJP	BJP	4
21	M	50s	Hindu Rajput	Middle Class	Mid-Level Gov't (Classroom Technician)	Public	Congress	BSP	BSP	1
15	M	30s	Hindu Rajput	Middle Class	Mid-Level Gov't (Clerk)	Public	BJP	BJP	BJP	2
17	M	40s	Scheduled Caste	Working Class	Administrative Gov't (Office Assistant)	Public	BJP	Congress	Congress	1
27	F	30s	Scheduled Caste	Working Class	Administrative Gov't (Cleaning)	Public	BJP	Congress	Congress	1
28	M	30s	Scheduled Caste	Working Class	Administrative Gov't (Cleaning)	Public	BJP	BJP	BJP	4
23	M	50s	Minority/Muslim	Working Class	Administrative Gov't (File clerk)	Public	Congress	Congress	Congress	2
2	M	20s	Punjabi Khatri	Middle Class	Small clothing shop	Unorganized	BJP	Congress	Congress	1
5	M	30s	Muslim/Minority	Lower Middle Class	Owns small furniture shop, Batla House	Unorganized	Congress	Congress	Congress	2
1	M	40s	Punjabi Khatri	Working Class	Owns small magazine stand	unorganized	BJP	Congress	Congress	2
3	M	60s	Kayastha	Working Class	Small stand sells backpacks	Unorganized	BJP	Congress	Congress	2
7	F	30s	Brahmin	Working Class	Small stand where sells food	Unorganized	Congress	Congress	Congress	1
31	M	60s	Brahmin	Working Class	Tailor	Unorganized	Congress	Congress	Congress	4
6	M	70s	Scheduled Caste	Poor	Small ironing stand	Unorganized	Congress	Congress	Congress	4
9	M	30s	Scheduled Caste	Poor	Mehndi stand	Unorganized	Congress	Congress	Congress	1
11	F	50s	Scheduled Caste	poor	Construction/bricks	Unorganized	Congress	N/A	N/A	N/A
4	F	40s	Muslim/Minority	Poor	Small tobacco stand	Unorganized	Congress	Congress	Congress	4
12	F	40s	Muslim/Minority	Poor	Not employed	Unorganized	Congress	BJP	Congress	2
10	M	40s	Muslim/Minority	Poor	Vegetable seller	Unorganized	BJP	Congress	Congress	1
						Total BJP Vote	19	10	6	

The change in BJP vote share in the New Delhi cases shows a pattern of decreasing support from 1999 to 2009. In the 1999 national election, 19 out of 35 New Delhi cases voted for the BJP. In the 2004 election, ten New Delhi cases voted for the BJP, whereas in the 2009 election, the number of voters for the BJP decreased to six. Table 5.18 presents a summary of the vote choices of the New Delhi cases in each national election.

Table 5.18 New Delhi Cases: vote choices, 1999-2009 elections

Election Year	BJP	Congress	Other
1999	19	14	2
2004	10	22	3
2009	6	27	2

The Delhi large-N analysis indicates that ethnic group identity, particularly being Hindu and upper caste, played a significant factor in the likelihood of voting for the BJP in the 1999 election, but that the latter became less of an influential factor in explaining vote choice in the 2004 and 2009 elections. In the New Delhi case studies, while the majority of upper caste Hindus voted for the BJP in 1999 (3 out of 5 Brahmins, and 5 out of 5 Punjabi Khatris), in 2009, only 2 upper caste Hindu voters voted for the BJP (1 Brahmin and 1 Punjabi Khatri), again suggesting that being upper caste had become less strongly associated with voting for the BJP from 1999 to 2009.

The New Delhi cases studies indicate some evidence of non-Hindu support for the BJP: one Muslim, a vegetable seller (case 10), voted for the BJP in 1999 (case 10), and an unemployed Muslim woman (case 12) voted for the BJP in 2004. The vegetable seller indicated that he would consider voting for any party in future elections if the party convinced him that they could more successfully address rising price levels than the Congress party. In general, the New Delhi cases reveal that Hindus are more likely than non-Hindus to vote for the BJP, affirming the role of religion on vote choice.

However, the New Delhi cases did not present a discernable pattern linking changes in the level of religiosity with voter support for the BJP. I could not identify a pattern linking higher levels of religiosity with increased voter support for the BJP.

Recall that table 3.2 posits four types of individual voting behavior based on the different ways in which ERV's mechanisms impact individual vote choice. These four hypothesized types of individual voting behavior result from differences in an individual voter's assessment of the perceived risks from ethnic group conflict and the perceived rewards from economic reforms and development, which in turn results in differences in the relative influence of ethnic and programmatic interests in explaining individual voter support for and ethnic party.

The New Delhi case study analysis provides the opportunity to explore whether certain combinations of socio-economic characteristics show distinct patterns of individual voting behavior predicted by ERV theory with regard to the reasons why a voter votes for the BJP.

My fieldwork interviewing voters for the New Delhi cases suggests different broad patterns of individual voting behavior with regard to understanding variation in voter support for the BJP over time. My analysis of the New Delhi case studies reveals four predominant patterns of urban voting behavior to explain changes in electoral support for the BJP in New Delhi from 1999-2009. These four patterns of individual voting behavior are referred to as the following: 1) Retrospective Programmatic Voting, 2) Weak Ethnic voting, 3) Strong Ethnic Voting, and 4) Party loyalty. The following table presents the number of New Delhi cases for each of the four types of vote patterns.

Table 5.19 Summary of Vote Patterns: All New Delhi cases

Vote Pattern	Number
Type 1: Retrospective Programmatic Voting	19
Type 2: Weak Ethnic Voting	8
Type 3: Strong Ethnic Voting	1
Type 4: Party Loyalty	6
Inconclusive	1
Total number of New Delhi cases	35

The following presents a discussion the nature of these four patterns of voting behavior and provides examples of individual New Delhi case studies that exemplify each pattern.[229]

1. Retrospective Programmatic Voting: The first pattern of voting behavior in the New Delhi cases, Retrospective Programmatic Voting, is characterized by voters who indicate that their assessment of party performance on specific programmatic issues (i.e. such as development, household financial conditions, or national security) is the main driver underlying their vote choices in the three national elections. Retrospective programmatic voting behavior best explains the vote choices of 19 New Delhi voters interviewed in this study.

While New Delhi cases from various ethnic (i.e., caste and religion) and income groups are represented in this category, a particularly strong finding is that nearly all (10/11) of the voters interviewed who work in the private sector fall into this pattern of Retrospective Programmatic voting behavior. I believe this is a significant finding: in a country associated with a history of political clientelism, the ability to work in the private sector means that a person's economic livelihood is not primarily based on access to state

---

[229] I used the following procedure for coding each New Delhi case using the data collected from the survey questionnaire. Based on the structure of the survey, the voters interviewed were able to indicate the main factors affecting their vote choice for each election. I recorded the responses of each New Delhi case for each of the three elections. I next labeled each of the voter's responses as either primarily influenced by ethnic factors, programmatic factors, or based on some other factor. Once each of the voter's responses was labeled, I identified four different patterns of voting behavior to explain variation in voter support for the BJP. For example, it became clear that some voters voted for the BJP based predominantly on retrospective programmatic concerns, while other voters voted for the BJP based on predominantly ethnic interests. A third group of voters was distinctive in that they strongly emphasized ethnic interests in explaining voter support for the BJP in one election, but just as adamantly emphasized that these concerns had taken a back seat to programmatic concerns in later elections. Finally, a fourth group of voters did not emphasize either ethnic interests or programmatic interests when explaining their politics choices, and instead talked about their loyalty and their personal or family relationship to the party.

employment. In addition, most private sector employment generally provides higher incomes than in the government or unorganized sectors.

Recall that ERV's second mechanism is based on Kitschelt's idea that structural changes associated with a strong political economy of development support programmatic voter-party linkage formation and retrospective programmatic demands, and posits that economic development and economic reforms create the conditions for new opportunities and expectations by voters, which in turn creates the possibility for an increasing number of voters to make retrospective programmatic demands on government and political leaders.

The finding that nearly all the New Delhi respondents from the private sector fall into this pattern of Retrospective Programmatic Voting suggests that, unlike poor citizens who often must discount future rewards and instead rely on direct patronage-based exchanges in turn for votes, these voters may be on a more firm footing to be able to demand future indirect collective goods and in turn to be more focused on retrospective programmatic interests in their vote choices.

Case 35 is a an upper caste Hindu woman who works as a Director of Human Resources at a large private multinational company and who falls into this category of voting behavior. This voter supported the BJP in the 1999 election, based on her assessment that the party could do better on issues relating to economic development, her concerns about corruption and the Congress party, and her favorable opinion of BJP party leadership under Atal Bihari Vajpayee. She did not vote in the 2004 election.

However, by 2009, this voter felt that the Congress party had been doing well at the national level since 2004, and also indicated that she viewed the BJP's politics as unnecessarily stoking Hindu-Muslim tensions. With regard to the BJP, she says, "With the BJP, it is possible that [Narendra] Modi comes to power...[I am] not ok with voting for Modi. The reason we are the second largest fastest growing economy is because all kinds of people [are] working to get it there. *There is economic value to all people working together to move the country forward.*"[230] Thus, she switched her vote to the Congress in the 2009 election, in hopes that the party would continue to deliver high levels of economic growth, but also because she associated the BJP with the potential for stirring up ethnic conflict, which she felt could have a negative impact on economic development.

Case 24 is an upper caste Hindu man who is a Partner at a private sector consulting firm. Similar to case 35, this voter voted for the BJP in the 1999 election because he believed that the Congress had become inadequate at governing and was functioning less like a party and more like a "family corporate fiefdom." At the time, he believed that the BJP under the leadership of Atal Bihari Vajpayee would be in an overall better position to govern.[231] Although this voter indicated that he did not care for the BJP's politics of *Hindutva*, he continued to vote for the BJP in the subsequent 2004 and 2009 elections, based on his view that the Congress party does not function well, and on his assessment that the BJP would be better at governing and better able to deliver on high levels of economic growth and development.

I found this pattern of Retrospective Programmatic Voting from New Delhi cases who were not employed in the private sector. For example, case 16 is a Department Chair at a public university in New Delhi. He is a Hindu from a scheduled caste. This voter

---

[230] New Delhi case study 35. The voter is making reference to Gujarat's Chief Minister Narendra Modi.
[231] New Delhi case study 24.

voted for the BJP in the 1999 and 2004 elections based largely on his concerns about employment, and his overall positive assessment of his local member of parliament (MP), a member of the BJP, who he believed was doing a good job promoting local economic development. In addition, he felt that Atal Bihari Vajpayee, as the leader of the BJP, was the right person to be Prime Minister and the most capable to lead the country.

This voter also expressed a strong dislike for the BJP's ideology of *Hindutva*, and indicated that he had become increasingly concerned about the BJP under the leadership of L.K. Advani in the run-up to the 2009 election saying, "Advani was responsible for the *Rath Yatra*...[the] demolition of the Babri Masjid...This was a dangerous move, just for the sake of politics."[232] In the 2009 election, he switched his vote to the Congress party based on his initial assessment of the performance of his new Congress MP, but similar to the Director of Human Resources, also because he associated some BJP leaders with the potential to provoke unwanted ethnic conflict.

My findings suggest that voters in this category place a high value not only on the role of economic growth and development but also on the importance of good governance. For some voters in this category, such as the Partner in the consulting firm, the role of ethnic conflict is not highlighted as a significant factor on vote choice. For other voters in this category, such as the Director of Human Resources or the Department Chair, ethnic conflict, rather than representing a group threat leading to a sense of heightened in-group identification, instead represents a potential negative influence on economic growth and development and to social stability in general. This pattern of Retrospective Programmatic Voting most closely resembles type 1 voting behavior in

---

[232] New Delhi case study 16.

table 3.2, in which a voter is generally more influenced by the opportunities posed by economic reforms and development than in-group threat posed by ethnic conflict, and thus vote choice and the evaluation of an ethnic party is predominantly influenced by retrospective programmatic interests.

While nearly all the New Delhi cases interviewed from the private sector fall into this category of Retrospective Programmatic Voting, voters from the public and unorganized sectors, as well as from different income levels and castes groups, also indicated that a retrospective assessment of government performance, on issues ranging from national and local development conditions, employment, price inflation and corruption, were key factors determining their vote choice and whether or not to vote to for the BJP. This suggests that the opportunities resulting from both a growing private sector as well as other changes taking place in New Delhi's very high political economy of development is supporting the conditions for voters to make retrospective programmatic demands on government and political leaders.

2. Weak Ethnic Voting: The second pattern of voting behavior, Weak Ethnic Voting, is quite different from the pattern described above. This pattern of voting behavior is characterized by New Delhi cases whose political choices are strongly influenced by ethnic identity and interests at one point of time, but whose political preferences distinctly change, such that they are more influenced by retrospective programmatic interests at a later point in time.[233] Weak Ethnic Voting best explains the voting behavior of eight New Delhi voters interviewed in this study.[234]

---

[233] Voters in this second category were very open about discussing their ethnic interests and the way in which these ethnic interests affected their decision to vote for the BJP.
[234] The eight New Delhi cases that fall into this category of weak ethnic voting behavior are cases 1, 3, 5, 8, 12, 15, 19 and 23.

While nearly all the voters working in the private sector fall into the category of Retrospective Programmatic Voting, the majority of voters in this pattern of voting behavior are either from the lower-middle class, are working class or poor, and half of the respondents work in the unorganized sector. Additionally, most of voters in this category are either from a middle or lower caste, or are a minority. Thus, this category of voters has a markedly different socio-economic profile from the cases in the first category.

A key characteristic of this group is that ethnic identity and interests are a distinguishing, if not the defining factor, driving their political choices at a particular point of time, (i.e., the 1999 election). Most notably, all of the New Delhi voters interviewed who are in this category and voted for the BJP in the 1999 election indicated that that their views and concerns about building the Hindu Ram temple were either an important factor or the driving factor in their vote choice.[235] However, in later elections, these voters indicated that their desire for the Ram temple to be built was no longer a factor in their vote choice. In the 2009 election, all voters in this category indicated that retrospective programmatic interests had become the primary factors influencing their vote choice.

Case 1 owns a small but thriving magazine stand in an outdoor market whose business has put him in Delhi's fast growing working class. He comes from a Punjabi Khatri family. In explaining his vote for the BJP in the 1999 election he noted that, "he is

---

[235] This finding is in contrast to the results of the large-N analysis for 1999, in which an indicator representing voter's preferences about whether or not the Hindu Ram temple should be built was not a statistically significant factor upon vote choice. As noted earlier, one explanation could be that the question about the Ram temple in the Indian NES survey is different from the survey question asked about the temple in the New Delhi case studies. The former NES survey question asks the respondent if she believes that the temple should be built, whereas the wording of the question for the case studies is more direct in asking if the temple was a factor in vote choice.

deeply devoted to Ram," and that this was the main issue for him and him family in their vote choice.

However, in 2004 after five years of the BJP-led government in power, this small business owner noted his dissatisfaction in that, not only did the BJP not take action about the Ram temple, but he was also motivated by Congress-leader Dr. Manmohan Singh's potential leadership. In the 2004 election, he switched his vote to Congress. Five years later, in the 2009 election, he notes that while the Ram temple is still important to him personally, it is no longer important to his political choice. Rather he says, "What is important is if parties can deliver on specific issues well. Development and growth are more important than religious issues."[236]

In addition, by the 2009 election, this voter's perception of ethnic conflict appears to have changed. He notes, "If people start fighting over religious issues, this can turn into conflict, and this can hinder progress." At this time, ethnic conflict is viewed less as a source of heightening in-group identification, and instead is viewed as having the potential to negatively impact economic growth and development, echoing similar concerns made by the Director of Human Resources.

Like the owner of the magazine stand, case 3 also works in the unorganized sector and operates a small but busy outdoor stand where he sells and fixes backpacks near a university. He is a middle caste Hindu whose small business also places him in Delhi's working class.

This small business owner voted for the BJP in the 1999 election, in part because he hoped that the party would take action and build the Ram temple, and also because he

---

[236] New Delhi case study 1.

felt that Atal Bihari Vajpayee would be a good leader. However, after five years of BJP rule, he was disappointed with the BJP's performance and was concerned about the role of BJP leader, L.K. Advani. He switched his vote to Congress in the 2004 election.

In the 2009 election, this voter emphasized his focus on party leadership in terms of being able to generate employment, and threw his political support behind the Congress party under the helm of Sonia Gandhi. In contrast to his views of the BJP in 1999, this voter now viewed the BJP under the leadership of L.K. Advani as "doomed," because "Advani would focus on making religious conflict."[237]

My findings suggest that voters in this category are influenced by both ethnic concerns, such as the Ram temple, and retrospective programmatic concerns, such as economic growth and employment. This pattern of Weak Ethnic Voting most closely resembles type 3 voting behavior in table 3.2, in which a voter is influenced by both the perceived risk of group threat from ethnic conflict and the opportunities posed by economic reforms and development, and as a result, changes in socio-economic conditions in turn change the relative importance of ethnic group identity and interests and retrospective programmatic interests on vote choice.

In conditions of moderate ethnic conflict in the 1999 election in Delhi, the political salience of ethnic group identity and interests for this type of voter appears to swamp out retrospective programmatic interests in explaining voter support for the BJP. However, in conditions of a very high political economy of development and a low level of ethnic conflict in the 2009 election in Delhi, retrospective programmatic interests supersede ethnic interests in these voters' political choices. Under the latter conditions,

---

[237] New Delhi case study 3.

these voters' perception of and relationship to ethnic conflict begins to resemble the views of some voters in the first category of retrospective programmatic voting.

3. Strong Ethnic Voting: The third pattern of voting behavior found in the New Delhi cases, Strong Ethnic Voting, is characterized by voters who indicate that ethnic group identity and interests are the predominant factor influencing their vote choice. For this type of voting behavior, the political salience of ethnic identity and interests persists in importance over time with regard to influencing political choices. Strong Ethnic Voting best explains the voting behavior of one New Delhi voter in this study.

Case 20 is an upper middle class, middle caste Hindu woman voter working in a highly skilled position in the public sector, who voted for the BJP in the 1999, 2004 and 2009 national elections. This voter indicates that while she is concerned about issues like corruption, development and national security, she emphasizes that she "connects" with the BJP's vision of *Hindutva*, which she associates with advocating for Hindus. The voter indicates that her continued support for the BJP over the three elections had less to do with the party's stated support for building Ram temple, and more broadly to do with her belief in the BJP's underlying support for Hindus and its vision of *Hindutva*. Of *Hindutva*, she says, "I connect to it. Other parties support other religions. [The] BJP is trying to protect Hindus."[238] For this voter, the notion that the BJP "protects" Hindus is a powerful influence in her support for the party over three national elections.

Although I interviewed only one New Delhi voter who fit into this third category of voting behavior, in interviews with other New Delhi case study respondents, two voters said that they knew of members of their own family, who were often older, and

---

[238] New Delhi case study 20.

who privately indicated that the BJP's explicit support for Hindus through advocating *Hindutva*, coupled with their belief that Congress focuses too much on Muslims, strongly influences their decision to vote for the BJP.[239]

In this pattern of Strong Ethnic Voting, the political salience of ethnic group identity and interests persists as a predominant factor guiding a voter's political choices. For this pattern of voting behavior, it appears that a voter's perception of group threat from ethnic conflict does not ebb and flow, as it does for weak ethnic voters, but rather it remains a strong ongoing concern influencing her vote choice. At the same time, this type of voter appears less focused on or influenced by the opportunities arising from changing conditions in the political economy of development.

This pattern of Strong Ethnic Voting most closely resembles type 2 voting behavior in table 3.2, in which the perceived threat from ethnic group conflict remains high, increasing an individual's sense of in-group identification, and thus vote choice and the evaluation of an ethnic party is predominantly influenced by ethnic group identity and interests.

4. Party Loyalty: The fourth pattern of voting behavior identified in the New Delhi cases, Party Loyalty, is characterized by voters who indicate a predominant focus on party loyalty, either stemming from the individual voter or the voter's family.[240] Six voters from the New Delhi cases fall into this category of party loyalty.

---

[239] New Delhi cases 35 and 24, who are both in their 30s and working in the private sector, indicated that they knew of family members who were from an "older generation," and who supported the BJP for these reasons.

[240] The survey questionnaire used for the case study analysis was not designed to identify or measure the strength of party identification in the way this term is used in the American politics literature. Rather, I am using the term, party loyalty, more simply to refer to respondents who indicate that party loyalty, rather than a particular ethnic or programmatic interest per se, is the driving factor in their support for a particular political party.

What is different about this category of voting behavior compared to the other three categories described above is that these voters generally do not emphasize either ethnic group identity and interests, or retrospective programmatic interests, as the key factors in their vote choice. Rather, their focus is almost entirely on voting for a particular party.

Cases 22 and 28 are BJP voters who fall into this category of party loyalty. Case 22 is a middle caste Hindu who works as a lab technician in a public institution of higher education. Case 28 is a scheduled caste Hindu who works as part of the cleaning staff at the same institution. Case 22 indicates that, while programmatic issues such as development, corruption, employment and prices are issues of concern, the most important factor in his vote choice is that his family always votes for the BJP. In addition, this voter indicated that the BJP's support for building the Ram temple was not a factor in his vote choice. Interestingly, he did not think that the BJP leader, L.K Advani would be a particularly good leader for India, because he associated him with the *Rath Yatra* to mobilize support for constructing the Ram temple in 1990 and the ensuing ethnic violence that followed. Yet, despite his concerns, this voter voted for the BJP in all three elections.[241]

Similarly, case 28 also indicates that he votes for the BJP because his family votes for the party. Unlike the previous voter, this voter was not able or willing to identify any particular political interests or concerns. Rather, he said that he is influenced by his uncle, who has a connection with the BJP and tells his family that they should vote for the party.

---

[241] New Delhi case study 22.

While neither of these voters indicated that patronage played a role in their vote choice, another New Delhi voter, case 27, noted during her interview that the BJP had distributed blankets to her neighborhood in the run-up to the 1999 election.[242] The New Delhi case studies do not provide clear evidence about the role and degree of patronage for these voters. For this category of voting behavior, it appears that neither mechanism posited in ERV theory adequately explains voting behavior, as neither ethnic group identity and interests nor retrospective programmatic interests play an important role in explaining voter support for an ethnic party. Rather, family or individual party loyalty appears to be the primary influence guiding voters' political choices. This pattern of Party Loyalty voting most closely resembles type 4 voting behavior in table 3.2, though it is important to note that it is unclear the degree to which party patronage plays a factor in these voters' political choices.

In summary, the above analysis of New Delhi case studies reveals four patterns of individual voting behavior to explain variation in voter support for the BJP: 1) Retrospective Programmatic Voting, 2) Weak Ethnic Voting, 3) Strong Ethnic Voting, and 4) Party Loyalty. I posit that ERV can explain the first three of these patterns of urban voting behavior in New Delhi, representing the different ways in which ERV's mechanisms impact individual voting behavior, through differences in an individual voter's assessment of and relationship to ethnic group conflict and economic reforms and development, which result in differences in the relative influence of ethnic group identity and interests and retrospective programmatic interests on vote choice and explaining individual voter support for an ethnic party.

---

[242] New Delhi case study 27 is a swing voter who fits the first pattern of voting behavior. She voted for the BJP in 1999 because she thought it could address rising prices, crime, and her concerns about employment for her adult children. She switched her vote to the Congress party in 2004 and 2009.

Chapter 6: Ethnic Politics and Voting Behavior in Gujarat and Ahmedabad

Located in western India, the state of Gujarat is a place of contrasts. Often considered the premier business state in India, the highly industrialized state is known for its long history of trade and corresponding mercantile culture of non-violent conflict resolution.[243] The state is the third most urbanized state in the country with over forty percent of Gujaratis living in urban areas.[244] Gujarat is also famous as the birthplace of Mahatma Gandhi[245] where, upon returning to India from South Africa, Gandhi chose the city of Ahmedabad to live and mobilize his vision of a non-violent independence movement against the British Raj.

Yet, in recent years, Gujarat, and in particular Ahmedabad, Gujarat's largest city, and India's fifth largest city, has become known for episodes of some of the most deadly Hindu-Muslim violence in India. This research project does not seek to answer the question of why Gujarat in particular has had such a stormy history of Hindu and Muslim

---

[243] Yagnik, Achyut and Suchitra Sheth, *The Shaping of Modern Gujarat: Plurality, Hindutva and Beyond.* New Delhi: Penguin Books, 2005. Located on the coast of the Indian ocean with multiple harbors and ports, the present area of Gujarat is believed to have a history of active maritime trade across Asia going back over a thousand years, (pgs. 18-38).

[244] Gujarat has twenty cities with a population of over 100,000 and four cities, Ahmedabad, Surat, Vadodara and Rajkot, with a population over one million. The 2011 Census of India estimates Gujarat's level of urbanization at 44 percent. See Census of India website, http://censusindia.gov.in/2011census/censusinfodashboard/stock/profiles/en/IND024_Gujarat.pdf Gujarat's urban population is projected to increase to two-thirds of the total population by 2030. After Delhi, the state of Tamil Nadu has the highest urban population with 53 percent. See, *India's Urban Awakening: Building Inclusive Cities, Sustaining Economic Growth*, McKinsey Global Institute: April 2010, p. 15.

[245] Gandhi was born in the town of Portbandar in 1869, which at the time was located in the British province of Bombay Presidency, but is now located in the state of Gujarat.

relations.[246] Rather, in this chapter I seek to examine voting behavior in Gujarat and Ahmedabad, in order to examine the factors affecting voter support for the BJP over time in an urbanized state with a historical context of violent ethnic conflict.

As a highly industrialized state with one of the country's fastest urbanization rates, and a political system dominated by the Congress and BJP parties, Gujarat shares some characteristics in common with Delhi that make it a good place for comparing urban voting behavior. Unlike in Delhi, where the BJP's fortunes went from capturing all the Lok Sabha parliamentary seats in 1999 to losing all the seats in 2009, the BJP in Gujarat has remained the dominant party in power for nearly two decades.

This chapter presents an empirical analysis of voting behavior in Gujarat and an in-depth analysis of voting behavior in Ahmedabad, and tests Ethnically Mediated Retrospective Voting (ERV) theory as a plausible means of explaining variation in urban electoral support for the BJP over the 1999, 2004 and 2009 national elections. The chapter is comprised of three main sections: 1) an overview of the history and political context of Gujarat relevant for this study, 2) an analysis of Indian National Election Study (NES) survey data of Gujarat voters for the 1999, 2004 and 2009 elections, and 3) an examination of case studies of individual voters and voting behavior in the city of Ahmedabad.

---

[246] Several authors have addressed this important topic. See, Varshney, Ashutosh, *Ethnic Conflict and Civic Life: Hindus and Muslims in India*. New Haven: Yale University Press, 2005. Wilkinson, Steven, *Votes and Violence: Electoral Competition and Ethnic Riots in India*. Cambridge: Cambridge University Press, 2004. Shani, Ornit, *Communalism, Caste and Hindu Nationalism: The Violence in Gujarat*. Cambridge: Cambridge University Press, 2007.

Gujarat

Gujarat's early industrialization and urbanization is strongly tied to its history as a center of cotton production and processing in the 1800s, followed by the rise of its textile industry in the mid-19th and early 20th century.[247] Two important factors in the development of Gujarat's textile industry are the American Civil War, in which demand for Western Indian cotton exploded, and the rise of textile mills, particularly in Ahmedabad, creating the capacity for cotton to be not only produced but also to be processed and manufactured locally.[248] From 1861 to 1946, the number of textile mills in Ahmedabad increased from one to seventy-four, resulting in large-scale urban migration for millwork, and the emergence of a large urban working class and a burgeoning smaller middle class.

From a political perspective, Gandhi's leadership and mobilization to achieve political independence and social reforms from his home base in the city of Ahmedabad resulted in the development of a strong state-level grass roots Congress party organization. The Indian National Congress Party under Gandhi's leadership working with Gujarat lawyer and Congress leader, Vallabhbhai Patel,[249] were integral pillars of Hindu-Muslim harmony in Gujarat in the first half of the 20th century.[250] By

---

[247] Yagnik and Sheth, p. 101. For a good introduction to the rise of the textile industry, see chapter 5, *Industrialization and Swadeshi*, pgs. 98-131.
[248] Ibid, p. 106. During the American Civil War, the South imposed its own cotton embargo disrupting cotton supplies to England. As a result, demand for cotton from Gujarat greatly intensified.
[249] Vallabhbhai (Sardar) Patel was a leader of the Indian National Congress known for his leadership in the Indian independence movement and the integration of post-independence India.
[250] Varshney, Ashutosh, *Ethnic Conflict and Civic Life: Hindus and Muslims in India,* chapter 9. Varshney identifies the role of Gandhi's political leadership, the Congress party, business guilds (mahajans) and labor unions as key factors in promoting intercommunal civic activity and in turn Hindu-Muslim peace in Ahmedabad in the first half of the 20th century.

the middle part of the 20th century, Gujarat had become an industrialized, urbanizing state with a strong Gandhian influence promoting Hindu-Muslim harmony.

However, over the past forty years, four primary countervailing forces have deeply affected the social fabric and political trajectory of Gujarat, and Ahmedabad in particular. These forces can be described as 1) the decline of the Congress party at the state level, 2) major episodes of Hindu-Muslim violent conflict, 3) the decline of the textile industry in the 1980s, and 4) the rise of the BJP in the 1990s to become the political dominant player in the state.

In 1969, Congress party infighting lead to a split of the party between Prime Minister Indira Gandhi and regional party leadership, marking a period of decline and weakening party organization in Gujarat.[251] The year, 1969, also witnessed the first of several of episodes of severe large-scale Hindu-Muslim violent conflict in Gujarat.[252] The 1969 riots in Ahmedabad are considered one of the worst cases of Hindu-Muslim violence in post-Independence India.[253]

The 1970s saw continuing cracks in the role and influence of the Congress Party in Gujarat. In 1974, the Nav Nirman riots across the state exposed deep frustration with Congress political leadership about rising prices of essential commodities and the widespread belief that the problem was the result of collusion

---

[251] Ibid, pgs. 241-242.
[252] For a detailed description of the 1969 riots in Ahmedabad, see Shah, Ghanshyam, "Communal Riots in Gujarat: Report of a Preliminary Investigation," *Economic and Political Weekly*, January 1970, pgs. 187-200. The number of people killed ranges from 1000 (Shah) to 600 (Varshney).
[253] Yagnik and Sheth, p. 230. It is important to note that the 1969 riots were not the first instance of violence in Ahmedabad. See, Spodek, Howard, "From Gandhi to Violence: Ahmedabad's 1985 Riots in Historical Perspective," *Modern Asian Studies*, 23(4), 1989. Spodek cites smaller outbreaks of violence in Ahmedabad in 1941, 1942, 1946, 1956, 1958 and 1964.

and price rigging by Congress politicians and traders.[254] What began as initial student protests in Ahmedabad turned into broad based protests and rioting across urban Gujarat, killing 100 people. The Nav Nirman riots deteriorated into a major political crisis, leading to the resignation of the Congress Chief Minister Chimanbhai Patel, and the imposition of presidential rule on Gujarat from the central government.[255]

The following year, in June 1975, Prime Minister Indira Gandhi declared an internal emergency lasting eighteen months and jailed her political opponents, including leaders of the Bharatiya Jana Sangh (BJS) party, the precursor to the BJP. The fallout from the Nav Nirman protests and Gandhi's internal emergency created an opening for the Jana Sangh party to broaden its base with frustrated and angry upper caste and middle class urban voters in Gujarat. The Jana Sangh, as part of a coalition of opposition parties, collectively called the Janata Party, defeated Congress and came to power in Gujarat in the 1975 state assembly election and again in the 1977 national election, which also marked the first time that a non-Congress government ruled in India.[256]

After the defeat of the Congress party in Gujarat to the Janata Party in the 1977 national election, Gujarat Congress leader, Madhavsinh Solanki, developed and successfully implemented the "KHAM" formula, a caste and religion based electoral

---

[254] Jones, Dawn and Rodney Jones, "Urban Upheaval in India: The 1974 Nav Nirman Riots in Gujarat," *Asian Survey*, 16(4), November 1976. Nav Nirman means "social reconstruction."

[255] Ibid, p. 1029. Christophe Jaffrelot notes that the Nav Nirman student protests were fused into a campaign by the Jana Sangh Party and the RSS's student wing, the Akhil Bharatiya Vidhyarthi Parishad (AVBP) against rising prices. See Jaffrelot, *The Hindu Nationalist Movement in India*, p. 258.

[256] *Statistical Report on General Election, 1975 to the Legislative Assembly of Gujarat*, New Delhi: Election Commission of India, http://eci.nic.in/eci_main1/ElectionStatistics.aspx. For background on the emergency see Frankel, *India's Political Economy 1947-2004*, pgs. 544-546, 649-652.The Janata Party coalition collapsed in 1980. For background on the 1975 assembly elections in Gujarat, see Shah, Ghanshyam, "The 1975 Gujarat Assembly Election in India," *Asian Survey*, vol. 16(3), March 1976.

strategy targeting the caste groups, Kshatriyas (a warrior caste), Harijans (Scheduled Castes, also known as Dalits), Adivasis (Scheduled Tribes), and Muslims.[257] The KHAM strategy worked extremely well electorally in 1980 against the newly created BJP (the first time the BJP competed electorally in Gujarat), with Congress winning both the national and state level elections in Gujarat.[258]

In 1985, Gujarat Chief Minister Solanki again targeted the KHAM caste and religion groups in the state assembly elections. Shortly before the state assembly election, Solanki announced an eighteen percent increase in the quota of reserved spaces in educational institutions and government jobs for OBCs from 10 percent to 28 percent.[259] The KHAM strategy again proved a successful electoral strategy for Congress, who won the Gujarat assembly election.

However, while the KHAM strategy worked well electorally for Congress in the 1980 and 1985 elections in Gujarat, socially the KHAM strategy created an enormous amount of resentment from the urban upper castes and middle class Gujaratis, notably, the Brahmins, Banias and Patels.[260] Beginning in February 1985 and for the following six months, Ahmedabad experienced another large scale major episode of widespread violent conflict and rioting, first directed at Dalits (scheduled

---

[257] Shani, Ornit, *Communalism, Caste and Hindu Nationalism: The Violence in Gujarat*, p. 74.

[258] Jaffrelot, p. 74. The BJP was created on April 6, 1980 from members of the Janata Party. See Jaffrelot, p. 315. The Congress party won all but one of Gujarat's twenty-six Lok Sabha parliamentary seats, and 140 out of 181 state assembly seats in 1980. See also Achyut and Sheth, p. 254.

[259] Shani, p. 79.

[260] Brahmins are traditional high caste Hindus. Banias are from the merchant or trading community and are also considered upper caste. The Patels are traditionally from a landowning caste and have been an upwardly mobile social group.

castes), but then turning into riots between Hindus and Muslims, killing about 275 people.[261] More Hindu-Muslim riots broke out the following year in Ahmedabad.

Also during this time, Gujarat experienced a period of de-industrialization in the 1980s resulting from a crisis in the textile mill industry. Writing about the mill crisis in Ahmedabad, Ornit Shani notes that between 1979 and 1984, twelve textile mills were closed, of which nine were closed in a period of six months, between 1983 and 1984, with an estimated 40,000-50,000 workers losing their mill jobs by 1985.[262] The rapid closure of textile mills created a major shock to the labor market, where mills were a predominant means of employment for many of the residents living in Ahmedabad.

The political turbulence created by Congress party infighting, the deep unpopularity and resentment of Congress policies particularly from the urban upper caste and middle class about the KHAM strategy and reservations, and the major economic upheaval created by the decline of the textile industry, created an opportunity for the newly created BJP to mobilize and gain a foothold in Gujarat.[263]

In the late 1980s, Gujarat became the staging ground for Hindu nationalist political mobilization efforts. During this time period, the BJP joined forces with the Hindu nationalist organization, Vishwa Hindu Parishad (VHP), in a sustained political mobilization effort centered on building the Ram temple in the city of Ayodhya.[264] In

---

[261] Spodek, p. 765.
[262] Shani, Ornit, *Communalism, Caste and Hindu Nationalism: The Violence in Gujarat*, p. 39. Shani notes that many workers lost their jobs due to technological advances of the power loom, see footnote 74, p. 39. The job loss estimates are taken from Varshney (40,000) and Shani (50,000).
[263] Varshney, p. 243.
[264] The Vishwa Hindu Parishad (VHP), also known as the World Hindu Council, was created in 1964 by the Rashtriya Swayamsevak Sangh (RSS) to promote and protect Hinduism. Throughout the

1987, the VHP launched an organized mass mobilization effort, the *Ram-Janaki Dharma Yatra*, taking place throughout Gujarat with the goal of "transcending caste and sect differences in the worship of Shri Rama and to affirm the unity of all Hindus."[265]

As described in Chapter Two, the most well known mobilization effort to "liberate Ram Janmabhoomi" and build a Ram temple at Ayodhya was initiated by BJP leader, L.K. Advani in the form of a *Rath Yatra* on September 25, 1990 in the city of Somnath, Gujarat.[266] Advani chose Somnath as the starting point of the *Rath Yatra* because it symbolized a place where Hindu temples had been both demolished and rebuilt.[267] After driving around India for nearly a month, Advani was arrested on October 23 in the state of Bihar. The BJP responded by launching a national protest movement, which in turn triggered ethnic riots across the country, killing about 100 people in Gujarat.[268]

The political impact of the yatras in Gujarat was dramatic: the yatras and associated Hindu-Muslim violent conflict that followed in their wake weakened the political effectiveness of the KHAM electoral strategy, and reshaped social and political alignments through the message of Hindu unity and pride. By 1990, the social and political identity of *Savarna* (upper caste Hindus) versus *Avarna* (lower castes Hindus and tribals) was reconstituted, emphasizing instead Hindus versus Muslims,

---

1980s, the VHP spearheaded efforts to build Hindu temples in order to bring Hindus of all castes together and build Hindu unity. See Jaffrelot, pgs. 193, 359-360.
[265] Yagnik and Sheth, p. 258.
[266] Jaffrelot, pgs. 416-420.
[267] According to L.K. Advani's website, Somnath was chosen as the starting point for his *Rath Yatra* because it was at Somnath that Hindu temples were plundered by Muslim invaders. However, in 1950, the Hindu temples were rebuilt. See http://www.lkadvani.in/eng/content/view/449/295/.
[268] Jaffrelot, p. 420.

through the BJP's advocacy of *Hindutva*. In a state undergoing major socio-economic changes, some upper caste middle class Gujaratis, no longer able to secure power through caste identities alone, "began to find security within the ideology of *Hindutva* through which they thought they could regain some measure of power and control."[269]

In the 1991 Lok Sabha election, the BJP won twenty out of twenty-six seats in Gujarat by focusing on *Hindutva* and support for building the Ram Temple, and also criticizing the Congress Party over corruption and rising prices.[270] The following year, after the Babri Mosque was torn down by Hindu nationalists at the disputed site in Ayodhya, Hindu-Muslim riots again broke out across Gujarat in December 1992, including Ahmedabad, but the worst riots and violence took place in the city of Surat.[271] Varshney estimates that over the course of four days, 197 people were killed in Surat, of which 175 were Muslims and 22 were Hindus.[272]

In 1995, for the first time in Gujarat a two party competition between the Congress and the BJP defined the state assembly elections. The BJP swept the state assembly elections, winning 121 out of 182 seats, and securing a greater percentage of votes in all geographical regions of the state.[273] The party did especially well in urban areas, capturing 53.2 percent of the urban vote share, compared to 30.2 percent by

---

[269] Yagnik and Sheth, p. 260.

[270] *Statistical Report on General Elections, 1991, to the Tenth Lok Sabha, Volume 1*, New Delhi: Election Commission of India, http://eci.nic.in/eci_main/StatisticalReports/LS_1991/VOL_I_91.pdf. See also Shah, Ghanshyam, "The BJP's Riddle in Gujarat," in *The BJP and the Compulsion of Politics in India*, Eds. Thomas Blom Hansen and Christophe Jaffrelot. Oxford: Oxford University Press, 1998, p. 257.

[271] Shah, p. 249. Yagnik and Sheth, p. 264.

[272] For an analysis of the different trajectories of ethnic violence in Ahmedabad and Surat over time, see Varshney, *Ethnic Conflict and Civic Life*, chapters 9-10.

[273] *Statistical Report on General Elections, 1995, to the Legislative Assembly of Gujarat*, New Delhi: Election Commission of India, http://eci.nic.in/eci_main/statisticalreports/SE_1995/StatisticalReport-GUJ95.pdf.

Congress.[274] Though the BJP did not explicitly focus on *Hindutva* in its 1995 campaign in Gujarat, survey research by Gujarati scholar, Ghanshyam Shah, suggests that the BJP's support for building the Ram temple and its advocacy of *Hindutva* were key factors for many who voted for the BJP in the election.[275]

Over the next three years, the BJP in Gujarat experienced a period of intense intraparty power struggles as different leaders fought to dominate the party.[276] Yet, despite the party infighting, the BJP was able to continue its dominance in Gujarat, winning both the 1996 and 1998 Lok Sabha national elections, as well as the 1998 state assembly election. The BJP continued to do well in urban areas, capturing 75 percent of the urban vote share compared to 19 percent by Congress in the 1996 national election.[277]

This somewhat lengthy background about the history and political context of Gujarat is included to highlight the major changes that have taken place in the state over the past four decades, most notably the socio-political history of episodes of major violent conflict between Hindus and Muslims and the rise of the BJP to become the dominant political party by the mid-1990s, which helps to set the stage for examining voting behavior in Gujarat and Ahmedabad in the 1999, 2004 and 2009 national elections.

In the lead up to the 1999 national election, tensions in Gujarat were heightened following instances of ethnic violence. Numerous instances of violence against Christians in South Gujarat beginning in December 1998 and continuing through the first part of

---

[274] Shah, Ghanshyam, "BJP's Rise to Power," *Economic & Political Weekly*, January 13-20, 1996, p. 166.
[275] Ibid, p. 169.
[276] For a discussion of the BJP's intra-party struggles during this time, see Shah, *The BJP's Riddle in Gujarat*, pgs. 261-265. Patel, Priyavadan, "Sectarian Mobilisation, Factionalism and Voting in Gujarat," *Economic & Political Weekly*, April 21-28, 1999.
[277] Patel, p. 2429.

1999 were reported by the media and human rights group organizations.[278] In addition, in July 1999, during the Kargil war with Pakistan, the Hindu nationalist organization, VHP, was accused of stoking communal tensions, which triggered two weeks of Hindu-Muslim riots in Ahmedabad.[279]

The BJP campaigned in Gujarat on a slogan of "abki bari, Atal Bihari" (this time, it's Atal Bihari) referring to support for BJP leader, Prime Minister Atal Bihari Vajpayee, at the center.[280] Yet, at the state level, the BJP faced a record of paralyzing intraparty factional infighting and a drastic economic slowdown: after seven years of eight percent average economic growth from 1991-1992 to 1998-1999, economic growth in Gujarat contracted eight percent in 1999-2000, to less than one percent.[281]

The 1999 election marked the increasing influence of BJP General-Secretary Narendra Modi in state-level party politics, who was put in charge of the BJP's state

---

[278] "Anti-Christian Violence on the Rise in India – New Report details politics behind extremist Hindu Attacks," *Human Rights Watch*, October 1, 1999, http://www.hrw.org/news/1999/09/29/anti-christian-violence-rise-india. Human Rights Watch reported that attacks on Christians increased significantly throughout the country when the BJP came to power, and that the highest number of reports of violence targeted at Christians occurred in Gujarat in 1998 and 1999. See also Engineer, Asghar Ali, "The BJP and its Roots in Gujarat," *Institute of Islamic Studies and Centre for Study of Society and Secularism*, http://www.csss-isla.com/arch%20231.htm.

[279] "CPDR Report Sees Saffron Hand in Ahmedabad Riots," *The Indian Express*, August 22, 1999. The news article summarizes a report by the Committee for the Protection of Democratic Rights (CPDR) which concludes that the VHP and Bajrang Dal fomented Hindu-Muslim conflict during a time of tension marked by 1) the Kargil conflict, 2) a cricket match between India and Pakistan, and 3) the annual Jagannath rath yatra on July 14th. Gandadhar, V., "We try to rebuild mutual faith and then another riot starts destroying our work," part of a three-part series on the July 1999 riots in Ahmedabad, *Rediff News*, August 5, 1999, http://www.rediff.com/news/1999/aug/05abd.htm.

[280] Patel, Priyavadan, "Sectarian Mobilization, Communal Polarization and Factionalism: Electoral Dominance of Hindutva and Voting in Gujarat," *Master's Thesis*, Department of Political Science, Faculty of Arts, The M.S. University of Baroda, 2003, p. 46.

[281] *The Reserve Bank of India's Handbook of Statistics on Indian Economy*, Table 4, Net State Domestic Product at Factor Cost – State Wise at current prices, http://rbidocs.rbi.org.in/rdocs/Publications/PDFs/004T_HBS120911.pdf. Montel, Ahluwalia, "State Level Performance Under Economic Reforms in India," paper presented at the Centre for Research on Economic Development and Policy Reform Conference on Indian Economic Prospects: Advancing Policy Reform at Stanford University, May 2000.

campaign, and who would soon become the state's Chief Minister.[282] The Congress Party joined forces with Shankarsinh Vaghela, once a primary actor within the BJP, but who notoriously revolted from the party to start his own short-lived Rashtriya Janata Party. However, Congress's aging leadership was unable to provide a compelling challenge to counter the BJP's Hindu nationalist mobilization. The BJP won the 1999 national election, increasing its vote share four percent, from 48.3 percent in 1998 to 52.5 in 1999, and adding one more parliamentary seat from 19 to 20 (out of 26 seats).[283]

It is essential to address the ethnic violence that ravaged Gujarat in 2002, considered by many to be one of worst episodes of ethnic violence in India since Partition. On February 27, 2002, 59 Hindu activists were attacked and killed in an arson fire on a train near the Godhra train station in Gujarat.[284] The next day, the VHP issued a statewide strike to protest the Godhra train attack and killing of Hindus. Over the ensuing days and months, over a thousand people were killed in ethnic violence across the state, directed mostly against Muslims.[285][286][287]

---

[282] V. Venkatesan, "A pracharak as Chief Minister," *Frontline*, October 13-26, 2001. Patel, *Master's Thesis*, p. 46.

[283] CSDS Team, "Clear line of cleavage in Gujarat," *Frontline*, November 27-December 10, 1999.

[284] The Commission of Inquiry, *Report of Justice GT Nanavati and Justice Akshay H Mehta, Part-I, Sabarmati Express Train Incident at Godhra*, September 18, 2008, http://home.gujarat.gov.in/homedepartment/downloads/godharaincident.pdf. Nine years later, 31 people, mostly Muslims, were convicted of criminal conspiracy and murder in the Godhra train killings. See, "Godhra verdict: 31 convicted in Sabarmati Express burning case," *Times of India*, February 22, 2011.

[285] "Gujarat riots toll to go up from 952 to 1,180," *Times of India*, February 16, 2009. The death toll figure increased by 228 people whose status changed from missing to deceased after seven years.

[286] Several studies have concluded that the 2002 riots in Gujarat were the result of pre-planned, organized attacks and a complicit state government apparatus that either directly or indirectly condoned the attacks on Muslims. See, Concerned Citizens Tribunal – Gujarat, *Crimes Against Humanity – An Inquiry into the Carnage in Gujarat, Vol. I*, Mumbai: Citizens for Justice and Peace, 2002. Human Rights Watch, *We Have No Orders to Save You, State Participation and Complicity in Communal Violence in Gujarat*, Vol. 14 No. 3, April 2002. Jaffrelot, Christophe, "Communal Riots in Gujarat: The State at Risk?," *Heidelberg Papers in South Asian and Comparative Politics*, South Asia Institute, University of Heidelberg, July 2003. Engineer, Asghar Ali, Ed. *The Gujarat Carnage*. New Delhi: Orient Longman, 2003. *International Religious Freedom Report 2003*, Bureau of Democracy

A few months after the riots started, Chief Minister Narendra Modi, on July 19th dissolved the state assembly and called for early state elections to be held in Gujarat, ten months before the elections were scheduled to take place.[288] However, the Indian Election Commission objected, declaring that an election in Gujarat could not be organized and conducted since so many voters were still living in relief camps.[289] After repeated appeals by BJP leaders to hold early elections in Gujarat, including a case brought by the BJP to the Supreme Court, the Election Commission set an election date for December. On December 12, 2002, the BJP won another landslide state election, capturing 126 out of 181 assembly seats.[290]

Two years later, Gujarati politics scholar, Priyavadan Patel, called the 2004 national election the first somewhat "normal" election the BJP had ever contested in Gujarat since coming to power (i.e. no Kargil war, no large-scale ethnic rioting, or

---

Human Rights and Labor, U.S. Department of State, http://www.state.gov/j/drl/rls/irf/2003/24470.htm.

[287] On April 10, 2012, the Supreme Court-appointed Special Investigation Team (SIT) declared that it found no evidence to prosecute Narendra Modi, top bureaucrats, or police officers in a massacre that took place in the Gulberg Society neighborhood of Ahmedabad, one of the worst affected areas in the 2002 riots. "SIT finds no proof against Modi, says court," *The Hindu*, April 10, 2012.

[288] Bunsha, Dionne, "Gujarat Game Plan," *Frontline*, August 3-16, 2002.

[289] Approximately 100,000 people were displaced and living in relief camps within the first week of the riots. Dasgupta Manas, "No plans to close camps: Modi," *The Hindu*, April 1, 2002. Jaffrelot, *The State at Risk*, p. 9.

[290] Kumar, Sanjay, "Gujarat Assembly Elections 2002 – Analysing the Verdict," *Economic & Political Weekly*, January 23, 2003. Using CSDS post-polling survey data, Kumar finds that the largest number of assembly seats and increase in vote share for the BJP occurred in districts affected by the riots (table 3). However, Kumar notes that though the ethnic riots appeared to have made a difference in the electoral outcome, they were not the entire story in the 2002 election. According to the survey data, twenty-nine percent of all voters indicated that they were satisfied with the state government's performance over the past five years, out of which seventy-seven percent voted for the BJP (table 5). All social groups except Muslims identified economic development as the most important priority for the new government (Muslims identified Hindu-Muslim harmony as their highest priority (table 15).

intense intra-party power struggles).[291] In the lead-up to the election, Hindu nationalist organizations such as the VHP stayed away from the electoral process.[292]

BJP Chief Minister, Narendra Modi, in addition to campaigning on the national "India Shining" slogan in 2004, focused on state and local level development progress on water, roads, power, and industrial development, while promoting a "Vibrant Gujarat" through the creation in 2003 of a new global investor's summit designed to attract foreign investment into the state.[293] The Congress Party focused on the BJP's development performance, seeking to frame the party as weak on development.[294] Congress's message earned it six more parliamentary seats, but it was not enough. The BJP won the 2004 national election in Gujarat, but its vote share decreased to 47.3 percent compared to 52.5 percent in the 1999 election. The BJP party captured a total of 14 seats, compared to Congress's 12 seats.

Within a period of ten years, the social and economic landscape in 1999 compared to 2009 in Gujarat changed significantly. The 1999 national election had taken place under conditions of low economic growth and a very high level of ethnic conflict and violence. Ten years later, the 2009 national election took place under conditions of high economic growth and a medium level of ethnic conflict. Over a period of two years, from 2007 to 2009, Gujarat had experienced double-digit levels of economic growth (i.e. 11.8

---

[291] Patel, Priyavadan, "Gujarat – Anti-incumbency Begins," *Economic & Political Weekly*, December 18, 2004 p. 5475.
[292] Desai, Darshan, "Divorce could be painful for BJP, VHP," *Times of India*, June 8, 2005.
[293] Timmons, Heather, "A Divisive Indian Official Is Loved by Business," *The New York Times*, February 8, 2011. "Is it Time to acknowledge the Gujarat 'miracle?," *The Economic Times*, January 16, 2011.
[294] Patel, "Gujarat – Anti-incumbency Begins," p. 5475.

percent in 2008-2009, and 16.9 percent in 2007-2008).[295] At the same time, while ethnic tensions were still present in Gujarati society, no accounts of large-scale ethnic violence had occurred.[296]

Narendra Modi focused the 2009 national election campaign again primarily on issues of development and the economy, emphasizing the growth of the state's domestic product during his tenure, while claiming that the development success in Gujarat could be unlocked across the country if the BJP came to power at the center.[297] Modi highlighted the success in bringing the Nano car project, touted as the people's car, to Gujarat as a means of bringing employment opportunities to the state.[298] The VHP again largely stayed out of the campaign process.

The Congress party sought to highlight the weaknesses of the BJP on development and focus on concern for *aam aadmi* (the common man).[299] However, the BJP's ability to point to higher growth rates and securing development projects like the Nano car, combined with Congress' weak party leadership, hindered its ability to pose a major threat to Modi's incumbent government. The BJP won the 2009 national election in Gujarat, capturing 15 out the states 26 Lok Sabha seats, and continued to perform well

---

[295] *The Reserve Bank of India's Handbook of Statistics on Indian Economy*, Table 4, Net State Domestic Product at Factor Cost – State Wise at current prices.

[296] Engineer, Asghar Ali, *India: Communal Riots: 2009*, South Asia Citizen's Web, January 2, 2010, at http://www.sacw.net/article1315.html.

[297] Jani, Mahashweta, "Gujarat: BJP Scrapes Through," *Economic & Political Weekly*, September 26, 2009, p. 135. Shah, Ghanshyam, "Modi's political craft: Replica of Assembly Elections," Unpublished Paper.

[298] The Nano car was conceived by Ratan Tata as a people's car for India's emerging middle class with a starting price of 100,000 rupees, or approximately US $2,200. After major violent protests by farmers in the state of West Bengal forced Tata Motors to shut down its Nano assembly plant, the company relocated its plant to Sanand, Gujarat. Siddiqui, Tanvir, "In Gujarat, BJP rides the Nano," *The Indian Express*, April 8, 2009. Berland Kaul, Allison, "Industrialization, Peasant Mobilization and the Conflict over Land Acquisition in India: The Case of the Nano Car," *Paper presented at the 2010 Annual Meeting of the American Political Science Association*, Washington, DC, September, 2-5, 2010. Interview with Mahashweta Jani, February 12, 2011.

[299] Shah, "Modi's political craft," p. 9.

in urban areas.[300] Table 6.1 summarizes the national election results for the Congress and BJP parties in Gujarat for the 1999, 2004 and 2009 national elections. The table shows the continued dominance of the BJP, though somewhat declining overall vote share, during the 1999-2009 timeframe in Gujarat.

Table 6.1 Gujarat National Election Results, 1999-2009

Lok Sabha National Elections	1999	2004	2009
Congress percentage of vote share	45.4	43.8	43.4
Congress M.P. seats won	6	12	11
BJP percentage of vote share	52.5	47.3	46.6
BJP M.P. seats won	20	14	15

Source: Election Commission of India.

In summary, this section offers a contextual narrative of the rise and political dominance of the BJP within the context of a two party rivalry in a highly industrialized, urbanizing state. Unlike in Delhi, in which we find a precipitous rise followed by a steep decline in the BJP's political fortunes during the 1999-2009 timeframe, the BJP has remained the dominant political force in Gujarat and in Ahmedabad. I posit that both ethnic and programmatic interests are central to understanding the nature of voter support for the BJP in Gujarat and in Ahmedabad over this timeframe. The following two sections examine voting behavior in Gujarat and in Ahmedabad and tests Ethnically Mediated Retrospective Voting (ERV) theory as a plausible means of explaining variation in urban electoral support for the BJP in the 1999, 2004 and 2009 national elections.

---

[300] The BJP won 54.6 percent of the urban vote share compared to 40.2 percent by Congress in the 2009 national election. Jani, "Gujarat: BJP Scrapes Through," p. 135.

Gujarat: Indian National Election Survey Analysis, 1999, 2004 and 2009

This section presents an analysis of voting behavior in Gujarat in three Indian national elections, 1999, 2004, and 2009, using survey data from the Indian National Election Studies (NES). This data comes from the same source that was used to analyze voting behavior in Delhi in the previous chapter.

For the following analysis, I again employ the typology of independent variables described in the research design chapter – one group representing indicators of ethnic group identity and interests, and a second group representing indicators of retrospective programmatic interests. [301] The dependent variable for this analysis is vote choice; a binary, or dichotomous, dependent variable coded 0 for individuals who voted for the Congress Party, and 1 for individuals who voted for the BJP.

Gujarat, 1999 Election

Under conditions of a drastic economic slowdown and recent violent ethnic conflict, the BJP swept the 1999 national election in Gujarat, increasing its vote share to 52.5 percent, the highest level since it came to power in the state in 1991.

The National Election Study conducted a post-poll election survey after the 1999 election in Gujarat using the same methodology and survey questionnaire that was used in Delhi. However, the sample size for the 1999 NES survey in Gujarat is larger than in Delhi. The 1999 NES in Gujarat sampled a total of 482 voters, of which 101 respondents refused to answer who they voted for, 6 respondents indicated that they did not remember

---

[301] Like the NES data used for Delhi, some of the survey questions asked are not always consistent over the years. Thus, while it is possible to make broad comparisons of the impact of these two types of indicators across space and time, the data limitations mean that it is not always possible to make comparisons of the impact of all the indicators across all three elections.

whom they voted for, and 3 respondents voted for a small regional party. Subtracting these respondents leaves a sample size of 372 respondents (compared to a sample size of n=63 for the Delhi 1999 NES).

With a sample size of over 300, the following analysis of the 1999 NES election survey data in Gujarat includes a logistic regression model using indicators of ethnic group identity and interests and retrospective programmatic interests. In addition, in order to compare voting behavior in Gujarat and Delhi in the 1999 election, I also discuss the differences in sample proportions for select indicators. A full list of the descriptive statistics for the Gujarat 1999 election analysis is listed in table 2, Appendix B.

The main logistic regression model includes indicators of ethnic group identity and interests (i.e., *caste, religion, Hindu Ram temple views*, and *Social Harmony*), and indicators of retrospective programmatic interests (i.e. *corruption, national security*, and *prices*). The model also includes indicators for age, class and religiosity. The indicator, *central government performance*, which is akin to a broad job approval rating of government performance, is not included in the model because it is significantly correlated with the indicator for *national security* (.52).[302] In addition, because the indicators for *social harmony* and *law and order* have moderately high correlation (.41), the main model includes the former indicator, while a second model includes the latter indicator. Table 6.2 on the following page provides the logistic regression results.

---

[302] A correlation matrix test indicated that the indicator for central government performance was significantly correlated with the indicator for national security: .52. When I ran the main model and included the variable, central government performance, stata dropped two variables from the model, indicating that the variables predict perfectly.

Vote choice 1999 = $ß_0 + ß_1 Age_i + ß_2$ Class (Rich)$_i + ß_3$Caste (Upper Caste)$_i +$
$ß_4$Religion (Hindu)$_i + ß_5$Religiosity$_i + ß_6$RamTempleviews$_i + ß_7$SocialHarmony$_i +$
$ß_8$Corruption$_i + ß_9$Prices$_i + ß_{10}$Security$_i + e_i$

Table 6.2 Logit Regression Results, Gujarat 1999 Election

	(1)	(2)
Age	-0.001	0.017
	(0.016)	(0.015)
Class (Rich)	0.938	1.728*
	(0.716)	(0.805)
Caste (Upper Caste)	1.406*	1.809**
	(0.572)	(0.627)
Religion (Hindu)	1.992*	1.424
	(1.182)	(1.037)
Religiosity	0.738	0.685
	(0.632)	(0.619)
Ram Temple Views	0.744**	0.348
	(0.292)	(0.254)
Social Harmony (Hindu-Muslim)	1.927**	-
	(0.539)	
Corruption	0.584	1.245**
	(0.521)	(0.479)
Prices	1.003	1.486
	(0.993)	(0.924)
Law & Order	-	0.923*
		(0.453)
National Security	2.827**	1.937**
	(0.599)	(.471)
Constant	-6.762**	-5.941**
	(1.628)	(1.378)
Observations	154	178
Pseudo R-squared	.45	.43

Source: Indian NES Survey (1999)
Significance: * = at 5%; ** = at 1%; standard errors are in parentheses.
Dependent Variable is vote choice, coded 0 for Congress, and 1 for the BJP

The results of the main model show that the ethnic identity and interests indicators for *caste (upper caste), religion (Hindu), Ram temple views,* and *Hindu-Muslim social harmony* have a positive and statistically significant impact on the likelihood of voting for the BJP, holding all else constant.[303] *Religiosity, age* and *wealth* are not statistically significant indicators of voter support for the BJP. The retrospective

---

[303] The p-value for the religion coefficient is .09 slightly above the 5% significance level.

programmatic indicator, *national security,* is also both positive and statistically significant on vote choice, while the indicators for both corruption and prices are not statistically significant.

In the second model, in column two, we find that the retrospective programmatic indicators for *corruption, prices, and law and order* have a positive statistically significant impact on the likelihood of voting for the BJP, holding all else constant. The ethnic identity and interest indicator for *caste (upper caste)* is again positive and statistically significant, while the indicators for *religion (Hindu)* and *Ram temple views* are no longer statistically significant. In this model, wealth is also a positive and statistically significant factor on voter support for the BJP. To interpret the substantive effects of individual indicators on vote choice, table 6.3 below presents the predicted probabilities calculated from the logistic regression results above.[304]

Table 6.3 Predicted Probabilities: Gujarat 1999 Election

	(1)	(2)
Age	n.s.	n.s.
Caste (Upper Caste)	.30	.37
Class (Rich)	n.s.	.33
Religion (Hindu)	.44	n.s.
Religiosity	n.s.	n.s.
Hindu Ram Temple views	.35	n.s.
Social Harmony (Hindu-Muslim)	.41	n/a
Price Levels	n.s.	n.s.
Corruption	n.s.	.28
National Security	.59	.44
Law & Order	n/a	.22

Source: Computed from the logit coefficients in table 6.2.
n.s. = not statistically significant; n/a = not applicable

The results of the predicted probabilities are revealing. It is useful to recall that the Gujarat 1999 national election had the highest level of ethnic conflict of the six

---

[304] Table 6.3 lists changes in the predicted probabilities of voting for the BJP as each indicator changes from its minimum to its maximum value, holding all other variables constant at their means, using prchange. See Long, J. Scott and Jeremy Freese, *Regression Models for Categorical Dependent Variables Using States Second Edition.* College Station: Stata Press, 2006, p. 169.

different elections scenarios studied in this research project (i.e. three national elections, 1999, 2004 and 2009, in two different locations, Gujarat and Delhi). Predicted probabilities in the main model show that the ethnic group indicator for *caste (upper caste)* increases the likelihood of voting for the BJP by 30 percentage points. The ethnic group indicator for *religion (Hindu)* increases the likelihood of voting for the BJP by 44 percentage points.

Table 6.3 also indicates the large effects of ethnic group interests on vote choice: voter opinion about building the Ram temple, and concerns about social harmony related to Hindu-Muslims relations each have significant substantive impacts on the likelihood of voting for the BJP, by 35 and 41 percentage points respectively. *These results suggest that ethnic group identity and interests were major factors in influencing voter support for the BJP in the 1999 national election in Gujarat.*

Predicted probabilities from the main model also show that a positive assessment of the incumbent BJP led government's performance on national security increases the likelihood of voting for the BJP by 59 percentage points. Although national security is considered a programmatic indicator for this research study, in practice, national security concerns can sometimes fuse with local ethnic group concerns, such as when the Kargil conflict with Pakistan was associated with stoking ethnic tensions and rioting in Ahmedabad July 1999.

The results in table 6.3 show that there is more to the story. Voters in Gujarat also cared about retrospective programmatic issues in this election, most notably, corruption. The predicted probabilities from the second model indicate the substantive impact of concerns about corruption on vote choice: a higher level of voter satisfaction with the incumbent government's efforts to reduce corruption increases the likelihood of voting for the BJP by 28 percentage points. This result is most readily understood in light of long standing voter concern and frustration in Gujarat about corruption in the Congress party (a major factor in the Nav Nirman riots).

The above analysis of 1999 Gujarat election survey data indicates that ethnic group identity and interests were very strong factors in explaining voter support for the BJP, but that voters were also influenced by programmatic concerns, notably concerns about corruption. How does this compare to voting behavior in the 1999 election in Delhi? By contrast, Delhi had experienced a moderate level of ethnic group conflict combined with a high level of economic growth during the 1999 election. The following table lists the differences in sample proportions of select ethnic indicators for Gujarat and Delhi for the 1999 election. Column three "Yes" presents the proportion of voters with a particular characteristic (i.e., upper caste), or who answered in the affirmative to a particular question and voted for the BJP, while column four "No" presents the proportion of voters who do not have the particular characteristic, or who answered in the negative to a particular question and voted for the BJP. The percentage can be derived by multiplying each proportion by 100.

Table 6.4 *Differences of sample proportions for select indicators for BJP voters, Gujarat and Delhi, 1999 election*

State	Indicator	Yes	No	Difference in proportions
Gujarat	Caste (upper caste)	.76	.36	-.40**
	Hindu Ram Temple views	.55	.41	-.14*
	Social Harmony (Hindu-Muslim)	.77	.34	-.43**
Delhi	Caste (upper caste)	.68	.24	-.44**
	Hindu Ram Temple views	.37	.29	-.08
	Social Harmony (Hindu-Muslim)	.56	.18	-.38**

Source: Indian NES Survey (1999)
Significance: * = at 5%; ** = at 1%
N = 372 for Gujarat; 63 for Delhi

If we first look at indicator for *caste (uppercaste)* we find that the difference in the sample proportions of upper caste versus non-upper caste voters who voted for the BJP is slightly higher for Delhi voters (.44) than for Gujarati voters (.40). However, if we look at the percentage upper caste voters who voted for the BJP in each state, we see that a higher percentage of upper caste voters voted for the BJP in Gujarat (.76) than in Delhi (.68). This suggests that, on average, a greater percentage of upper caste voters voted for the BJP in Gujarat than in Delhi in the 1999 election.

The table also highlights differences regarding ethnic group interests relating to *Hindu Ram temple views* and *Hindu-Muslim social harmony* between voters in Delhi an in Gujarat. We find that the percentage of voters who highlighted the importance of building the Ram temple and improving Hindu-Muslim social relations and voted for the BJP is markedly higher in Gujarat (55 percent and 77 percent), than in Delhi (37 percent and 56 percent). These results suggest that ethnic group interests relating to the Ram temple and Hindu-Muslim relations were more distinguishing factors of voter support for the BJP in Gujarat than in Delhi in the 1999 election.

The analysis of voting behavior in Delhi in the previous chapter examined what level of government (i.e. central versus state) voters indicate they are most concerned about when they vote in the national election. The NES survey indicates that Delhi voters in general in the 1999 election were more focused on the work of the central government than the state government. A similar analysis of voting behavior in Gujarat indicates that that BJP voters placed more emphasis on the work of the central government than Congress voters.

Table 6.5 Gujarat voter priorities in 1999: central versus state level government

	Neither	State level	Both	Central level	Other
All Voters	22.31	30.91	20.16	26.34	0.27
BJP voters	16.38	32.20	17.51	33.90	0.00
Congress voters	27.69	29.74	22.56	19.49	0.51

Source: Indian NES Survey (1999)

Table 6.5 shows that BJP voters placed a higher level of importance on the work of the central government than Congress voters (33.9 percent versus 19.49 percent), likely reflecting the role of the incumbent BJP-led government in addressing BJP voters' ethnic group interests relating to the Ram temple and Hindu-Muslim relations, and national security concerns at that time. This suggests that different voters may prioritize different levels of government performance when voting in a national election.

In summary, this analysis of voting behavior shows that ethnic group identity (i.e. upper caste and Hindu) and ethnic group interests (i.e. Hindu Ram temple, and Hindu-Muslim social relations) were major factors in explaining voter support for the BJP in the 1999 election in Gujarat. In addition, it is likely that nationally security concerns overlapped to a degree with ethnic group concerns particularly during this election, in which the Kargil conflict was associated with Hindu-Muslim rioting in the state. The analysis also showed that retrospective programmatic concerns relating to corruption was also an important factor in vote choice.

In the context of Gujarat's weak political economy of development marked by a drastic economic slowdown in 1999, and a very high level of ethnic conflict arising from the Kargil conflict with Pakistan and Hindu-Muslim riots in Gujarat, these empirical findings of voting behavior in Gujarat in 1999 support ERV theory's prediction that the relative influence ethnic group identity and interests are strong factors in explaining voting behavior and voter support for the BJP, while retrospective programmatic interests are somewhat less influential, most closely represented by scenario 2 in table 3.1.

Gujarat, 2004 Election

After widespread Hindu-Muslim rioting and violence gripped Gujarat in early 2002, followed by a BJP sweep in the state's assembly election, a period of less ethnic violence but continued heightened ethnic tensions followed in the lead up to the 2004 national election. Within a period of five years, Gujarat's economy had rebounded from a growth rate of less than one percent in 1999-2000, to a growth rate of 8.9 percent in 2004-2005.[305] Within a period of eleven years, the state's poverty level declined from a quarter (24.2 percent) of its population in 1993-95, to 12.5 percent by 2004-2005.[306] The BJP won the 2004 national elections in Gujarat, but it lost six Lok Sabha seats, decreasing from 20 to 14, and reducing its vote share by five percent.

---

[305] *The Reserve Bank of India's Handbook of Statistics on Indian Economy,* Table 4, Net State Domestic Product at Factor Cost – State Wise at current prices.

[306] *Reserve Bank of India's Handbook of Statistics on Indian Economy,* Table 162: Number and Percentage of Population Below Poverty Line. The 2004-2005 poverty level is the most recent available.

The 2004 post poll national election survey includes 1106 respondents in Gujarat and uses the same methodology and questionnaire that was used for the 2004 NES in Delhi. Of the 1106 voters sampled, 193 respondents declined to answer who they voted for, and 19 indicated that they didn't know who they voter for. Seventeen respondents voted for a small regional party. Subtracting these respondents leaves a sample size of 877 respondents who either voted for the BJP or the Congress party.

Since the questionnaire used for the 2004 NES in Delhi and in Gujarat is the same and the sample size is appropriate, the analysis of the 2004 NES in Gujarat is able to employ the same logistic regression model and indicators that are used for the Delhi 2004 analysis to test for the effects of ethnic group identity and interests and retrospective programmatic interests on the likelihood of voting for the BJP.

The following model includes indicators of ethnic group identity and interests: (i.e., *caste, religion, ram temple views,* and *social harmony*), and indicators of retrospective programmatic voting (i.e., *personal financial conditions, employment, development, corruption, national security* and *central government performance*).[307] The indicator for *central government performance* is included in the main model in column one. This indicator is removed in the second and third models, in order to better ascertain which retrospective programmatic issues are driving vote choice. Because of the moderately high correlation between indicators for *national security* and *corruption* (.49), and for *national security* and *development* (.55), I retain the indicators for *corruption* and

---

[307] As noted in Chapter Four, due to the differences in the survey questions asked between the 1999 and 2004 Indian NES surveys, some of the indicators included in the 2004 model are different from the indicators used in the 1999 model. Specifically, survey questions about a voter's retrospective assessment about price levels and law and order are included in the 1999 NES survey, but are not included in the 2004 NES survey, whereas questions about voter's retrospective assessment about employment and development are included in the 2004 NES survey but not in the 1999 NES survey.

development, in model two and remove the indicator for *national security.* In model three, I retain the indicator for *national security,* and remove indicators for *development* and *corruption* The models include indicators for *age, class* and *religiosity.* Table 6.6 provides a summary of the regression results for all three models, with main model results listed in the first column.

Vote choice 2004 = $\beta_0 + \beta_1 Age_i + \beta_2$ Class (Rich)$_i + \beta_3$Caste (Upper Caste)$_i + \beta_4$Religion (Hindu)$_i + \beta_5$Religiosity$_i + \beta_6$RamTempleviews$_i + \beta_7$SocialHarmony$_i + \beta_8$PersonalFinance$_i + \beta_9$Employment$_i + \beta_{10}$Corruption$_i + \beta_{11}$Development$_i + \beta_{12}$NationalSecurity$_i + \beta_{13}$Central Government Performance$_i + e_i$

Table 6.6 Logit Regression Results, Gujarat 2004 Election

	(1)	(2)	(3)
Age	-0.002	-0.001	-0.000
	(0.007)	(0.006)	(0.006)
Class (Rich)	0.566	0.389	0.193
	(0.443)	(0.388)	(.387)
Caste (Upper Caste)	0.987**	0.882**	1.064**
	(0.238)	(0.208)	(0.201)
Religion (Hindu)	0.500	0.705*	0.739**
	(0.325)	(0.295)	(0.245)
Religiosity	-0.099	0.012	-0.173
	(0.151)	(0.131)	(0.126)
Ram Temple Views	-0.048	-0.048	-0.033
	(.081)	(0.071)	(0.067)
Social Harmony (Hindu-Muslim)	-0.071	-0.009	0.023
	(0.144)	(0.128)	(0.119)
Personal Financial Conditions	0.368*	0.840**	0.756**
	(0.197)	(0.171)	(0.158)
Employment	0.239	0.459**	0.641**
	(0.151)	(0.134)	(0.124)
Corruption	0.642**	0.817**	-
	(0.167)	(0.149)	
Development	0.289	0.427**	-
	(0.183)	(0.163)	
National Security	0.785**	-	0.931**
	(0.187)		(0.147)
Central Government Performance	0.844**	-	-
	(0.125)		
Constant	-9.905**	-6.478**	-6.119**
	(0.951)	(0.791)	(0.723)
Observations	614	667	721
Pseudo R-squared	.35	.26	.25

Source: Indian NES Survey (2004)
Significance: * = at 5%; ** = at 1%; standard errors are in parentheses.
Dependent Variable is vote choice, coded 0 for Congress, and 1 for the BJP

The logit coefficient estimates in the main model, column one, show that ethnic group identity indicator for *caste (upper caste)*, and retrospective programmatic indicators for *personal financial conditions, corruption, national security* and *central government performance* each have a positive and statistically significant impact on the likelihood of voting for the BJP, holding all else constant. The retrospective programmatic indicators for *employment* and *development* are not statistically significant on vote choice. In addition, the ethnic group identity and interests indicators relating to *religion (Hindu), ram temple views,* and *social harmony* are not statistically significant on vote choice. The indicators for *age, wealth,* and *religiosity* are also not statistically significant.

In model two, column two, in which *central government performance* is removed to better ascertain which retrospective issues are influencing vote choice, all of the retrospective programmatic indicators included in the model, *personal financial conditions, employment, corruption,* and *development*, are positive and have a statistically significant impact on the likelihood of voting for the BJP, holding all else constant. In this model, *religion (Hindu)* is also positive and statistically significant on vote choice.

In model three, in which the indicator, *national security* is retained, and indicators for *development and corruption* are removed, I find that *national security* is positive and statistically significant on vote choice. Additionally, I find no changes in the direction or statistical significance of the common variables between model two and model three. Table 6.7 presents the predicted probabilities calculated from the logistic regression results above.

Table 6.7 Predicted Probabilities: Gujarat 2004 Election

	(1)	(2)	(3)
Age	n.s.	n.s.	n.s.
Class (Rich)	n.s.	n.s.	n.s.
Caste (Upper Caste)	.24	.22	.26
Religion (Hindu)	n.s.	.16	.16
Religiosity	n.s.	n.s.	n.s.
Ram Temple views	n.s.	n.s.	n.s.
Social Harmony (Hindu-Muslim)	n.s.	n.s.	n.s.
Personal Financial Conditions	.17	.38	.34
Employment	n.s.	.22	.31
Corruption	.30	.37	n/a
Development	n.s.	.20	n.a
National Security	.34	n/a	.40
Central Government Performance	.53	n/a	n/a

Source: Computed from the logit coefficients in table 6.7.
n.s. = not statistically significant; n/a = not applicable

Predicted probabilities calculated for the main model in column one show the substantive influence of ethnic identity on vote choice: the ethnic group identity indicator for *caste (upper caste)* increases the likelihood of voting for the BJP by 24 percentage points. The predicted probabilities for retrospective programmatic indicators relating to *personal financial conditions, corruption, national security* and *central government performance* indicate a strong substantive impact on the likelihood of voting for the BJP. A positive assessment in reducing corruption levels increases the likelihood of voting for the BJP by 30 percentage points. Thus, similar to the 1999 election, corruption continues to be an important factor on vote choice. The indicator representing voter's overall assessment of *central government performance* has the greatest impact on the likelihood of voting for the BJP, increasing the likelihood of voting for the BJP by 53 percent points.

In model two, in which *central government performance* and *national security* indicators are removed, the predicted probabilities for each of the retrospective indicators for *personal financial conditions, development, employment,* and *corruption* indicate strong substantive effects on the likelihood of voting for the BJP. In this model, the predicted probabilities for both ethnic group identity indicators, *caste (upper caste)* and *religion (Hindu)*, increase the likelihood of voting for the BJP by 22 and 16 percentage points, respectively. In model three, column three, the predicted probability for *national security* increases the likelihood of voting for the BJP by 40 percentage points.

These results suggest that under conditions of both a high level of ethnic conflict and a high political economy of development, retrospective programmatic interests have strong substantive effects on the likelihood of voting for the BJP, while ethnic group identity continues to have a significant impact on vote choice.

How do these results compare over space and time? I again employ a simple comparative analysis examining differences in sample proportions of ethnic indicators relating to caste and religion for the Gujarat 1999, Gujarat 2004, and Delhi 2004 elections. Column three "Yes" presents the proportion of voters with a particular characteristic (i.e., upper caste) and voted for the BJP, while column four "No" presents the proportion of voters who do not have the particular characteristic, and voted for the BJP.

Table 6.8 *Differences of sample proportions for Ethnic Indicators for BJP voters, Gujarat 1999, Gujarat 2004 and Delhi 2004 elections*

State/Year	Indicator	Yes	No	Difference in proportions
Gujarat 1999	Caste (upper caste)	.76	.36	-.40**
	Religion (Hindu)	.49	.21	-.28**
Gujarat 2004	Caste (upper caste)	.56	.36	-.20**
	Religion (Hindu)	.45	.21	-.24**
Delhi 2004	Caste (upper caste)	.47	.28	-.19**
	Religion (Hindu)	.42	.28	-.14**

Source: Indian NES Survey (1999, 2004)
Significance: * = at 5%; ** = at 1%
N = 372 for Gujarat 1999; 877 for Gujarat 2004; 791 for Delhi 2004

The results of the sample proportions above indicate that ethnic identity relating to being upper caste or Hindu is more of a distinguishing feature of voter support for the BJP in Gujarat in the 1999 election compared to in the 2004 election. The results also suggest that ethnic identity relating to being upper caste or Hindu is more of a distinguishing feature of voter support for the BJP in Gujarat than in Delhi in the 2004 election. With Gujarat experiencing a much higher level of ethnic conflict than Delhi in both the 1999 and 2004 elections, these results support ERV's prediction that the relative influence of ethnic group identity on vote choice and explaining voter support for the BJP would be generally stronger in Gujarat than in Delhi.

In summary, the analysis of voting behavior in the 2004 national election in Gujarat shows that the effects of ethnic group identity associated with being upper caste and Hindu continues to be significantly associated with voter support for the BJP in Gujarat, although the above comparative analysis examining differences in sample proportions of ethnic indicators relating to caste and religion over time suggests that being upper caste or Hindu was more of a distinguishing feature associated with BJP support in the 1999 election than compared to in the 2004 election in Gujarat.

The results from the logistical regression analysis and predicted probabilities also indicate that a range of retrospective programmatic concerns, relating to personal financial conditions, development, employment, corruption and national security, had strong substantive effects on the likelihood of voting for the BJP in the 2004 election in Gujarat.

Under conditions marked by a lessoning of violent ethnic conflict (i.e. no Kargil War, no ethnic rioting in the state) but continued heightened ethnic tensions, and a stronger political economy of development with high economic growth, these empirical findings of voting behavior in the 2004 election in Gujarat, I argue, support ERV theory's prediction that retrospective programmatic interests would play a stronger role in explaining voter support for the BJP, while ethnic group identity and interests also continue to have a strong, though relatively less extreme, influence in explaining voter support for the BJP, compared to in the 1999 election, most closely represented by scenario 1 in table 3.1

Gujarat, 2009 Election

The 2009 national election witnessed a continuing dominance of the BJP in Gujarat. The state experienced five years of strong economic growth from 2004 to 2009, and although violent ethnic conflict was significantly abated, ethnic tensions between Hindus and Muslims remained a prevalent aspect of Gujarati society. The BJP, which had become deeply associated with the state's chief minister, Narendra Modi, captured an additional seat and won the 2009 election.

The 2009 post-poll national elections survey used for the following analysis sampled 954 respondents in Gujarat. Subtracting the 31 respondents who indicated that they voted for a small regional party leaves a sample size of 923 respondents who either voted for the BJP or the Congress party. A full list of the descriptive statistics for the Gujarat 2009 election analysis is listed in table 6, Appendix B.

As noted in the analysis of voting behavior in Delhi in the 2009 election in Chapter 5, the interview schedule used in the 2009 NES is different from the 2004

NES, with important implications for data analysis.[309] Due to the nature of the 2009 election survey data, which includes variables with very different sample sizes, the first logistic regression model includes only variables which have the full sample size to test for the effects of ethnic group identity interests and retrospective programmatic interests on the likelihood of voting for the BJP. Then, to better ascertain which retrospective issues are influencing vote choice, I remove the indicator *central government performance*, and add individual indicators of retrospective programmatic voting to the model, which each have a much reduced sample size. The results are listed in models, 2, 3, and 4.

The main logit model in column one includes indicators of ethnic group identity: (i.e., *caste* and *religion*), and one indicator of retrospective programmatic voting (i.e., *central government performance*). The model also includes indicators for *age*, *class* and *religiosity*. Table 6.9 provides a summary of the logistic regression results.

---

[309] While the same set of survey questions was asked to all respondents in the 2004 NES, by contrast, five sets of questionnaires, including both common questions and unique questions, were randomly administered to respondents in the 2009 NES. Thus, some survey questions (i.e. class, caste, religion, religiosity, age, central government performance) were administered to all respondents, while others (including many which were asked to all respondents in 2004) were randomly administered to one-fifth of all respondents. As a result of this split sample interview schedule, the Gujarat 2009 survey data used in this analysis includes some variables with a sample size of 1000, and other variables with a sample size closer to 200.

Vote choice 2009 = $\beta_0 + \beta_1 Age_i + \beta_2$ Class (Rich)$_i + \beta_3$Caste (Upper Caste)$_i$ + β_4Religion (Hindu)$_i + \beta_5$Religiosity$_i + \beta_6$Central Government Performance$_i + e_i$

Table 6.9 Logit Regression Results, Gujarat 2009 election

	(1)	(2)	(3)	(4)
Age	-0.000	-0.00	-0.006	-0.005
	(0.005)	(0.012)	(0.023)	(0.016)
Class (Rich)	0.7323**	1.766*	1.588*	0.210
	(0.264)	(0.803)	(0.809)	(0.579)
Caste (Upper Caste)	1.115**	1.067**	1.235**	1.131**
	(0.199)	(0.366)	(0.410)	(0.423)
Religion (Hindu)	1.823**	1.196*	1.367**	1.043*
	(0.297)	(0.508)	(0.196)	(0.539)
Religiosity	0.182	0.002	0.082	-0.343
	(0.099)	(0.174)	(0.196)	(0.297)
Personal Financial Conditions	-	0.284* (0.169)	-	-
Development	-	-	0.230 (0.193)	-
Terrorism	-	-	-	-0.490* (0.235)
Central Government Performance	-1.213** (0.107)	-	-	-
Constant	1.071*	-2.490	-2.651*	1.315
	(0.552)	(1.062)	(1.310)	(1.366)
Observations	826	183	149	120
Pseudo R-squared	.26	.11	.12	.12

Source: Indian NES Survey (2009)
Significance: * = at 5%; ** = at 1%; standard errors are in parentheses.
Dependent Variable is vote choice, coded 0 for Congress, and 1 for the BJP

The results of the main model in column one show that the ethnic identity indicators for *caste (upper caste)* and *religion (Hindu)*, as well as the indicator for wealth are each positive and have a statistically significant impact on vote choice, holding all else constant. In addition, the retrospective programmatic indicator, *central government performance* is negative and also have a statistically significant impact on the likelihood of voting for the BJP, holding all else constant. Again, we find that *religiosity* is not a statistically significant factor on voter support for the BJP.

Model two, column two, shows that when the indicator, *personal financial conditions,* is included in the model, it is positive and statistically significant on vote choice. In model three, column three, when the indicator *development* is included, we find that it is not statistically significant on vote choice. Lastly, in model four, column four, when the indicator *terrorism* is included, representing voter assessment of government performance in addressing the 2009 Mumbai terrorist attacks, it is negative and has a statistically significant impact on the likelihood of voting for the BJP. Table 6.10 presents the predicted probabilities calculated from the logistic regression results above.

Table 6.10 Predicted Probabilities, Gujarat 2009 election

	(1)	(2)	(3)	(4)
Age	n.s.	n.s.	n.s.	n.s.
Class (Rich)	.17	.38	.35	n.s.
Caste (Upper Caste)	.26	.26	.30	.27
Religion (Hindu)	.40	.27	.32	.24
Religiosity	n.s.	n.s.	n.s.	n.s.
Personal Financial Conditions	n/a	.27	n/a	n/a
Development	n/a	n/a	n.s.	n/a
Terrorism	n/a	n/a	n/a	-.35
Central Govt. Performance	-.68	n/a	n/a	n/a

Source: Computed from the logit coefficients.
n.s. = not statistically significant; n/a = not applicable

The predicted probabilities in the main model show that ethnic identity indicators for *caste (upper caste)* and *religion (Hindu)* increase the likelihood of voting for the BJP by 26 and 40 percentage points respectively. This suggests that being upper caste and Hindu continues to have strong effects on the likelihood of voting for the BJP in Gujarat. Additionally, a high level of wealth also significantly increases the likelihood of voting for the BJP by 17 percentage points. The retrospective programmatic indicator, *central government performance*, has a large negative impact on vote choice: a high level of satisfaction with the performance of the incumbent Congress-led UPA government is associated with a 68 percentage point decrease in the likelihood of voting for the BJP.

The results of model two, when the retrospective programmatic indicator, *personal financial conditions,* is added to the model, is initially somewhat surprising: *personal financial conditions* is associated with a 27 percentage point <u>increase</u> in the likelihood of voting for the BJP. In other words, the predicted probabilities suggest that a positive assessment of government performance related to personal financial conditions is associated with a 27 percentage point increase in the likelihood of voting for the BJP. If voters in Gujarat are focused <u>only</u> on central government performance, then it is hard to explain why a positive assessment of the Congress-led central government performance on this programmatic issue would be associated with a higher likelihood of voter support for the BJP in the 2009 election.

However, a look at the priorities of BJP and Congress voters indicates important shifts with regard to emphasizing the work of state government versus the central government over time. In the 1999 election, BJP supporters in Gujarat on average indicated that they placed a significantly higher degree of importance on the work of the incumbent-led BJP government at the center than Congress supporters (33.9 percent versus 19.49 percent).

In the 2009 election, the priorities shifted: BJP voters on average placed greater importance on the work of the BJP-led state level government, whereas Congress supporters now placed greater importance on the work of the Congress-led central government. Table 6.11 summarizes Gujarati voters' priorities with regard to the work of the state and central government in the 2009 election.

Table 6.11 Gujarat voter priorities in 2009: central versus state level government

	Neither	State level	Both	Central level	Other
All Voters	3.25	30.23	22.10	26.87	1.19
BJP voters	3.42	45.30	22.65	11.54	1.26
Congress voters	3.08	14.73	21.54	42.64	1.28

Source: Indian NES Survey (2009)

The table shows that 45 percent of BJP voters were more focused on the work of the state level government in the 2009 election in Gujarat, compared to 11 percent of BJP voters who prioritized the work of the central government. Congress voter priorities were the complete inverse of BJP voters in Gujarat: over 42 percent of Congress voters focused on the work of the central level government, while about 14 percent of Congress voters indicated that they focused more on the work of the state level government.

Further analysis of BJP voters in the 2009 election in Gujarat indicates that BJP voters who indicated that personal financial conditions in India were either "better" or "much better" compared to five years ago were on average more likely to emphasize the work of state level government rather than the central level government.[310] Thus, I posit that the positive value of the predicted probability for *personal financial conditions* is, in part, a retrospective programmatic assessment of state level performance of the BJP-led government.[311] This is again suggestive of an interesting extension of ERV that different voters may prioritize and focus on different levels of government performance when voting in a national election.

---

[310] A cross tabulation of the relationship of the variable *personal financial conditions* with the variable *voter priorities*, regarding central versus state level government, shows that forty-three percent of BJP voters who indicated that personal financial conditions were "better" were focused on the work of the state level government. Only 9 percent of BJP voters who indicated that personal financial conditions were "better" emphasized the work of the central level government. The remaining BJP voters either focused on both levels of government or declined to specify.
[311] In the next section focusing on case studies of individual voters in Ahmedabad, I find that fifty percent of voters interviewed indicate that their opinion of BJP Chief Minister Narendra Modi affects their vote choice in the national elections.

In the results of model three, when the retrospective programmatic indicator *development* is added to the model, only ethnic identity indicators for caste and religion, and a high level of wealth, have any substantive effects on the likelihood for voting for the BJP. The results of model four, show that *terrorism* is associated with a large negative substantive effect on voter support for the BJP: the more satisfied one is with government performance in handling the 2009 Mumbai terror attacks, the less likely one is to vote for the BJP by 35 percentage points. This suggests that a retrospective programmatic assessment of government performance on issues relating to terrorism and national security continues to be a very important factor of vote choice and distinguishing voter support for the BJP in Gujarat.

As noted in the Delhi 2009 election analysis, the 2009 NES survey administered a distinctly different question on the Ram temple issue compared to the 1999 and 2004 surveys. The table below presents the results from the 2009 NES survey question: What would you suggest be built on the site [at Ayodhya]?[312]

Table 6.12 What should be built at the Ayodhya site? (Gujarat 2009)

	Neither	Mosque	Temple	Both	No opinion
All Voters	13	9	29	28	20
Congress voters	9	5	9	12	11
BJP voters	4	4	20	16	9

Source: Indian NES Survey (2009)
Figures above are in number of respondents.

The results show that a larger number of BJP voters surveyed favor a Hindu temple to be built at the Ayodhya site over other options. By comparison, BJP voters

---

[312] In the 1999 and 2004 survey, a different but related question was asked: On the site where Babri Masjid was situated only Ram temple should be built (agree, no opinion, disagree). This question was asked to all survey respondents in the 2004 survey, whereas the Ayodhya-related question was asked to only one-fifth of the respondents in the 2009 survey. The sample size for this question is 99.

surveyed in the 2009 election in Delhi were more inclined to favor both a temple and a mosque to be built at the Ayodhya site. Although this is a very small sample size, it is somewhat suggestive that the ethnic group interest relating to building the Ram temple was a factor for some BJP voters in the 2009 election in Gujarat.[313]

The analysis of 2009 election survey data for Gujarat shows that ethnic group identity indicators for r*eligion (Hindu)* and *caste (upper caste)* have a strong impact on the likelihood of voting for the BJP. Additionally, the analysis has shown that retrospective programmatic indicators relating to *central government performance*, *personal financial conditions*, and *terrorism* also have statistically significant and strong substantive effects on the likelihood of voting for the BJP. In addition, the analysis indicates that a high level of wealth is associated with a higher likelihood of voting for the BJP.

How do these results compare over time? Table 6.13 presents the results of the difference in sample proportions for indicators of *caste* and *religion* in the 1999, 2004 and 2009 elections for BJP voters in Gujarat. Column 3 presents the proportion of voters with a particular characteristic (i.e. being upper caste) who voted for the BJP, while column 4 presents the proportion of voters who do not have the characteristic (i.e. non upper-caste) and voted for the BJP.

---

[313] However, *Ram temple views,* was not statistically significant in the previous analysis of the 2004 election in Gujarat. Thus, we cannot say with this very small sample size that this finding holds any statistical significance.

Table 6.13 Differences of sample proportions for indicators of caste and religion for BJP voters, Gujarat 1999, 2004 and 2009 elections

Year	Indicator	Yes	No	Difference in proportions
1999	Caste (upper caste)	.76	.36	-.40**
	Religion (Hindu)	.49	.21	-.28**
2004	Caste (upper caste)	.56	.36	-.20**
	Religion (Hindu)	.45	.21	-.24**
2009	Caste (upper caste)	.69	.43	-.26**
	Religion (Hindu)	.54	.27	-.27**

Source: Indian NES Survey (1999, 2004, 2009)
Significance: * = at 5%; ** = at 1%
N = 372 (1999); 877 (2004); 923(2009)

While the differences with respect to these ethnic indicators for BJP voters markedly narrowed between the 1999 election and the 2004 election, the 2009 results show a slight increase in the degree of difference in upper caste versus non-upper caste voter support for the BJP, and Hindu versus non-Hindu voter support for the BJP.

If we look at the indicator for *caste (upper caste)*, we find that 76 percent of upper caste voters voted for the BJP in the 1999 election. Five years later, this percentage of upper caste voters who voted for the BJP was markedly reduced to 56 percent in the 2004 election. Yet, by the 2009 election, the number of upper caste voters who voted for the BJP increased to 69 percent. Though we find a marked decrease in the proportion of upper caste voters who voted for the BJP from 1999 to 2004, this overall trend from 1999 to 2009 suggests that being upper caste continues to be a distinguishing characteristic of BJP voters in Gujarat.

The same is true when we look at the results for the indicator for *religion (Hindu)*. Though we find a slight decrease in the proportion of Hindu voters who voted for the BJP from 1999 to 2004, the overall trend indicates a generally consistent proportion of Hindus who voted for the BJP from 1999 to 2009.

By contrast, the percentage of Hindus who voted for the BJP in the 2009 election in Delhi is markedly lower than in Gujarat (i.e. 42 percent in Delhi versus 54 percent in Gujarat), and has decreased incrementally over the 1999-2009 timeframe. Thus, within the context of the BJP's ethno-political mobilization efforts to support the construction of the Ram temple, which was keenly felt in Gujarat, and ongoing ethnic tensions between Hindus and Muslims, we find that Hindus continue to be a strong base of support for the BJP in Gujarat.

The analysis of voting behavior in the 2009 election in Gujarat shows that, while being upper caste or Hindu was more of a distinguishing feature associated with BJP support in the 1999 election compared to the 2004 election in Gujarat, the relative influence of ethnic group identity continues to play a significant impact on voting behavior and explaining voter support for the BJP in Gujarat in the 2009 election. In addition, the analysis shows retrospective programmatic interests, in particular relating to personal financial conditions and national security, were also important factors influencing voter support for the BJP.

Under conditions of a high level of political economy of development and a medium level of ethnic conflict, which characterized the context of the 2009 election in Delhi, ERV predicts that retrospective programmatic interests would have a strong influence in explaining voter support for the BJP, while ethnic group identity and interests would also have a strong, though somewhat less extreme, influence in explaining voter support for the BJP. Though the overall level of ethnic conflict declined from 1999 to 2009, these findings suggest that ethnic identity continues to be a strong, though less extreme, factor influencing voting behavior in Gujarat. In summary, these empirical results indicate the strong influence of both ethnic and programmatic interests in explaining voter support for the BJP in Gujarat in 2009. These empirical results I argue support ERV theory as a plausible means of explaining voter support for the BJP in Gujarat in the 2009 election, most closely represented by scenario 1 in 3.1.

Ahmedabad: Case Studies Analysis, 1999-2009

This section presents an analysis of case studies of 37 voters in Ahmedabad, the largest city in Gujarat and the fifth largest city in India. The first section of this chapter addressed the history of episodes of violent ethnic conflict that have taken place in Gujarat. Ahmedabad, in particular, has experienced several episodes of large-scale ethnic violence over the past four decades, most notably in 1969, 1985-86, 1990, 1992 and 2002.[314]

Ahmedabad has long been divided economically into the more affluent and newer western bank, and the older working class and poorer eastern bank, with the Sabarmati River separating the two sections.[315] However, after the 2002 riots, ghettoization increased markedly, with the east side home to Muslims and Dalits, and the west side home to Hindus.[316] Thus, unlike the New Delhi cases, which are examples of urban voting behavior in a large Indian city with low to moderate levels of ethic conflict and violence, the Ahmedabad cases provide insight into urban voting behavior in the context

---

[314] This list does not include every episode of ethnic violence in Ahmedabad over the past 40 years.
[315] Burman, "The Two Banks of the River," *Economic & Political Weekly*, September 18, 1976. See also Yagnik and Sheth, *The Shaping of Modern Gujarat*, pgs. 229-230. The eastern bank itself has two sections, the "old city" built in the 15th century during the era of the Gujarat Sultanate near the river, and the eastern belt on the east side of the old city, developed in the 20th century to house laborers working in the textile mills. The two sections of the eastern bank together are distinctly different economically and socially from the more affluent west bank.
[316] Interview with Mahashweta Jani, February 12, 2011.

of a large Indian city, in which the city's residents have been profoundly impacted by multiple episodes of high levels of ethnic conflict and violence.

The data for the Ahmedabad cases was collected using the same survey questionnaire that was used for the New Delhi cases studies, in which voters were asked about the factors affecting their vote choices in the 1999, 2004 and 2009 national elections. Voter identification and interviews took place in different areas of Ahmedabad, on both the east side and west side of the city.

Like the New Delhi cases, I use a purposive sampling design to identify cases, in which individual voters were identified based on a combination of socio-economic characteristics (i.e., religion, caste, class/income, nature of employment). Table 6.14 provides a summary list of the socio-economic characteristics represented in the Ahmedabad cases.[317]

Table 6.14 Summary of socio-economic characteristics of Ahmedabad case studies

Caste		Religion		Class		Sector	
Brahmin*	6	Hindu	32	Rich	4	Private	11
Bania*	8	Muslim	4	Upper Middle	7	Public	14
Patels**	6	Christian	1	Middle	11	Unorganized	12
Scheduled castes***	7			Working	7		
Tribals****	5			Poor	8		
Others/No caste	5						
Total	37		37		37		37

*Upper castes for this research project include Brahmins and Bania, (including one from Punjab).
**Patels are upwardly mobile middle caste Hindus.
**Scheduled castes are lower caste Hindus.
***Tribals, like scheduled castes, are a historically disadvantaged population.

Ahmedabad's ethnic social composition is different from New Delhi. In particular, the ethnic social composition of New Delhi (and Delhi) includes Punjabis who immigrated to the area during Partition and have become a part of the city's business and

---

[317] Age and gender were not purposively sampled.

trading community. They are often associated with supporting the BJP. Ahmedabad (and Gujarat) also has its own prominent "bania"[318] merchant and trading community, but in addition, it also has an ethnic group known as the Patels, or Patidars.

The Patels are historically from agricultural and landowning communities, whose wealth and social status increased in the 20th century, partly as a result of their participation in India's Green and White Revolutions to increase agricultural and milk production.[319] Many members of the Patel community left their original communities and have since become part of the urban educated middle class. Patels are estimated to make up about twenty percent of the population.[320] Together, the Brahmins and Banias, and the Patels, resented the reservation policies advocated by the Congress party in the 1980s, and were considered an important political voting block for the newly emerging BJP during that time. All three castes are included in the Ahmedabad case study sample. Table 6.15 on the following page presents the details of each voter interviewed for this study and their corresponding vote choices for the 1999, 2004 and 2009 national elections.

---

[318] I am using the now commonly used term Bania. However, the original term for this caste group is Vaniya. Yagnik and Sheth note, "Traders were called Vanik or Vanijah, which evolved over the centuries to Vaniya, a caste term which today refers to both Hindus and Jains...The commonly used 'Baniya" is a corruption of Vaniya used first by the Portuguese and then by the Dutch and English as a collective noun for all Gujarati traders irrespective of religion," p. 21.
[319] Ibid, p. 235.
[320] Patel, Priyavadan, "Sectarian Mobilization, Communal Polarization and Factionalism," p. 14.

Table 6.15 Ahmedabad Cases

Case No	M/F	Age	Caste/Religion	Class	Occupation	Sector	1999 Vote	2004 Vote	2009 Vote	Vote Type
16	M	30s	Bania	Rich	Owner, Large Travel Company	Private	BJP	BJP	BJP	2
25	M	50s	Punjabi	Rich	Owner, Company Selling Eco-Friendly Bags	Private	BJP	BJP	BJP	1
31	M	50s	Kashmir Pandit/Brahmin	Rich	Owner, Health Care Consulting Firm; Former Air Force Cdr.	Private	BJP	Congress	Congress	1
32	M	50s	Keralite Brahmin	Rich	Owner of Multiple Companies	Private	BJP	BJP	BJP	1
29	M	50s	Bania	Upper-middle Class	Owner, Local Accounting Firm	Private	Congress	Congress	Congress	1
27	M	60s	Brahmin	Upper-middle Class	Owner/Consultant, Engineering & Design Firm	Private	BJP	BJP	BJP	4
12	M	30s	Brahmin	Upper-Middle Class	Owner, Local Transport Company	Private	BJP	BJP	BJP	2
26	M	30s	Bania/Jain	middle class	Owner, Local Driving School	Private	N/A	BJP	BJP	1
14	M	20s	Bania	middle class	Office Clerk, National Car Rental Company	Private	N/A	BJP	BJP	2
30	M	40s	Patel	Lower middle class	Client Relations, Accounting Firm	Private	BJP	BJP	BJP	2
3	M	40s	Scheduled Caste	Poor	Night Watchman	Private	Congress	Congress	Congress	4
24	F	40s	Muslim	Upper-middle Class	Senior Academic Researcher, Higher Education	Public	Congress	Congress	Congress	4
11	F	30s	Scheduled Caste	Upper-middle Class	Senior Officer, Government Life Insurance Corporation	Public	Congress	Congress	Congress	1
10	F	50s	Patel	Upper-middle class	Retired Nurse	Public	BJP	BJP	BJP	1
13	M	50s	Christian	Upper-middle Class	Senior Executor, Higher Education	Public	BJP	BJP	N/A	1
22	M	40s	Muslim	Middle Class	Mid-Level Gov't (Clerk, Government Telephone Office)	Public	BJP	BJP	BJP	2
17	F	40s	Bania	Middle Class	Mid-Level Gov't (Project Administration, Higher Education)	Public	BJP	N/A	BJP	4
9	F	50s	Brahmin	Middle Class	Mid-Level Gov't (Principle, Public School)	Public	BJP	BJP	BJP	3
8	M	50s	Patel	Middle Class	Mid-Level Gov't (Science Teacher, Public School)	Public	BJP	BJP	BJP	1
5	M	50s	Muslim	Lower Middle Class	Mid-Level Gov't (Skilled Clerk, Public Trust)	Public	Congress	Congress	Congress	4
7	M	40s	Muslim	Working Class	Low-Skilled Gov't (Clerk)	Public	Congress	Congress	Congress	1
6	M	50s	Scheduled Caste	Working Class	Low-Skilled Gov't (Messenger)	Public	Congress	Congress	Congress	1
4	M	60s	Patel	Working Class	Low Skilled Gov't (Acountant)	Public	BJP	BJP	BJP	1
2	F	60s	Patel	Working Class	Low Skilled Gov't (Messenger)	Public	Congress	N/A	N/A	N/A
1	F	40s	Scheduled Caste	Poor	Low Skilled Gov't (Cleaning)	Public	BJP	Congress	Congress	3
28	F	30s	Scheduled Caste	Middle Class	Housewife, not working	Not Working	BJP	Congress	Congress	1
15	M	30s	Bania	Middle Class	Owns medium sized family-run curbside grocery store	Unorganized	BJP	BJP	BJP	2
33	M	60s	Muslim	Lower Middle Class	Auto Rickshaw Driver	Unorganized	Congress	Congress	Congress	3
23	M	60s	Bania	Working Class	Pan Stall/Tobacco Stand	unorganized	BJP	BJP	BJP	3
34	F	30s	Devipujak/Tribal	Working Class	Two fruit stands	Unorganized	BJP	BJP	BJP	3
36	F	60s	Devipujak/Tribal	Working Class	Two vegetable stands	Unorganized	Congress	Congress	BJP	1
18	M	70s	Patel	Poor	Tiny food stand (Lari)	Unorganized	Congress	BJP	BJP	1
19	F	40s	Scheduled Caste	Poor	Vegetable Seller	Unorganized	Congress	BJP	BJP	1
20	M	50s	Devipujak/Tribal	poor	Vegetable Seller	Unorganized	Congress	BJP	BJP	1
21	M	60s	Scheduled Caste	Poor	Cobbler	Unorganized	Congress	Congress	Congress	4
35	F	40s	Devipujak/Tribal	Poor	Garlic seller	Unorganized	Congress	Congress	Congress	1
37	F	40s	Devipujak/Tribal	Poor	Vegetable Seller	Unorganized	Congress	Congress	BJP	1
						Total BJP Vote	19	20	22	

Table 6.15 shows that voter support for the BJP in the Ahmedabad cases remained strong and even gained in strength from 1999 to 2009. In the 1999 election, nineteen voters voted for the BJP; five years later, the number increased to 20. In the 2009 election, the number of voters increased to 22. By contrast, voter support for the BJP in the New Delhi cases reduced sharply during the same timeframe. Table 6.16 shows the contrast in voter support for the BJP in the Ahmedabad and New Delhi cases in the 1999, 2004 and 2009 national elections. These patterns of voter support for the BJP in the New Delhi and Ahmedabad case studies broadly reflect the trends in voter support for the BJP in Gujarat and Delhi during this timeframe.

Table 6.16 Ahmedabad and New Delhi Cases: number of BJP voters

Election Year	Ahmedabad	New Delhi
1999	19	19
2004	20	10
2009	22	6

A couple of general points of comparison between the Ahmedabad cases and the New Delhi cases are worth noting. First, in the New Delhi cases, a majority of upper caste Hindus switched their vote away from the BJP from 1999 to 2009. By contrast, in the Ahmedabad cases, I found continued upper caste support for the BJP during the 1999 to 2009 timeframe. In the 1999 election, 11 out of 14 upper caste respondents voted for the BJP. In the 2009 election, 12 out of 14 upper caste respondents voted for the BJP. The majority of the upwardly mobile Patels, 4 out of 6, also consistently voted for the BJP. Only one upper caste respondent, an upper income Kashmiri Brahmin, switched his vote away from the BJP to Congress during this timeframe. Thus, the upper caste Brahmins and Banias, and the Patels, are a strong vote block for the BJP for the Ahmedabad voters interviewed for this study.

In addition to this generally stable trend of upper caste support for the BJP, the Ahmedabad cases indicate that several lower income voters, from a scheduled caste or tribe, switched their support *toward* the BJP in later elections. In particular, five low-income respondents working in the unorganized sector voted for the Congress party in the 1999 election, but indicated that they switched their vote to the BJP in later elections.[321] Taking together these two trends, we find in the Ahmedabad cases both a stable trend in upper caste support for the BJP, combined with individuals from other

---

[321] The five cases that switched their vote from the Congress party to the BJP are cases 36, 18, 19, 20 and 37.

caste and income groups in the city, namely lower income and lower caste voters, who shifted their support toward the BJP.

A second notable difference between the New Delhi cases and the Ahmedabad cases is the presence (or absence) of Muslim voter support for the BJP. Two Muslim respondents interviewed in New Delhi indicated that they voted for the BJP. By contrast no Muslim respondents interviewed in Ahmedabad indicated that they had voted for the BJP in any of the three national elections.

Lastly, a notable similarity is that the Ahmedabad cases do not present a pattern linking higher levels of religiosity with increased voter support for the BJP, for either the voters who consistently voted for the BJP over the three elections, or the voters who switched their vote to the BJP.[322] This result suggests that religiosity is not a particularly good indicator of BJP support in Ahmedabad, and is consistent with similar results found in the New Delhi cases.

In the New Delhi case studies analysis, I discovered four patterns of urban voting behavior to explain changes in electoral support for the BJP from 1999 to 2009: 1) Retrospective Programmatic Voting, 2) Weak Ethnic voting, 3) Strong Ethnic Voting, and 4) Party loyalty. My analysis of the Ahmedabad case studies finds these four predominant patters of urban voting behavior to explain changes in electoral support for the BJP in Ahmedabad from 1999 to 2009. The following table presents a summary of

---

[322] Of the 18 Ahmedabad case respondents who consistently voted for the BJP in all three national elections, eight voters indicated that religion had remained the same level of importance, while another eight voters indicated that religion had increased in importance. Two voters declined to answer the question. For the five swing voters, one voter indicated that religion was not important to him, one voter indicated that religion had increased in importance, and a third voter indicated that religion had remained the same level of importance. Two swing voters declined to comment.

the number of voters for each of the four types of vote patterns for the New Delhi and the Ahmedabad case studies.

Table 6.17 Summary of Vote Patterns: Ahmedabad and New Delhi Cases

Vote Pattern	Ahmedabad	New Delhi
Type 1: Retrospective Programmatic Voting	19	19
Type 2: Weak Ethnic Voting	6	8
Type 3: Strong Ethnic Voting	5	1
Type 4: Party Loyalty Voting	6	6
Inconclusive	1	1
Total	37	35

The above table shows that the number of retrospective programmatic voters as well as loyal party voters is the same. However, the number of strong ethnic voters is clearly different: the Ahmedabad cases include five strong ethnic voters, whereas the New Delhi cases include only one strong ethnic voter. What do these four patterns of voting behavior look like with regard to electoral support for the BJP over time? Table 6.18 shows the number of voters for each voting pattern of respondents who voted for the BJP in the 1999 and the 2009 elections in New Delhi and in Ahmedabad.

Table 6.18 Vote Patterns of BJP voters in Ahmedabad and New Delhi, 1999 & 2009

City/Vote Pattern	1999 Election	2009 Election
Ahmedabad		
Type 1: Retrospective Programmatic Voting	7	11
Type 2: Weak Ethnic Voting	6	6
Type 3: Strong Ethnic Voting	4	3
Type 4: Party Loyalty Voting	2	2
Total BJP Vote	19	22
New Delhi		
Type 1: Retrospective Programmatic Voting	11	2
Type 2: Weak Ethnic Voting	5	1
Type 3: Strong Ethnic Voting	1	1
Type 4: Party Loyalty Voting	2	2
Total BJP Vote	19	6

Table 6.18 begins to uncover the differences in the voting patterns underlying electoral support for the BJP over time in each city. In the 1999 election, ethnic voting – both weak ethnic and strong ethnic voting – explains more than half of voter support for the BJP in the Ahmedabad cases, but about one-third of voter support for the BJP in the New Delhi cases. In the 2009 election, ethnic voting continues to explain nearly half of all voter support for the BJP in the Ahmedabad cases, but about one-third of voter support for the BJP in the New Delhi cases. This suggests that ethnic voting is generally more influential in explaining voter support for the BJP in the Ahmedabad cases than in the New Delhi cases. The following section provides a discussion of the four patterns of voting behavior in the context of the Ahmedabad cases and provides examples of individual Ahmedabad voters interviewed who exemplify each pattern.

1. Retrospective Programmatic Voting: The first pattern of voting behavior, Retrospective Programmatic Voting, is characterized by voters who indicate that their assessment of party performance on specific programmatic issues is the main driver in their vote choices. Nineteen Ahmedabad case respondents fall into this category of voting behavior. A particularly strong finding in the New Delhi cases is that nearly all the voters from the private sector fall into this pattern of voting behavior. By contrast, though a majority of Ahmedabad respondents with an upper-middle class income or higher and working in the private sector fall into this category of voting behavior, we also find that several very low income respondents working in the unorganized sector also display this pattern of voting behavior.

Case 25 is an upper caste Hindu who owns a large business, representing a very high income voter from the private sector, and falls into this category of Retrospective

Programmatic Voting. When asked if the dispute over the Ram temple in Ayodhya was a factor in his vote choice, this entrepreneur and business owner responded that he "recoiled from it," as well at the BJP's use of *Hindutva*.[323] Instead, he voted for the BJP in the 1999 election, because he felt that, "India's security was in better hands with the BJP than in Congress." In the following 2004 and 2009 elections, this large business owner continued to vote for the BJP, but he said that his ongoing support was largely based on his positive perception of the party's ability to handle the economy.

I also found this pattern of Retrospective Programmatic Voting from Ahmedabad respondents who were employed in the public sector. Case 8 is a science teacher who voted for the BJP in all three national elections. This voter indicated that political corruption and national security were the main factors in his vote choice in the 1999 and 2004 elections, while a focus on employment and rising prices were the overarching interests influencing his vote choice in the 2009 election. Expressing a similar view with other Ahmedabad voters interviewed for this research, the respondent linked his opinion and assessment of Chief Minister Modi's performance at the state level to his vote choice in the national elections: "If the BJP performs at the Center level like [it does] at the State," he noted, "the BJP at the Center is fine."[324][325]

These two cases provide examples of Retrospective Programmatic Voting behavior from Ahmedabad voters who work in either the private or public sector, and

---

[323] Ahmedabad case study 25.

[324] Ahmedabad case study 8.

[325] The survey questionnaire for the Ahmedabad case study includes the following question: " Does your opinion of Chief Minister Modi affect your vote choice in the National/Lok Sabha election?" The response was nearly split between the number of respondents who responded that their opinion of Modi did affect their vote choice in the national elections (17/37) and the number of respondents who said their opinion of Modi did not affect their vote choice in the national elections (16/37). Four case respondents did not answer this question.

with at least a middle class income or higher, whose support for the BJP is largely based on retrospective programmatic interests.

In addition to these cases of middle or higher income retrospective programmatic urban voters working in the private or public sector, my case study research identified a different type of voter in Ahmedabad, who I suggest can be considered a "burgeoning" retrospective programmatic voter, with a distinctly different socio-economic profile: the very low-income urban voter who works in the unorganized sector. This type of urban voter was interviewed both in New Delhi and Ahmedabad (i.e. 12 voters, six for each city) and represents individuals with very low levels of income, (i.e. approximately U.S. $1-2 dollars per day).[326]

The case study interviews revealed that an underlying commonality for this group of voters in both cities is their near total emphasis on prospects for improved livelihood. When asked their views about ethnic identity and interests such as *Hindutva* or the Ram temple, these voters indicated that they did not focus on these issues when voting, but instead were concerned about items such as water, sanitation (specifically, access to toilets), and electricity.

Five Ahmedabad case respondents from this socio-economic group switched their vote away from the Congress to the BJP in later elections.[327] All five of these voters interviewed make a living as small food or vegetable vendors, and the majority are poor (though one is working class) and lower caste. Cases 36 and 37 are voters who operate small vegetable stands and fall into this category of "burgeoning" retrospective

---

[326] In the New Delhi cases, though two Muslim voters from this socio-economic stratum voted for the BJP in a single election, these voters more often voted for the Congress party.

[327] The five cases that switched their vote from the Congress party to the BJP are cases 36, 18, 19, 20 and 37.

programmatic voting. Case 36, a widow in her 60s, whose family income from two vegetable stands provides the equivalent of approximately $3-4 dollars per day, indicated that she had long associated the Congress party with Indira Gandhi, and voted for the Congress in the 1999 and 2004 elections. But she also indicated that toilets and electricity had recently come to her neighborhood and she gave the BJP credit for these improvements and voted for them in the 2009 election, saying that she was "starting to link changes she sees in the neighborhood to who is in power – BJP or Congress." She said that her opinion of Narendra Modi had influenced whom she votes for in the national election.

Similarly, case 37, who operates one vegetable stand and earns about $1-2 dollars per day, had also associated the Congress party with Indira Gandhi and working for the poor. But she switched her voted to the BJP in the 2004 election. "After Modi came, it was only about him." Like case respondent 36, this voter linked Modi's coming to power with bringing water and toilets to her neighborhood. Thus, she associated the BJP with Narendra Modi, and Narendra Modi with the possibility of a better livelihood.

While none of these voters indicated that political patronage, such as money, gifts, employment, or other direct, immediate, exclusive payoff, played a role in their vote choices, my findings do not provide clear evidence about the role of patronage for these voters.

Unlike middle and higher income programmatic voters who highlighted concerns about broader issues such as development, inflation, or national security as primary factors in their vote choice, these low income urban voters emphasized concerns relating to better access to public goods provisions, such as water, sanitation, and electricity, and said they switched their vote to the BJP in later elections because they thought that the party was making improvements in these areas and was more likely to make these conditions better than the Congress party. I am using the term "burgeoning" retrospective programmatic voting in the sense that these voters display an emerging awareness of the link between their vote and a form of reward or punishment for government performance of access to public goods. These voters did not display a broader awareness or concern about public policy positions and outcomes.

My findings suggest that for the voters from these two different socio-economic groups in this category, retrospective programmatic issues are the main factors influencing their vote choices, and the predominant means of explaining electoral support for the BJP. Though a majority of Ahmedabad respondents within the highest level of income and working in the private sector fall into this category of voting behavior, this research suggests that very low-income voters can display burgeoning retrospective programmatic voting. This pattern of Retrospective Programmatic Voting most closely resembles type 1 voting behavior in table 3.2. In the Ahmedabad cases, Retrospective Programmatic Voting appears to be influenced by the perceived rewards from economic development and growth, but also for some voters, by linking improvements in public service provisions to which party is in power.

2. Weak Ethnic Voting: The second pattern of voting behavior, Weak Ethnic Voting, is characterized by voters who are strongly influenced by ethnic identity and interests at one point of time, but whose political preferences change, such that they vote based on retrospective programmatic interests at a later point of time. In the New Delhi cases, the majority of voters in this category are from a middle or lower caste, have lower incomes than retrospective programmatic voters, and half of the respondents work in the unorganized sector.

However, the distribution of weak ethnic voting behavior in the Ahmedabad cases is more widespread among socio-economic groups. Of the six weak ethnic voters in Ahmedabad, four voters are upper caste and work in the private sector, one voter is upper caste middle class and works in the public sector, and one voter is upper caste middle class and works in the unorganized sector. This distribution of Weak Ethnic Voting suggests that, under conditions of a high level of ethnic conflict, the relative political salience of ethnic group identity and interests can supersede retrospective programmatic interests, including for some high income voters who share similar socio-economic characteristics with retrospective programmatic voters. However, similar to weak ethnic voters in the New Delhi cases, in later elections, as Gujarat experienced increasingly higher levels of economic growth and development, this category of Ahmedabad voters became less focused on ethnic issues and identified programmatic issues, particularly development, concerns about rising prices, and corruption, as much stronger factors influencing their vote choice.

Cases 15 and 30 are voters who fall into this category of Weak Ethnic Voting. Case 15 comes from a bania (merchant) family and owns a medium-sized curbside grocery store. Case 30 is a Patel who manages client relations for a private accounting firm. Both of their stated incomes place them in a middle class income group. These two voters emphasized that the Ram temple issue along with positive views of BJP party leadership under Atal Bihari Vajpayee were key factors in their support for the BJP in the 1999 election.[328]

In later elections, however, these voters indicated that they shifted their focus and that concerns about development had become a much more important factor influencing their vote choice. They both linked Chief Minister Modi's performance at the state level with improved development conditions, and indicated that their opinion of Modi and his performance at the state level in turn affected their vote choice in national elections. Responding to a question about his views about the BJP in the 2009 national election, the grocery story owner said, "When I go to vote, I think more about Gujarat and what Modi is doing."[329] The narratives of these two Ahmedabad voters, who indicate the importance of the Ram temple issue as a key political issue in the 1999 election, but distinctly change their focus to programmatic issues such as economic development when voting in later elections, is very similar to the narratives of weak ethnic voters in the New Delhi cases.

The Ahmedabad case studies also include weak ethnic voters who indicated that the BJP's advocacy of *Hindutva*, rather than the Ram temple issue, was a critical factor in their support for the party in the 1999 election. Cases 12 and 22 are voters who indicated the importance of *Hindutva* in voting for the BJP in the 1999 election, but then went on to focus on programmatic issues in the later elections. Case 12 is an upper caste Hindu who owns his own transport business where he manages about sixty employees. He explained that his father was a member of the Hindu nationalist organization, the RSS, and it [*Hindutva*] is "in his blood." When asked why he voted for the BJP in the 1999 election,

---

[328] Ahmedabad case studies 15 and 30.
[329] Ahmedabad case study 15.

he said, "It's not Ram Mandir per se, because Ram is not an end. It's *Hindutva*, there were concerns that Hindus were losing their identity. It was important to gather them."[330]

Case 22 is an upper caste Hindu and a clerk in a government telephone office, who also indicated that *Hindutva* was important to him in the 1999 election. He spoke of his support of *Hindutva* in terms of both responding to Muslim extremism and Congress' use of Muslims as vote banks. He noted, "Congress always gives more to Muslims. We felt that it [*Hindutva*] was necessary."[331] For these two voters, the BJP's advocacy of *Hindutva* was a key factor in their support for the party in the 1999 election.

Yet, like other weak ethnic voters, these two respondents indicated that programmatic issues began to take precedence in later elections. The transport business owner said that when the BJP came to power in 1999, they didn't deliver on their promises relating to their (Hindu nationalist) goals. By the 2009 election, his focus had shifted to economic development, concerns about rising prices, and corruption in politics.

The government telephone office employee also noted that during their five-year term in power the BJP did not deliver on their promises. In later elections, he noted that concerns about rising prices and corruption in politics, which he strongly associated with the Congress party, were the predominant factors influencing his vote choice. Both of these voters continued to vote for the BJP in later elections, but for distinctly different reasons, namely, a focus on programmatic issues including, economic development, rising prices and political corruption.

In this second pattern of voting behavior, Weak Ethnic Voting, I posit that a very high level of Hindu-Muslim conflict in Ahmedabad in the lead up to the 1999 election in

---

[330] Ahmedabad case study 12.
[331] Ahmedabad case study 22.

turn heightened the political salience of ethnicity on vote choice. While some weak ethnic voters in Ahmedabad identified a strong desire to see the Ram temple built as a key motivator in their support for the BJP in the 1999 election, others expressed deep concerns about Hindu identity and unity through their support of the BJP's position on *Hindutva*.

My findings suggest that voters in this category of Weak Ethnic Voting are influenced by both ethnic concerns, such as the Ram temple and *Hindutva*, and retrospective programmatic concerns, such as economic development, managing prices and combating political corruption in their vote choices. Similar to the New Delhi cases, this pattern of Weak Ethnic Voting most closely resembles type 3 voting behavior in table 3.2, in which a voter is influenced by both the perceived risk of group threat from ethnic conflict and the opportunities posed by economic reforms and development, and as a result, changes in socio-economic conditions in turn change the relative importance of ethnic group identity and interests and retrospective programmatic interests on vote choice.

For this type of voting behavior, the conditions of a very high level of Hindu-Muslim conflict in the 1999 election in Ahmedabad, lead to a heightened political salience of ethnic group identity and interests, which appears to swamp out retrospective programmatic interests in explaining voter support for the BJP. In the subsequent 2004 and 2009 national elections, as the severity of ethnic conflict was reduced somewhat, combined with a high political economy of development, which many voters associated with BJP Chief Minister, Narendra Modi, retrospective programmatic interests appear to supersede ethnic interests in these voter's political choices.

3. Strong Ethnic Voting: The third pattern of voting behavior, Strong Ethnic Voting, is characterized by voters for whom the political salience of ethnic identity and interests persists in importance over time. The majority of Ahmedabad respondents who fall into this category of Strong Ethnic Voting come from the working class and work in the unorganized sector. As a group, the strong ethnic voters in the Ahmedabad cases have similar socio-economic characteristics to weak ethnic voters in the New Delhi cases (i.e., lower caste or minority, working class income, and work in the unorganized sector), though one voter is from the middle class and works in the public sector. Strong Ethnic Voting best explains the voting behavior of five Ahmedabad voters in this study.

Case 23 is a Hindu from a bania family who operates a small but thriving paan stall (similar to a tobacco stand) located on a busy street. His steady business puts him in a working class income group. For this paan stall operator, the BJP's advocacy of *Hindutva* is a key factor in his ongoing support for the party. Of *Hindutva*, he notes, "It was absolutely necessary at that point in time…Congress was appeasing Muslims so much…It was only the BJP that stopped this."[332] Unlike weak ethnic voters who turned their focus to programmatic issues in later elections, this voter emphasized that his concerns about Hindu-Muslim relations and support for *Hindutva* continued to strongly influence his vote choice and support for the BJP in the 2004 and 2009 elections.

Case 34 is a woman from the Devipujak community who manages two fruit stands with her husband at an outdoor large market. For this voter, internal security between Hindus and Muslims in the city and particularly in the market where she works is of paramount importance. She explained that for a long time, she did not feel safe in

---

[332] Ahmedabad case study 23.

the market, and she attributed the BJP's coming to power with more internal security between Hindus and Muslims.[333] She emphasized the importance of the BJP's ability to bring security between Hindus and Muslims as the key factor in her continued support for the BJP.

Case 9 is a middle class Hindu woman who works as a Principal in a public high school. Like several weak ethnic voters, this voter discussed her desire to see the Ram temple built as the main reason why she supported the BJP in the 1999 election.[334] However, unlike the pattern of weak ethnic voters, she noted that the Ram temple issue continued to be an important issue for her politically in the 2004 and 2009 elections and was the main factor influencing her continued support for the BJP.

In this pattern of Strong Ethnic Voting, the political salience of ethnic group identity and interests remains heightened and is the predominant factor influencing a voter's political choices. My findings in Ahmedabad suggest that, for many voters who are in this category of voting behavior, the perception of group threat from ethnic conflict remains a persistent ongoing concern influencing their vote choice. My case study research in Ahmedabad did not provide a clear explanation why some very low income voters working in the unorganized sector in Ahmedabad display burgeoning retrospective programmatic voting behavior, while other low income voters working in the unorganized sector display strong ethnic voting behavior. I hope to conduct further research to explore the factors influencing burgeoning retrospective programmatic voting

---

[333] Ahmedabad case study 34.
[334] Ahmedabad case study 9.

behavior for some low income voters versus strong ethnic voting behavior for other low income voters.[335]

This pattern of Strong Ethnic Voting exhibited in Ahmedabad most closely resembles type 2 voting behavior in table 3.2, in which a voter perceives a persistent high level of risk from ethnic conflict, and thus vote choice and the evaluation of an ethnic party is predominantly influenced by ethnic group identity and interests.

3. Party Loyalty: The fourth pattern of voting behavior, Party Loyalty, is characterized by voters who identify the importance of party loyalty as a key factor in their vote choices. Similar to the New Delhi cases who fall into this category of voting behavior, the Ahmedabad voters interviewed in this study indicated that either strong family party loyalty or individual party loyalty is the most important factor in their vote choice. Party Loyalty best explains the voting behavior of six Ahmedabad voters in this study

Cases 27 and 17 are two Ahmedabad voters who fall into this category of party loyalty. Case 17 works as a project administrator at a local university. When asked about what influences her vote choice, she indicated that it is highly influenced by her family. While she links Modi with improving development conditions in Gujarat, her overriding

---

[335] For example, one line of possible future research might explore if differences in an individual voters' direct exposure with ethnic conflict in a particular neighborhood or section of a city over time is correlated with differences in the political salience of ethnic group identity and interests on vote choice. We might hypothesize that low income voters in a neighborhood or section of the city which have had less direct exposure with ethnic conflict are more likely to display an emerging awareness of the link between their vote and a form of reward or punishment for government performance of access to public goods, than low income voters who continue to experience group threat from ethnic conflict in their neighborhood or section of the city.

sentiment is her, "love for the [BJP] party," which she expressed several times as the main reason why she votes for the BJP.[336]

Case 27 votes for the BJP because of his personal sense of loyalty to the party and party ideology. This voter is an upper caste Hindu who owns his own engineering and design consulting firm and expressed deep concerns about the legacy of corruption in the Congress party. By contrast, he identified BJP leader Atal Bihari Vajpayee who is "unpurchaseable."[337] This voter did not identify specific ethnic or programmatic issues as key factors in influencing his support for the BJP. Rather, he emphasized ideological loyalty in describing why he votes for the BJP.

For this fourth category of voting behavior, neither mechanism posited in ERV theory adequately explains the voting behavior of these two respondents. Rather, a different mechanism related to a voter's individual or family loyalty to a particular party appears to be guiding these voters' political choices. This pattern of Party Loyalty most closely resembles type 4 voting behavior in table 3.2, in which some other type of interests other than ethnic or programmatic interests, such as party loyalty, influences vote choice and the decision to vote for an ethnic party.

In conclusion, the Ahmedabad case studies reveal four patterns of voting behavior to explain variation in voter support for the BJP: 1) Retrospective Programmatic Voting, 2) Weak Ethnic Voting, 3) Strong Ethnic Voting, and 4) Party Loyalty. Similar to the New Delhi voters interviewed for this study, I posit that ERV is able to explain three out of four patterns of voting behavior (i.e., retrospective programmatic voting, weak ethnic voting, and strong ethnic voting), which represent differences in an individual voter's

---

[336] Ahmedabad case study 17.
[337] Ahmedabad case study 27.

assessment of the potential threat from ethnic group conflict and the reward from economic reforms and development, and have a subsequent role in the relative influence of ethnic group identity and interests and retrospective programmatic interests on vote choice and the nature of support for an ethnic party at the individual level.

Chapter 7: Conclusion

In many new and maturing democracies, and in countries struggling to establish democracy, ethnic parties are an important actor in electoral politics. Existing research has shown that ethnic parties and ethnic political participation can be a stable and peaceful presence in democracies. Yet, examples exist of ethnic parties associated with ethnic conflict or ethnic violence.

The Bharatiya Janata Party is an example of an ethnic party, which has been associated with ethnic violence in the past. The seeds of this study began with a focus on the BJP, the only ethnic party that competes at the national level in India, in order to understand what factors influence voter support for this ethnic party.

Since urban areas often represent the focal point of socio-economic changes relating to economic growth and development, examining voting behavior through a focus on urban voter support for the BJP, I posited, would provide a unique lens for a research project seeking to understand the factors affecting voter support for an ethnic party in a rapidly developing country context.

Existing theories to explain why voters vote for the BJP focus predominantly on either ethnic factors, such as caste or religion, or programmatic factors, such as the economy or corruption. Yet, my initial field research suggested that both ethnic and programmatic factors influence voter support for this party. Additionally, I found variation in the relative influence of ethnic interests and programmatic interests in explaining voter support for the BJP over space and time.

This final chapter provides a summary of this dissertation study and its key findings. I begin with a brief review of the main questions guiding this study and the theoretical framework I offer to address these questions. I next discuss the research findings as they relate to an examination of voting behavior over space and time. I conclude with a discussion of the implications of these findings for the study of Indian politics and questions for future research on the study of voting behavior and the nature of voter support for ethnic parties in developing country contexts.

My interest in voting behavior and understanding the factors that influence voter support for an ethnic party, such as the BJP, in a rapidly developing country context gave rise to three broad questions guiding this dissertation study. First, how do ethnic and programmatic interests influence voting behavior and help us understand variation in voter support for an ethnic party such as the BJP? Second, what conditions increase the salience of ethnic factors in voters' political choices? Third, what conditions increase the salience of programmatic factors in voters' political choices?

To answer these questions, I present a theory of voting behavior, Ethnically Mediated Retrospective Voting (ERV), which posits the conditions under which ethnic interests and retrospective programmatic interests influence voters' political choices, as a means of explaining variation in voter support for the BJP.

ERV can be understood as a theory of retrospective voting which is adapted to explain voting behavior and the factors affecting voter support for an ethnic party in a rapidly developing country context, which aims to account for the impact of 1) changes in the perceived level of ethnic group conflict, and 2) changes brought about by rapid economic growth and reform, on voters' political choices.

ERV first posits that an increase in the perceived level of ethnic group conflict in turn creates the conditions for an increase in the political salience of ethnic group identity and interests. Second, ERV posits that changes resulting from economic reform and economic growth create the conditions for increasing retrospective programmatic demands by voters.

The mechanisms of ERV together posit different generalized scenarios of voting behavior to explain voter support for an ethnic party in different socio-economic conditions, listed in table 3.1 These scenarios of voting behavior represent the ways in which ERV's two mechanisms predict the relative influence of ethnic and programmatic interests in explaining overall voter support for an ethnic party under different socio-economic conditions.

This dissertation also tests the proposition that ERV's mechanisms impact individual voting behavior in different ways. I posit four types of individual voting behavior, listed in table 3.2, based on differences in an individual voter's assessment of in-group threat from ethnic group conflict and the reward from economic growth and development, which in turn affects the relative influence of ethnic group identity and interests and retrospective programmatic interests on vote choice and explaining individual voter support for an ethnic party.

I employ a mixed-method strategy of data collection and analysis referred to as "nested analysis," which includes data analysis of voting behavior in the states of Delhi and Gujarat in three Indian national elections, 1999, 2004 and 2009, using Indian National Election Survey (NES) data, and case study analysis of individual urban voters and their voting behavior in the cities of New Delhi, Delhi and Ahmedabad, Gujarat. This research design provides the means to examine both the way in which ethnic and programmatic interests influence voter support for the BJP at the societal level, and also how these factors influence voting behavior and voter support for the BJP for the individual voter.

Summary of Research Findings

My findings indicate that ethnic interests and retrospective programmatic interests are both important factors in explaining voter support for the BJP over space and time. The analysis of voting behavior in Delhi and Gujarat indicates that the condition of a high level of perceived ethnic conflict is associated with a heightened political salience of ethnic identity and interests. In particular, in the 1999 election, which had the highest level of ethnic conflict for each state, the relative influence of ethnic interests on vote choice and explaining voter support for the BJP was markedly higher in both Gujarat and Delhi than compared to in the 2004 and 2009 elections.

Additionally, I find that in Gujarat, which has a socio-political history of episodes of ethnic violence between Hindus and Muslims, and which also keenly felt the BJP's ethno-nationalist mobilization strategy during the 1990s, the relative influence of ethnic group identity and interests in explaining voter support for the BJP is comparatively higher than in Delhi, which has generally experienced low to moderate levels ethnic conflict between Muslims and Hindus.

The analysis of voting behavior in Delhi and Gujarat also indicates that the condition of a strong political economy of development is associated with an increase in retrospective programmatic demands guiding voters' political choices. I find that during the 2009 election, which witnessed the strongest levels of economic growth and development in both Delhi and Gujarat, the relative influence of retrospective programmatic interests on vote choice and explaining voter support for the BJP is higher in both Delhi and Gujarat than compared to in the 1999 election. The analysis of voting behavior in Delhi and Gujarat indicate that retrospective programmatic concerns on issues such as development and personal financial conditions had particularly strong effects on vote choice in the 2009 election. Though it is difficult to make direct comparisons of the strength of retrospective programmatic variables over time due to differences in models in the large-N analysis, the findings from the case study analysis in both cities suggest an increasing influence in the role of retrospective programmatic interests to explain individual voter support for the BJP from 1999 to 2009.

In addition to finding evidence of the effects of ERV's individual propositions on voting behavior, the findings from the large-N analysis of voting behavior over time in Delhi and Gujarat provide evidence to support the proposition that ERV's combined mechanisms are able to explain changes in the relative influence of ethnic interests and retrospective programmatic interests on voting behavior and voter support for the BJP at the societal level under different socio-economic conditions, as hypothesized in table 3.1.

In the context of a high political economy of development, and a moderate level of ethnic group conflict, which characterized the context of the 1999 election in Delhi, my findings indicate that both ethnic group identity and interests and retrospective programmatic interests were strong factors in explaining voting behavior and voter support for the BJP, most closely represented by scenario 1 in table 3.1

Ten years later, under conditions of a very high level of political economy of development and a low level of ethnic conflict, which characterized the context of the 2009 election in Delhi, my findings indicate that the relative influence of retrospective programmatic interests were strong factors in explaining voting behavior and voter support for the BJP, while the political salience of ethnic group identity and interests were less influential, most closely represented by scenario 3 in table 3.1

In the context of a weak political economy of development combined with a very high level of ethnic conflict in Gujarat in the 1999 election, my findings indicate that the relative influence ethnic group identity and interests were strong factors in explaining voting behavior and voter support for the BJP, while retrospective programmatic interests were somewhat less influential, most closely represented by scenario 2 in table 3.1

Ten years later, in the context of a high political economy of development, and a medium level of ethnic group conflict in Gujarat in the 2009 election, my findings indicate that the influence of both ethnic group identity and interests and retrospective programmatic interests were strong factors in explaining voting behavior and voter support for the BJP, most closely represented by scenario 1 in table 3.1

These findings suggest that ERV provides a plausible means for explaining changes in the relative influence of ethnic and programmatic interests on voting behavior and voter support for an ethnic party, such as the BJP, in different socio-economic conditions.

The findings from the case study analysis of individual voting behavior over time in New Delhi and Ahmedabad provides evidence to support the proposition that ERV's mechanisms impact individual voter's political choices in different ways, as hypothesized in table 3.2.

In both the New Delhi and the Ahmedabad case studies, I find evidence of four patterns of individual voting behavior which explain changes in electoral support for the BJP, namely, 1) Retrospective Programmatic Voting, 2) Weak Ethnic Voting, 3) Strong Ethnic Voting, and 4) Party Loyalty. These patterns of voting behavior illustrate differences in an individual voter's assessment of and relationship to ethnic group conflict and economic reforms and development, which in turn result in differences in the relative influence of ethnic group identity and interests and retrospective programmatic interests on vote choice and explaining individual voter support for an ethnic party.

The case study findings of voters who engage in Retrospective Programmatic Voting in New Delhi and Ahmedabad suggest that they place a high value on the role of economic reforms and development, and also on the importance of good governance. This pattern of Retrospective Programmatic Voting most closely resembles type 1 voting behavior in table 3.2, in which a voter is generally more influenced by the opportunities posed by economic reforms and development than in-group threat posed by ethnic conflict, and thus vote choice and the evaluation of an ethnic party is predominantly influenced by retrospective programmatic interests.

Voters who engage in Weak Ethnic Voting in the Ahmedabad and New Delhi cases are influenced by both ethnic concerns, such as *Hindutva* or the Ram temple, and retrospective programmatic concerns, such as economic development or personal financial conditions. This pattern of Weak Ethnic Voting most closely resembles type 3 voting behavior in table 3.2, in which a voter is influenced by both the perceived risk of group threat from ethnic conflict and the opportunities posed by economic reforms and development, and as a result, changes in socio-economic conditions in turn change the relative importance of ethnic group identity and interests and retrospective programmatic interests on vote choice.

For voters who engage in Strong Ethnic Voting in the Ahmedabad and New Delhi cases, I found that ethnic interests are the predominant factor influencing a voter's political choices. For these voters, the perception of group threat from ethnic conflict does not appear to ebb and flow, as it does for weak ethnic voters, but persists as a strong ongoing concern over time. This pattern of Strong Ethnic Voting most closely resembles type 2 voting behavior in table 3.2, in which the perceived threat from ethnic group conflict remains generally high, increasing an individual's sense of in-group identification, and thus vote choice and the evaluation of an ethnic party is predominantly influenced by ethnic group identity and interest

For voters in the category, Party Loyalty, neither ethnic interests nor retrospective programmatic interests play a strong role in explaining voter support for an ethnic party. For these particular voters, the focus is almost entirely on voting for a particular party. This pattern of Party Loyalty voting most closely resembles type four voting behavior in table 3.2, in which some other type of interests other than ethnic or programmatic interests influence vote choice and the decision to vote for an ethnic party.

By comparison, the findings from both the large-N analysis of voting behavior in Delhi and Gujarat, and the case study analysis of voting behavior in New Delhi and Ahmedabad, indicate that the degree of a voter's religiosity is not a good predictor of voter support for an ethnic party.

Contributions to the study of Indian Politics

In this section, I discuss two areas in which my research findings seek to engage the study of Indian electoral politics and voting behavior in India going forward. First, the research findings suggest the possibility of testing ERV as a plausible means for examining and explaining voting behavior and the nature of voter support for ethnic parties in other Indian states.

For example, Bihar is one of India's poorest and largest states, with a current population of 100 million. For fifteen years, the state was governed by the Rashtriya Janata Dal Party, a party associated with the interests of OBCs and Muslims. During this time, Lalu Prasad Yadav and his wife, Rabri Devi, alternatively ruled the state largely through caste-based patronage politics. By 2004, the last year of their long tenure, Lalu Prasad Yadav was under investigation for multiple corruption charges, while the state's economic growth rate was less than one percent.

In 2005, the Rashtriya Janata Dal party lost to the BJP-Janata Dal (United) alliance. During the BJP-Janata Dal (U) alliance's tenure, from 2005 to 2009, Bihar's average state GDP increased dramatically to 11 percent.

In the 2010 state assembly election, the BJP-Janata Dal (U) alliance won a second term. Post-election analysis focused on the alliance government's positive performance on development issues, such as improving the state's transportation infrastructure, the coalition's ongoing focus on development issues during the 2010 campaign, and a strategy to appeal to certain ethnic groups (particularly low caste Hindus and Muslims) through various welfare measures, as key factors behind the incumbent's ability to win a second term.

ERV posits that under the condition of a strong level of economic reforms and development, an increasing number of voters can engage in retrospective programmatic appeals in their political choices to explain voting behavior and in turn voter support for an ethnic party. Thus, under the conditions of an increasingly stronger political economy of development in Bihar over the past five years, we could hypothesize that an increasing number of voters in Bihar engaged in a retrospective programmatic assessment of the BJP-Janata Dal (U) tenure during the 2010 state assembly elections, which contributed to continued support for the BJP-Janata Dal (U) alliance. However, a much more in-depth empirical analysis of survey data from the recent state elections in Bihar is needed to parse out the way in which both ethnic and programmatic interests influenced voter support for the BJP-Janata Dal (U) alliance in order for this coalition to win a second term.

Second, the research findings suggest that voters in India may prioritize and focus on different levels of government performance when voting in a national election.

For example, in Gujarat, BJP voters in the 1999 election were on average more focused on the work of the BJP-led central government. Ten years later, BJP voters in the 2009 election were on average significantly more focused on the work of the BJP-led state government led by the popular Chief Minister, Narendra Modi.

In Delhi, both BJP and Congress voters in the 1999 election were generally more focused on the work of the central government. Five years later, Congress voters had become much more focused on the work of the Congress-led state government. These findings suggest a possible extension of ERV, that Indian voters make retrospective programmatic assessments of different levels of government. More research is needed to understand the factors influencing a voter's decision to focus on the work of one level of government over another level of government at a given point of time.

Final Thoughts

The findings of this study shows that ethnic interests and programmatic interests are both critical factors in explaining why voters vote for an ethnic party, such as the BJP. If we focus only on the role of ethnic interests or on the role of programmatic interests, we are missing a critical part of the complexity of voting behavior and explaining voter support for an ethnic party in a developing country.

This complexity of voting behavior is evident both at the societal level and at the level of the individual voter. At the societal level, this study finds that changes in socio-economic conditions related to ethnic conflict and the political economy of development impact the relative influence of ethnic interests and programmatic interests in explaining overall voter support for an ethnic party.

The findings also suggest that individual voters may assess the potential threat from ethnic group conflict and the reward from economic reforms and development differently, which in turn results in differences in the relative influence of ethnic and programmatic interests on vote choice and explaining individual voter support for an ethnic party.

In developing and testing Ethnically Mediated Retrospective Voting as a means of explaining voter support for the BJP in two highly urbanized areas in India, this study seeks to broaden the way in which we conceptualize voting behavior and our understanding of the nature of voter support for an ethnic party in a developing country context. While this dissertation has sought to provide answers to questions about the nature of voter support for an ethnic party, many questions remain.

In this study, party system competition is held constant, as both Gujarat and Delhi have a two party system. Wilkinson indicates that the nature of party system competition and the effective number of parties competing for votes at the town and state level play a pivotal role in determining the electoral incentives for political elites to prevent or allow violence. A question for further research is to examine how the nature of party systems and party competition impacts the salience of ethnic interests and programmatic interests on voting behavior and the nature of voter support for an ethnic party.

This study also sought to examine the role of programmatic voter-party linkages in explaining voting behavior and voter support for an ethnic party in two highly urbanized areas in India. Scholars have begun to study voter-party linkage formation and change in countries such as Argentina, Brazil, and India. A question for future research is to examine how changes in programmatic voter-party linkage formation impacts the nature of voter support for an ethnic party in other developing country contexts.

While the scope of this dissertation is designed to focus on explaining voting behavior and why voters vote for an ethnic party in two highly urbanized locations in India, ERV could be a useful framework for examining voting behavior and the nature of voter support for ethnic parties in other developing country contexts.

As more election survey data and other forms of data are generated about voting behavior in developing countries in the future, scholars will be in an increasingly better position to conduct research and analysis about voting behavior and to gain more insight into the factors influencing electoral support for ethnic parties in developing countries.

www.ingramcontent.com/pod-product-compliance
Lightning Source LLC
LaVergne TN
LVHW011933070526
838202LV00054B/4622